The User-Friendly Old Testament:
A Modern Approach to Ancient Scripture

"I can hardly wait to give [this book] to my beloved family members and dear friends. . . . Marilyn manages to draw [universal truths] from an ancient text . . . and pulse new life into its passages. . . . This truly is a 'user-friendly' guide to potentially daunting scripture."
  —Saskia C., musician

"[Marilyn] Faulkner takes a history and turns it into a manual for life! [She includes] just the right recipe of historical connections, spiritual insight[s], and alarmingly pertinent application[s]. Finally, the Old Testament has lessons for me, here and now."
  —Elizabeth I., youth group leader

"[This book] makes the reader feel like the ancients are as close as neighbors who feel, think, and respond to life in a familiar way to our own lives. . . . There isn't a better book on the Old Testament to turn to today that can help all members of the family, no matter the age, to discover the treasures in the . . . Old Testament."
  —Laura B., doctoral candidate in Hebrew studies

"Marilyn has a gift to relate the scriptures to our own lives. . . . The story of David especially touched my heart. I want to implement the idea of using the five smooth stones of prayer, faith, service, forgiveness, and love in my own life. Reading the Old Testament in a 'user-friendly' version is exactly what I need!"
  —DeeAnne B., office manager

"With her well-informed but easily accessible [and] down-to-earth style, Marilyn Faulkner brings these stories alive with her modern-day parallels and lessons for life that are suddenly very relevant in today's world. . . . *The User-Friendly Old Testament* will be a welcome companion text for me in my own study, and in preparing future lessons for youth . . . and adult groups."
  —Gary G., physician

"I loved the discussion of Job, and comforting others. If I hadn't read anything else, the four tips for providing comfort would have been worth getting the book. I really enjoyed having the Old Testament stories presented in ways that I might actually be able to follow them!"

—Angela A., single mother

THE USER-FRIENDLY BOOK OF MORMON: TIMELESS TRUTHS FOR TODAY'S CHALLENGES

"*User-Friendly* perfectly describes Marilyn Faulkner's fresh new approach to the Book of Mormon. It not only trumps the best of what's out there, but creates a unique new approach rich enough to be a lesson manual all its own."

—Kieth Merrill, Academy Award-winning producer and director

"I can't wait to study the Book of Mormon with Marilyn's questions in mind: 'Where am I in this story? Where is Jesus in this story?' Has the Book of Mormon ever been applied in a more practical, personal, and friendly way? I doubt it!"

—Wendy Ulrich, PhD, MBA psychologist, and author of *Weakness Is Not a Sin*

"I love how Marilyn views the Book of Mormon not only as the word of God but also as a literary masterpiece. Through this perspective, we can truly discover the relatability of the characters, their actions, and what it all means to us today."

—Melanie, Amazon Review

BACK TO THE BEST BOOKS: HOW THE CLASSICS CAN CHANGE YOUR LIFE

"The rich pleasures and profound lessons of literature come alive in this stimulating collection of essays on great novels. Faulkner's readings of the classics are sympathetic but sharp-eyed and alive to both philosophical content and literary quality. Like any good critic, she makes readers want to hit the books. A fine introduction to a well-chosen canon."

—Kirkus Reviews

"Marilyn makes each book sound so enticing, and her observations are so interesting, that you will want to go out and purchase every book she reviews—even the ones you have already read!"

—Kathy G., Amazon Review

THE USER-FRIENDLY

OLD
TESTAMENT

A MODERN APPROACH TO ANCIENT SCRIPTURE

THE USER-FRIENDLY

OLD TESTAMENT

A MODERN APPROACH TO ANCIENT SCRIPTURE

MARILYN GREEN FAULKNER

CFI, an imprint of Cedar Fort, Inc.
Springville, Utah

ISBN 13: 978-1-4621-2010-9

Published by CFI, an imprint of Cedar Fort, Inc., 2373 W. 700 S., Springville, UT 84663
Distributed by Cedar Fort, Inc., www.cedarfort.com

LIBRARY OF CONGRESS CATALOGING-IN-PUBLICATION DATA

Names: Faulkner, Marilyn Green, 1953- author.
Title: The user-friendly Old Testament : timeless truths for today's
   challenges / by Marilyn Green Faulkner.
Description: Springville, UT : CFI, an imprint of Cedar Fort, Inc., [2017] |
   Includes bibliographical references and index.
Identifiers: LCCN 2017037627 (print) | LCCN 2017042361 (ebook) | ISBN
   9781462127696 (ebook) | ISBN 9781462120109 (pbk. : alk. paper)
Subjects: LCSH: Bible. Old Testament--Introductions. | Church of Jesus Christ
   of Latter-day Saints--Doctrines. | Mormon Church--Doctrines.
Classification: LCC BS1140.3 (ebook) | LCC BS1140.3 .F38 2017 (print) | DDC
   221.6/1--dc23
LC record available at https://lccn.loc.gov/2017037627

Cover design by Katie Payne
Cover design © 2017 by Cedar Fort, Inc.
Edited and typeset by Chelsea Holdaway

Printed in the United States of America

10 9 8 7 6 5 4 3 2 1

Printed on acid-free paper

For Craig,
my reason to smile every day.

Contents

Contents

Prologue

IT'S A BRAVE NEW WORLD

In the last few decades, whether we like it or not, all of us have been obliged to embrace the digital age, and we find ourselves facing a confusing array of devices with their attendant charge cords, pass codes, and *modi operandi*.

In response, I've learned to seek out devices that are reviewed as "user-friendly." This is a relatively new term, coined to describe complex machines or systems that are readily accessible without special skills or lengthy sets of instructions. In other words, given a little time, patience, and a few helpful suggestions (usually from someone at least half my age), I can eventually get the hang of using them.

MAKING THE SCRIPTURES USER-FRIENDLY

Whether you are reading the family Bible, or scrolling through an endless array of Bible maps and supplementary content on that miraculous little phone, certain things remain the same. Even though the Bible that sat on my nightstand as a child is easily accessible on every one of my devices, it's still a rather difficult book. And the best way to understand it, in my experience, is to find a way to relate it to your life. After all, the scriptures are meant to change us, and the only real key to change is through making a personal connection to the story. I've found that this is usually done by finding a personal, or "parabolic," element in the text.[1]

For example, in Genesis, we read that Adam and Eve made choices that caused them to be banished from the garden and driven into the lone and dreary world. Now, as readers, we can go through every verse, making sure that we know the Hebrew root of "Adam," or trying to determine where the Garden of Eden was located. All of that is interesting, but it may not be life-changing. It's got to become meaningful to you.

How does the story of Adam's family apply to your life? What choices have you made that took you out of a state of innocence and into a greater knowledge of good and evil? Were they sins or transgressions? Are you wasting time now, wishing you could get back to the "good old days" before you made so many mistakes? Are you, like Cain, assuming a victim mentality and blaming others for the way things are going? Or, like Sister Eve, are you thankful for your painful experiences because they have brought you wisdom? Like faithful Adam, are you waiting for messengers from God? And what will you do if a message does come? Where are you in this story?

You don't have to understand everything in the scriptures, any more than you have to understand how to program the motherboard of your computer. You just need to learn how to turn on the device and make it work for you.

THE USER-FRIENDLY OLD TESTAMENT

So if you have found the Old Testament hard going in the past, we will approach it in a way that is a little more "user-friendly." Rather than worry about understanding every verse, we'll delve into the lives of some of the iconic figures of the text, and see what they have to teach us about life, the Savior, and ourselves. I hope that as we do so the narrative and spiritual power of the Old Testament will become evident, and that you will be inspired to explore more of its stories on your own. We will also take a look at the "wisdom literature" and the big prophetic books in the same way. We'll just stop here and there and try to learn a lesson or two that can apply to our lives today. For example, Esau has something to teach you about your issues with your dishonest brother or critical sister. Potiphar's wife may hold the key to overcoming your struggle with pornography. Job can help you understand why your child died—even after all the fasting, faith, and prayer. There is so much in the Bible to enrich your life right now.

Here are four guidelines I like to follow when studying the Old Testament:

1. Understand the context
2. Learn the lingo
3. Use a modern perspective
4. Keep the focus on Jesus

In order to help achieve these objectives, I will offer some information about the historical context of the stories. I'll explain some of the literary devices: the tools that our authors used to make the text memorable and meaningful. I'll share some quotes from modern thinkers and religious leaders that illuminate the topics we will discuss, and I will randomly stop here and there to share what I think might interest you along the way. Finally, I will attempt to relate every story to the Atonement of Christ, and explore how our understanding of Him is enlarged by the text.

I hope that this will build your confidence in making the Old Testament your own book. You see, it doesn't matter as much if you know Biblical Hebrew, or if you can trace the wanderings of the Israelites on a map. What matters more is if you can understand the language that God uses to speak to you, and if you can see His hand in your own sojourn in the wilderness.

MANUFACTURER'S WARNING: THIS BOOK IS NOT FOR THE FAINT OF HEART.

Though the Old Testament is full of stories that appeal to children, it is, in its original form, a book for adults. It will shock you with its frank treatment of human weakness, sexuality, and sinfulness. It will cause you to question your assumptions, and ask you to rethink just about everything you have ever thought about God. What the *Jewish Study Bible* reminds us about Genesis applies to much of the Bible:

[The vehicle of Genesis] is . . . narrative. The theology must be inferred from stories, and the lived relationship with God takes precedence over abstract theology. Those who think of stories . . . as fit only for children . . . [will] miss the complexity and sophistication of the stories of Genesis. . . . [These stories] have occupied the attention of some of the keenest thinkers in human history.[2]

So be prepared to do some mental work, because, like every great work of literature, the Old Testament demands the best of us. As a work of scripture, the Bible asks us to change our minds and our behavior in response to its warnings. Scripture study should do, even more intensely, what German novelist, Franz Kafka, described as the function of all great literature: "I think we ought to read only the kind of books that wound or stab us. If the book we're reading doesn't wake us up with a blow to the head, what are we reading for? . . . A book must be the axe for the frozen sea within us. That is my belief."[3]

Though it may not always be easy reading, the ultimate objective of the Old Testament is to increase the happiness, peace, and productivity of our lives. In that most important sense, it truly is user-friendly.

NOTES

1. "Parabolic" is a term used by some commentators to refer to a personal, symbolic application of the Bible stories. I first encountered this term in the excellent little volume, *The First Christmas: What the Gospels Really Teach About Jesus's Birth*. (Marcus J. Borg and John Dominic Crossan, "Part One: Parable, Overture, and Context," in *The First Christmas: What the Gospels Really Teach About Jesus's Birth* (New York: HarperCollins, 2007.)

2. Adele Berlin and Marc Zvi Brettler, eds., *The Jewish Study Bible: Featuring the Jewish Publication Society TANAKH Translation* (New York: Oxford University Press, 2004), 8–9.

3. Franz Kafka in Greg Mills, *Why States Recover: Changing Walking Societies into Winning Nations, from Afghanistan to Zimbabwe* (London: C. Hurst & Co., 2014), xii.

Introduction

Do We Need to Believe the Bible in Order to Believe *in* the Bible?

This question is not as obtuse as it may seem on the surface. What I am asking here is fundamental to our study of the Bible; namely, can you really believe *in* the Bible without believing that it is a work of factual history?

Since the advent of biblical criticism in the nineteenth century, just about every part of the Bible has come into question for most intellectuals. Nowadays, in the secular world, we are told that the books weren't written by the people they are named for, and that the miracles recounted were simply legends, or symbolic stories. There was no David, no Abraham, and Adam and Eve are simply characters in a fairy tale for adults.

In a rather violent theological reaction, as the Bible becomes less accepted as a historical document, evangelical Christians have doubled down and become even more fanatical about every word of the Bible being true. So you can actually go to your local natural history museum and view skeletons of dinosaurs, and then go down the street to hear a sermon that such creatures never actually existed, because the Bible doesn't mention them, and nothing could have predated Adam and Eve. It's a strange world for the thoughtful believer. Can we accept the Bible as God's word without accepting it as completely factual?

You will be happy to know that I have an answer to this question. And the answer is yes, and no.

Yes, you can believe in the Bible without believing in every detail of it as factual history. Here is how. The Bible is the greatest work of literature in the Western world. It contains the accumulated wisdom and spiritual heritage of the Judeo-Christian civilization; and, as such, is a priceless treasure. The Bible contains poetry, songs, prayers, lamentations, histories, and sermons, and exemplifies the way that our culture thinks and feels and reaches up to God. It is one of the most important books we have, and it contains an inexhaustible supply of principles to live by. You can believe in all of that without buying the story of Eve actually talking with a snake. The Bible can be a guiding presence in your faith, without being your guide to history.

> " The Bible—banned, burned, beloved. More widely read, more frequently attacked than any other book in history. Generations of intellectuals have attempted to discredit it; dictators of every age have outlawed it and executed those who read it. Yet soldiers carry it into battle believing it more powerful than their weapons. Fragments of it smuggled into solitary prison cells have transformed ruthless killers into gentle saints.
> —Charles Colson[1]

WHAT CONSTITUTES A BELIEVER?

So, if partial faith can still be called faith, how much do we need to believe in the Bible in order to be called a believer? Having been raised in a deeply Christian faith that is considered *not* to be Christian by much of the Christian community, I'm a little sensitive on this issue. When we begin to make judgments about what constitutes a believer—rejecting those who do not believe in miracles, for example, or those who may have a different view of the Trinity—we are treading on dangerous ground. A believer is one who believes, one whose heart responds to the message of scripture and values it as a guide for living. And so, whatever level of belief you have in God, or scripture, or miracles, you may identify yourself as a believer if your heart is drawn to these things.

Just exactly how much or how little of what the Bible asserts is actually factual will long be a matter of debate. Modern scholar Bart Ehrman said, "Even though I do deal with the Bible as a historian, I do not personally think that it is the *only* way to deal with the Bible, and I find it unsettling when readers think that once the Gospels are shown to have discrepancies, implausibilities, and historical mistakes, we should just get rid of them and move on to other things."[1] Just because something isn't completely factual, doesn't mean it can't be true. It even appears that the ancients had a different view of the relationship between facts and the truth; they believed that facts (such as numbers of people, years of life, or days of rain) were there to serve the truth, and thus were a bit more malleable than we literal-minded moderns would find acceptable. Context is crucial to understanding just what we are being asked to believe from the scriptures;

> Take away [the] rich social fabric [that religion has always been] and what you are left with [are] people who are uncertain about who they really are.
>
> –David Brooks[3]

many of our debates arise from confusion about context. For example, our ancestors may not have felt compelled to believe that Methuselah lived for more than a thousand years. They may have understood that number to be symbolic rather than literal. There is so much about these texts that we simply do not understand.

I hesitate to label anyone as a nonbeliever if they label themselves as a sincere seeker after truth. I am also convinced that in any congregation you would be hard put to find many people who really believe everything they are being taught. I think we all get to be called believers, if we can believe anything at all.

One thing we can all agree upon is that the story of the Jews has a universal appeal, beautifully expressed by Simon Schama:

What the Jews have lived through, and somehow survived to tell the tale, has been the most intense version known to human history of adversities endured by other peoples as well; of a culture perennially resisting its annihilation, of remaking homes and habitats, writing the prose and the poetry of life, through a succession of uprootings and assaults. It is what makes this story at once particular and universal, the shared inheritance of Jews and non-Jews alike, an account of our common humanity.[4]

OUR BASIS FOR BELIEF IS CONSTANTLY SHIFTING

One last thought about this business of belief. Though God doesn't change, people do, and our reasons for believing what we believe are often transitory. When I was a missionary for The Church of Jesus Christ of Latter-day Saints in Japan, we served in a small congregation that was basically unraveling. The leaders had pretty much stopped attending and were feuding with each other; as missionaries, we were frustrated and confused about how to go forward. Our district leader suggested that we go back to the members of the branch, and teach them the basic missionary discussions. In those days that meant a six-lesson treatment of the doctrines of Christianity and the claims of The Church of Jesus Christ of Latter-day Saints as the rightful repository of the restored authority of Christ in modern days, through our founder—the prophet Joseph Smith.

So that is what we did. All of our branch members were fairly recent converts to the Church; none of them had been raised in it (as had most of the missionaries), so there was no cultural connection to our religion for them like there was for me. Each member had, at some point, simply decided to believe in the claims of the missionaries and the teachings in the scriptures. The remarkable thing that emerged from going back to these people and teaching them the basic doctrines again, was that—for nearly all of them—their decision to join the Church did not necessarily stem from their belief in all of the doctrines. Certainly most of them had experienced some kind of spiritual awakening, or insight, that had led them toward the decision. But for some of them, it was the community of believers that drew them in. For others, it was an answer to one question or another that had brought them into fellowship with the Church. Very few of them could actually say that they believed everything, or even nearly everything, that we as missionaries were teaching. Yet they found something in the faith that kept them coming.

That experience was illuminating. It taught me that all of us believe things for a variety of reasons, many of which are more emotional than a matter of divine revelation. And those reasons for belief can shift as our life experiences change.

> The psychological dangers through which earlier generations were guided by the symbols and spiritual exercises of their mythological and religious inheritance, we today (in so far as we are unbelievers, or, if believers, in so far as our inherited beliefs fail to represent the real problems of contemporary life) must face alone, or, at best with only tentative, impromptu, and not often very effective guidance. This is our problem as modern, "enlightened" individuals, for whom all gods and devils have been rationalized out of existence.
>
> –Joseph Campbell[5]

WATERING THE SEED OF FAITH

But my experience in this little branch had two parts. Instead of just accepting whatever level of belief existed in the minds and hearts of the members, we treated each of them as if they were approaching the faith for the first time. We taught them the basic doctrines of the Atonement of Christ, the need for a Savior, the importance of covenants, and the value of scripture. We prayed with them and encouraged them to read and pray on their own—asking God if what they were learning was true. We challenged them to examine their lives and repent of wrongdoing. In short, we gave them the whole experience of investigating the Church all over again, and invited them to accept the faith as new converts.

The results were, not to oversell it, pretty amazing. I came away from that experience converted in a way that I hadn't been before. Most of these people, when invited to take a fresh look at their belief system, found it for the first time. One by one, they embraced it with joy. Up until that time, I suppose I had an idea that faith, like many things, was an accident of birth, experience, and opportunity; some people become believers because their background just predisposes them to do so. As a result of that experience on my mission and other experiences since, I have come to believe in the literal truth of the divine Jesus. I believe that His divinity isn't just a jumble of trumped-up claims created to enslave people's minds, but that there really is a Savior, and He really is mighty to save. His saving power is universal; it leaps over cultural boundaries and seeps through the barriers of tradition. There is a divine reality behind the scriptures that gives them an actual power—regardless of how interpreters and redactors may have confused the details through nearly two hundred translations—and I rely on those scriptures as guides for my life. I understand now that even though, like the members of that little Japanese branch, our first steps toward belief may be driven by emotion or social connection, we should not discount the doctrine as a result. There is a potent power there.

HELP THOU MY UNBELIEF

Rather than succumbing to our doubts, I think we need to challenge ourselves when it comes to faith. Jesus compared faith to a tiny seed that could grow into a great tree. Most of us spend many hours every week nourishing other seeds—seeds of doubt, skepticism, pessimism, and even despair. Yet we may feel hesitant to pour even a little water on the seed of faith, lest we look gullible or silly. But that seed is real, and it can grow. Reading the Bible with a heart open to what God wants to teach us can help it grow.

All along the way there will be things that will seem so fantastic as to be laughable. Questions will abound. Credulity will be strained. But then, there will be moments when we simply stop and think, in the words of the ancients, "There art thou" (see Psalm 139:8). It may be the moment that the wronged elder brother Esau folds the trickster Jacob in his arms—in a perfect foreshadowing of the parable of the prodigal son. It may be in the courage of the defiant Job, who will not accept any easy answers, yet says, "Though he slay me, yet will I trust in him" (Job 13:15). Or it may be in the vision of thousands of angels surrounding a city that appeared to be lost to an enemy, and Elisha's simple, yet stunning, affirmation that, "They that be with us are more than they that be against us" (2 Kings 6:16).

As we read the Bible, we stand on the shoulders of giants; and for a moment, we can see a little further down the road. We are allowed to be that fly on the wall and hear the conversation between Joseph and Potiphar's wife (the conversation that neither thought anyone heard), and feel the thrill when he gets himself out of there. We grow frustrated at the flaws in weak characters like Saul and Samson, and mourn the even more tragic flaws in the great ones like David and Solomon. We find our loved ones, and ourselves, everywhere we look.

And we find beauty: poetic language unsurpassed anywhere in literature, wrenching cries from the heart, enthralling narratives, and even humor. We find villains and heroes, and sometimes God appears to assume both of those roles! There are so many questions to ask, and so many answers offered; the layers of meaning multiply as our understanding grows.

So whether you are a literal believer or a literary skeptic, I invite you to join me in examining some of the iconic stories that have shaped our culture and our collective faith. As you read, I'd invite you to close your eyes now and then and open your heart to what God may be trying to say to you.

Remember the beautiful story of the father who begs Jesus for help with his disabled son? Perhaps he just viewed Jesus as another charismatic preacher, or a magician, or maybe simply as a last resort for a desperate parent. When he cried out for help, Jesus probably surprised him by turning the problem back over to him, saying,

If thou canst believe, all things *are* possible to him that believeth. And straightway the father of the child cried out, and said with tears, Lord, I believe; help thou mine unbelief. (Mark 9:23–24; emphasis added)

As we read, we can pray that the Lord will help us in our unbelief, since He understands that the whole business of life is very confusing. In fact, it is meant to be. The Bible is like the *New York Times* crossword—the Sunday version, of course—it is meant to make you work. If the answers were printed at the bottom of the page, where would the fun be in that?

The Old Testament is not for the faint of heart, but it can become a starting point of a believing heart. As you open its pages, you join millions of fellow humans who have pondered its passages and found divine guidance. Angels will hover near, whispering their interpretations. (Pardon the pun, but I imagine they have spirited discussions about scripture as well!) And you will be in good company. Jesus was a great student of the scriptures, as well as their inspiration. You may find, as did those lucky two whom he joined on the road to Emmaus, that your view of Bible stories can be illuminated when you look through His divine lens.

And beginning at Moses and all the prophets, he expounded unto them in all the scriptures the things concerning himself.
And their eyes were opened, and they knew him. . . .
They said one to another, Did not our hearts burn within us, while he talked with us by the way, and while he opened to us the scriptures? (Luke 24:27, 31–32)

NOTES

1. Charles W. Colson, *Loving God* (Grand Rapids, MI: Zondervan, 1987), 55.
2. "Video of How Jesus Became God," Bart Ehrman, *The Bart Ehrman Blog*, accessed August 21, 2017, ehrmanblog.org/video-of-how-jesus -became-god-part-1-of-3/.

3. David Brooks in, Jeffrey R. Holland, "Bound by Loving Ties" (Brigham Young University Education Week devotional, August 16, 2016), www.lds.org/prophets-and-apostles/unto-all-the-world /bound-by-loving-ties?lang=eng&clang=pes#_edn16.
4. Simon Schama, *The Story of the Jews: Finding the Words 1000BC–1492AD* (New York: HarperCollins, 2014).
5. Joseph Campbell, *The Hero with a Thousand Faces*, 3rd ed. (Novato, CA: New World Library, 2008), 86–87.

Chapter One

FROM THE GARDEN TO THE FLOOD

Begin at the Beginning:
An Overview of Genesis

So many of the greatest Bible stories are included in Genesis that it is tempting simply to write this whole book about it and be finished. I won't succumb to that temptation, but we will spend an inordinate amount of time on this first book of the Bible. Here are a few themes introduced in Genesis that will recur throughout the Bible.

1. It's not easy being green. The innocence of the Garden of Eden sounds idyllic, but once Adam and Eve left the garden, they were able to grow in many ways. It's interesting that while we all long for it, innocence actually becomes a negative in the long run. Experience may be painful, but it is the only way to become a spiritual adult. This is a nice reminder for when we find ourselves longing for the good old days, before we made all those mistakes!

2. We are never alone. Adam and Eve left the garden, but God went with them. The book of Genesis describes a God who takes walks in the garden, literally breathes life into Adam, and personally shuts the door of the ark. The Bible authors want us to feel His closeness. Enoch's vision, recorded by Joseph Smith in the book of

Moses, describes a God who—even though He's omniscient, and it seems like He should know better—actually weeps over us. He reacts to our emotions with emotions of His own: a startling and life-altering perspective.

3. We can't go back, but we can go forward. There isn't a way back to Eden and innocence, but there is a way forward—through repentance. Even Cain is offered protection and a way to move on. No matter what happens—even in the worst storm—God will help us build an ark to cover and protect ourselves, and our loved ones, until we land safely home.

> When people talk about destiny, they tend to forget that it isn't deprived [sic] from [free will], [free will] to both accept it or destroy it. . . . You cannot violate the spiritual laws of the universe. You will always pay a heavy price for being ignorant about this fact. You have the [free will] to do whatever you wish in the paradise of life, but only as long as you don't violate the sacred rules, when eating the fruit of selfishness, the tree of good and evil. That need to explore discernment will cost you your happiness, and expel you from the paradise destined to you."
>
> —Robin Sacredfire[1]

These are only a few of the themes we can find in this most amazing of anthologies. Through its stories, I believe that the authors are trying to teach us what God is like. And the way we learn to know Him is by understanding how He is both Master of the universe and a close, personal friend to every living soul.

LESSONS ABOUT GOD, FAMILY, AND OURSELVES

As you read, notice how the biblical narrative goes from big to little and back again. Unlike traditional history—which focuses mainly on key events and famous figures—scriptural history concerns itself with big events and little people. The widow who feeds Elijah is as important as the prophet himself. Though Bathsheba had no rights, nor any standing in Israelite society, she gets the justice due to her in the scriptural account of David's betrayal.

Even God himself is portrayed in both the most expansive and the most intimate of terms. The Bible begins with two descriptions of the Creation. One is cosmic in scope: God speaks from the outer reaches of the universe, and the world forms from the void. This is a majestic, though distant, creator. But just when we are settling into a reverent, worship-from-a-distance mode, we have a description of the Creator actually fashioning a man and a woman from the dust of the earth. Amy-Jill Levine tells us that Adam's name, *Ah-dama,* is a Hebrew pun on the word mud; so Adam is "a man from the mud, or a human from the humus."[2] This God takes a rib right out of Adam's chest and fashions Eve. He walks in the garden in the cool of the day. This is a personal God, not a distant deity.

Both aspects of the Creation are important because they show us two sides of God's nature: His power over the cosmos, and His intensely personal and intimate interaction with His creations. Genesis is the beginning of learning about who God is and how He works.

Another theme to notice in the Bible is the illusion of secrecy—how many times people do things that impact history when they think no one is watching. One of the pleasures of great stories is that they give us a "God's-eye view" of human actions. Even though Cain thinks no one sees him when he kills Abel, God sees, and we get to see what God sees. Moses buries the Egyptian, and we are right there. David orders the death of Uriah and thinks that no one will find out, but we know that people will be talking about it for the next few thousand years. Every action has consequences, and though we may successfully hide our sins for a time, everything will eventually be revealed. All of this serves to heighten our appreciation of Christ's Atonement, which not only releases us from guilt, and mitigates (where possible) the effects of our sins, but also erases our sins from the mind of God.

You might also notice how family relationships are at the center of everything. Bruce R. McConkie said, "Almost the whole message of the book of Genesis in the Old Testament is family. It is family, family, family."[3] Family relationships require forgiveness and reconciliation. Everybody knows it is easier to be our best selves outside the walls of our homes; your family knows the worst of you. (Someone has said, "Of course your family can push your buttons; they installed them!"[4]) Genesis is the ultimate soap opera, and just about every type of family interaction is included in its stories—from sibling rivalry to marital betrayal. Parental styles range from cluelessness to cruelty to Christlike love. Nearly every great historical occurrence is told through the experiences of a family; and, in many cases, the family relationships are the tipping points that change history.

As we place ourselves in these stories, the lessons of Genesis hit home. For example, if you go to church every Sunday, but have a sister you haven't spoken to in years, then Genesis has a message for you. If you read your scriptures, but make fun of your crazy Aunt Marilyn (I'm just saying), you haven't quite got the picture yet. And most of all, if you betray your spouse, your children, your siblings, or your faith, Genesis will show you how that betrayal can destroy more than those intimate relationships. The consequences can be far more widespread and eternal. Genesis is where we start learning about how important the family really is, and how we must preserve those sacred ties no matter what.

If I were writing a book of scripture, I'd probably preach a lot more than Genesis does. As Adam and Eve leave the garden, you'd kind of think that there'd be fifty chapters of people praying and fasting and showing lots of examples of really good works. But instead, Genesis gives us fifty chapters of families squabbling, moving, having children, and occasionally engaging in physical combat with each other. In short, they are having the very kinds of problems that we have. Once in awhile, characters experience great moments of clarity where they receive some kind of vision about their lives and what they're supposed to be like, and we are lifted up right along with them. Then, they just get back into the day-to-day challenges. It's breathtaking in its honesty, and it is totally relatable. Once you get past the idea that everyone ought to be perfect, Genesis is an incredible world in microcosm where you can meet just about every kind of human being.

Okay, these are just a few things to think about. Remember, the point is not to get every detail right. The point is to get the point—the lesson that God wants you to learn today about your life—and to put yourself in the story as we go.

> By the way, if you get mad at your Mac laptop and wonder who designed this demonic device, notice the manufacturer's icon on top: an apple with a bite out of it.
>
> –Peter Kreeft[5]

God Saw That It Was Good: Our Divine Heritage

GENESIS 1–2

One of my most memorable educational experiences happened during the years that I was studying for my master's degree in literature. I was a wife and mother—as well as a student—so at times, there were scheduling challenges. One year, our family vacation fell during the first week of school, causing me to miss the beginning session of a graduate seminar on comparative world literatures. The teacher kindly offered to meet me for lunch and teach me the material. So one afternoon, Dr. Donald Shojai, who had immersed himself in the literatures of the world for decades, told me five of the major creation myths—one after the other. It was an unforgettable journey through time with a master storyteller.

As I listened to the sacred stories that had formed the foundation of each culture, I couldn't help but notice a unique feature of the creation narrative as found in Genesis. In the other creation myths, the gods first create the earth, and then they form men and women as an afterthought, almost as a sort of domestic staff meant to serve them. But in Genesis, God creates the earth and everything in it with one purpose: to be a setting for humankind. Men and women are not an afterthought; they are the very object of the Creation. And the God of Genesis is not power hungry; He immediately gives man dominion over

> "We believe that the creation of a woman was the crowning and final and most glorified moment of human creation. That we start with light & dark and land & sea and we move through fish & fowl & beasts of the field and we get to Adam and it's still not good enough. And only when Eve was created–that is our theology, that the crowning creation and the glory of the human experience came with the creation of Eve.
>
> –Jeffrey R. Holland[6]

the new world. The earth and all that are within it are there for the benefit of the human race. These humans are not a species remote from God; they are closely related to Him in both form and function. "God created man in his own image, in the image of God created he him, male and female created he them" (Genesis 1:27).

Finally, rather than regretting that He had made these troublesome creatures, God looked out upon His creation and saw that "it was very good" (Genesis 1:31). Since we are God's creations, this means that we are good. This idea is so familiar to us now that we may not realize how revolutionary it was when these scriptures were first disseminated. The idea that human beings are—by nature— good, was not generally accepted by the ancient civilizations that coexisted with the Hebrews. This is, perhaps, the most revolutionary idea of the Bible.

Today's creation myths don't vary widely from those taught to Babylonian and Syrian children thousands of years ago. Evolutionary biology has once again reduced humankind to a subset of creation; humans, we are told, are driven by certain basic needs and instincts, and the strongest creatures survive to pass along the traits necessary for survival. As a result, to call humans either "good" or "bad" is rather like calling a hyena "bad" because it feeds on carrion, or an eagle "bad" because it snatches a sparrow out of the sky. Humans are simply creatures; and, in the end, will act in their own selfish interest. While the Bible version of the Creation may be interpreted to include the evolutionary view of creation, it also takes it up a notch. Genesis invites us to imagine a nature for ourselves that is higher than that of the animals. We are literally children of God.

Our creation was not simply an accident. Whatever the process that brought us to our current state, the process was in God's hands, and our nature is akin to His. That idea is huge. And, since our Western justice system and code of laws was built on the principles taught in the Bible, that huge idea has infiltrated its way into Western thought, resulting in a shared culture that values the individual and recognizes our rights to "Life, Liberty, and the pursuit of Happiness."[7]

WHAT IT MEANS TO BE A CHILD OF GOD

Perhaps we don't realize how important it is to believe in the divine nature within us. Years ago, I had a friend, who wasn't a member of the Church, with whom I shared a daily walk. Our daughters were friends, and we often discussed the tricky details of raising teenage girls. One day, she surprised me by saying, "Your girls seem to have an inner confidence that my girls lack. They laugh things off that devastate my daughters. How do you help them have such a secure sense of self?"

I responded, "Well, I don't know. They certainly have their insecurities. But one thing I know that makes a huge difference is what they are taught at church. For example, once a week, from the time they are twelve years old, my girls stand up in their youth meeting and recite the Young Women theme, which begins, 'We are daughters of our Heavenly Father, who loves us, and we love Him.' I can't help but believe that saying that sentence out loud, week after week, has an impact on them. They are taught to believe that they are of divine origin—that they are really something greater than they appear to be right now. I think that gives them a feeling of worth that transcends the ups and downs of their current lives. It's not about what they do; it's about who they are."

She was quiet for a minute and then said, "That is an amazing thing. I know that kind of teaching would be great for my girls too." Then she smiled and said, "But it's not worth it; you're all way

> It was no accident that one of the first things God asked of Adam was for him to name the animals he saw around him. Why do you suppose God asked man to do that? Because once you have a name, you have the beginning of understanding, and once you have understanding, you lose fear. God didn't want man to be fearful. He wanted man to be brave.
>
> –John E. Kramer[8]

too busy in your church!" We laughed and kept on walking, but I thought to myself that for me, at least, it seemed worth the effort we were expending to raise them in a faith that teaches them to value themselves so highly. And looking at them now, I know that it was.

YOU ARE HOLDING A GREAT MAN

President Henry B. Eyring shared this touching moment from his own child-rearing experience:

I remember once a seven- or eight-year-old son of ours jumping on his bed hard enough that I thought it might break. I felt a flash of frustration, and I moved quickly to set my house in order. I grabbed my son by his little shoulders and lifted him up to where our eyes met.

The Spirit put words into my mind. It seemed a quiet voice, but it pierced to my heart: "You are holding a great person." I gently set him back on the bed and apologized.

Now he has become the great man the Holy Ghost let me see 40 years ago. I am eternally grateful that the Lord rescued me from my unkind feelings by sending the Holy Ghost to let me see a child of God as He saw him.[9]

The source of President Eyring's perspective about his son is rooted in Genesis: "And God saw every thing that he had made, and, behold, it was very good" (Genesis 1:31). When God looks at you, He sees something very good. When you view your children

> I believe that, notwithstanding the fact the spirits of men, as an incident to mortality, are deprived of memory and cast out of the presence of God, there still persists in the spirit of every human soul a residuum from his pre-existent spiritual life which instinctively responds to the voice of the Spirit until and unless it is inhibited by the free agency of the individual.
> –Marion G. Romney[10]

and grandchildren and the other young people you know through His eyes, you can see it too—even when they are teenagers! If you can communicate that vision to them, their lives will rise to meet it.

The Creation and Personal Creativity

GENESIS 1–2

Joseph Smith taught the revolutionary doctrine that the worlds were created by faith. In reference to Hebrews 11:3, which states that, "through faith . . . the worlds were framed," the *Lectures on Faith* states:

> By this we understand that the principle of power, which existed in the bosom of God, by which the worlds were framed, was faith; and that it is by reason of this principle of power, existing in the Deity, that all created things exist—so that all things in heaven, on earth, or under the earth, exist by reason of faith as it existed in Him.
>
> Had it not been for the principle of faith the worlds would never have been framed, neither would man have been formed of the dust—it is the principle by which Jehovah works, and through which he exercises power over all temporal, as well as eternal things. Take this principle or attribute, (for it is an attribute) from the Deity and he would cease to exist.[11]

In response to this, J. Reuben Clark Jr. said, "As I think about faith, this principle of power, I am obliged to believe that it is an intelligent force. Of what kind, I do not know. But it is superior to and overrules all other forces of which we know."[12]

In other words, God—in conjunction with some laws of nature that are way over our heads—creates by faith. He begins by believing in a vision. What actions combine with His vision and belief are a divine mystery, but we know that vision and belief are a crucial part of it. Creation is rooted

> What does a person need to be creative? Some of the markers I see are curiosity, eagerness to learn, courage to be innovative, willingness to work hard, a desire to be a problem solver, and the ability to learn from mistakes. These are the same tools required to excel in just about any discipline. . . .
> —Claudine Bigelow[13]

in faith, which is a real force (an intelligent force, according to J. Rueben Clark, Jr.) that is initiated in the mind of God. This is another life-changing concept when you think about it. It means that each of us, as a child of God, has the ability to visualize and believe, and then bring into being hitherto uncreated things. That is what creativity means. It starts with a vision and a leap of faith.

My husband, Craig, was an entrepreneur before you could major in it in college. He created his first little business when he was eleven (ironing shirts for missionaries at twenty-five cents apiece), and has never stopped since. At one point, our first publishing company grew to the point where we needed to buy our own printing presses, which meant that it was time to build our own facility. So we purchased an acre of land in a business district, and I thought we would build a modest-sized building. But one day, as we walked the property together, Craig told me that he wanted to build a structure that was double the size of what we needed at the time, and far more costly than I had anticipated.

As I watched him describe the project, face alight with animation, I said, "But that is a much larger building than we need! What are you going to do with all that space?" He stopped and looked at me, somewhat confused, and replied, "But can't you see it? I can see the whole thing, and I know how we will fill every corner of that building." The ability to visualize that which does not, as yet, exist, is a hallmark of the creative mind. Every act of creativity begins with vision, faith, and the courage to breathe life into the clay.

CREATIVITY IS A DIVINE ATTRIBUTE

Since God is, by essence, a creator, creativity must be a godly attribute. As we consciously add more creative experiences to our daily lives, we change in good ways. Creativity is sometimes discouraged in children, because it is usually disorderly and messy; coloring within the lines and adhering to time-honored traditions is much more comforting to the generation in charge. But encouraging creativity in our children, and in ourselves, can be life-changing.

Beginning with Genesis, the Bible is filled with stories of people who took a creative approach to righteousness. Adam names animals (see Genesis 2:19), Abraham negotiates with God (see Genesis 18:23–33), Noah builds a boat (see Genesis 6:22), and so on. In every case, the creative individual is following the model set in Genesis by the great Jehovah. People who are willing to take a creative approach to righteous living—to do a thing in a different way than everyone else is doing it—move the world forward. I call this quality "creative morality," and I admire people who bring a creative approach to doing what is right. We can bring creativity to every area of our lives.

Mothers are some of the most creative people I know because they are faced with the nearly impossible task of raising children—a task that is like herding kittens that can also talk back. Every mother knows that very little that you learn while raising your first child is useful, because the next one will be totally different and crash all of your theories! So mothers are constantly reinventing the wheel. And sometimes they come up with remarkable ideas.

It's hard to believe that the brash, audacious Richard Branson—entrepreneur, adventurer, and founder of Virgin Airlines—was a shy, introverted child who would cling to his mother's skirts and refused to speak to anyone. Instead of following the accepted pattern for child-rearing, Eve Branson took a truly creative approach. One day she dropped seven-year old Richard off in a field three miles from their home. "You will now walk home," she said, "You will have to talk to people to find your way home." Hours later, Branson finally arrived home to a mother frantic with worry. (She had forgotten to factor in the time he would spend examining bugs and rocks!) From then on, he lost his fear of people and began his journey to a remarkable career that has impacted the lives of many.[15] The future success

> The desire to create is one of the deepest yearnings of the human soul.
> —Dieter F. Uchtdorf[14]

of a great entrepreneur was founded in the unique approach of a creative mother.

CREATIVITY AS A SOURCE OF JOY

God describes His own purpose in this way: "For behold, this is my work and my glory—to bring to pass the immortality and eternal life of man" (Moses 1:39).

Promoting our progress and well-being is not only the work and glory of God; it is also His joy. When the Nephites gathered around Christ after His Resurrection, hanging on His every word and begging for His blessing, He said, "My joy is full" (3 Nephi 17:20). Even in the midst of His greatest trials, Jesus took joy in little children, in the love of His followers and friends, and in His relationship with His father. His great desire was to impart that same joy to us. He said, "These things have I spoken unto you, that my joy might remain in you, and that your joy might be full" (John 15:11).

Whenever we are involved in the effort of creation, we are taking part in the work and glory of God. The Creation didn't finish with the introduction of Adam and Eve into the garden. Every time a man or woman creates something beautiful, it continues God's work of Creation. Every time we learn and grow, the Creation continues. And with every child that is born and loved and taught, the Creation grows more glorious. A beautiful poem titled, "Song of Creation," imagines a mother and father in Heaven, engaged in the joyful project of creating the earth together:

Who made the world, my child?
Father made the rain
silver and forever.
Mother's hand
drew riverbeds and hollowed seas,
drew riverbeds and hollowed seas
to bring the rain home.[16]

We can't control whether our lives will be free of sorrow, but no matter what our circumstances, we can bring joy into our lives through creativity. The poet Maya Angelou said, "Everybody born comes from the Creator trailing wisps of glory. We come from the Creator with creativity. I think that each one of us is born with creativity."[17] Tapping into our own inner reservoirs of creativity is a way to kindle the divine spark within.

> God is creating at every moment of the world's existence in and through the perpetually endowed creativity of the very stuff of the world.
>
> –Arthur Peacocke[18]

Adam's Family Learns That Life Is Not Fair

GENESIS 3–5

As Adam and Eve leave the Garden of Eden, the scriptures record nothing of their feelings. We assume that they were upset, fearful, and perhaps even confused. But they might have also felt curious, adventurous, and excited to experience something different. Most of us experience all of those emotions during a move to a new environment.

Though exiled to the lone and dreary world, it appears from the text that Adam and Eve, and their family, could still hear God's voice. Cain does not seem at all surprised to have a conversation with the Lord: "And the Lord said unto Cain, Where is Abel thy brother? And he said, I know not: Am I my brother's keeper?" (Genesis 4:9).

However, Cain is deeply dismayed at the idea that being sent away from the place where his father dwells will mean that he will no longer be in God's presence:

My punishment is greater than I can bear.
    Behold, thou hast driven me out this day from the face of the earth; and from thy face shall I be hid. . . . (Genesis 4:13–14)

This comment, I believe, tells us something important about Cain's faithful parents. As Adam and Eve faced a fallen world, they chose to react with obedience, faith, and optimism. By so doing, they remained, to a certain extent, in God's presence. Cain chose the opposite—focusing on his own selfish desires and shifting responsibility for his actions to someone else. When commanded to provide a sacrifice, we are told that he brought an

> "People are always blaming their circumstances for what they are. I don't believe in circumstances. The people who get on in this world are the people who get up and look for the circumstances they want, and, if they can't find them, make them.
> —George Bernard Shaw[19]

offering from "the fruit of the ground," but not the choicest, first-lings of the flock, as did Abel (see Genesis 4:3–4). But when God rejected his offering, Cain was angry. We must assume that this was one episode in a long history of resentment between the brothers that eventually resulted in the first murder.

WHERE AM I IN THIS STORY?

As we look at the dynamics of Adam's family, we might ask ourselves the question: Who am I in this story? Do I sound more like Cain, or more like Adam and Eve? Do I respond to God's commands by giving my best effort, or only a half-hearted show of duty? When family members need my help, do I hope someone else will take care of them? Am I my brother's (or sister's) keeper? And when a sibling gets all the favorable treatment, am I bitter?

How often do we fall prey to the idea that life is unfair? At one time or other, most of us have said something like this: "I've worked hard; I've done everything that God asked, and nothing is working out!" In my experience, I've felt that most people who lose faith in God do so, not because there are doctrinal issues, but because their feelings are hurt. They are offended because God seems to have rejected them, and so they reject Him—in essence, banishing themselves from His presence.

It is significant to me that the scriptures do not elaborate on why God rejected Cain's offer, He just does. And in the same way, most of us will never understand, in this life at least, why one person dies of cancer at a young age, while the guy next door smokes two packs a day and just turned ninety. Or why one business fails and another succeeds—though the failing business owner may have worked twice as hard. Or why some women who long to be mothers cannot

> Between stimulus and response there is a space. In that space is our power to choose our response. In our response lies our growth and our freedom.
>
> –Victor Frankl[20]

have a child while so many others are blessed with children they go on to neglect or even abuse.

With every horrifying new report of natural disasters, killings, and unspeakable wickedness, we are tempted to ask, what kind of a God would allow the random suffering and cruelty that exists in this world? Yet, rather than focusing on the unanswerable questions, Adam and Eve simply focused on doing what God asked them to do; by doing this, they placed themselves in a position to receive a deeper understanding about why the world is the way it is. And even if they couldn't understand the reasons for everything, they had the comfort of God's presence to make life worthwhile. This is something that Cain, preoccupied with his own needs, could never understand.

THE STORY OF THE TWO SONS OF ADAM, FROM THE QURAN

"Recite to them the story of the two sons of Adam; truly when they offered an offering, and it was accepted from one of them, and was not accepted from the other, that one said, 'I will surely kill thee;' he said, 'God only accepts from those who fear. If thou dost stretch forth to me thine hand to kill me, I will not stretch forth mine hand to kill thee; verily, I fear God, the Lord of the worlds; verily, I wish that thou mayest draw upon thee my sin and thy sin, and be of the fellows of the Fire, for that is the reward of the unjust.' But his soul allowed him to slay his brother, and he slew him, and in the morning he was of those who lose. And God sent a crow to scratch in the earth and show him how he might hide his brother's shame, he said, 'Alas, for me! Am I too helpless to become like this crow and hide my brother's shame?' and in the morning he was of those who did repent" (Qur'an 5:30-34; E. H. Palmer, translator).

TOOLBOX: THE SUBVERSIVE NATURE OF SCRIPTURE

There is a secret ingredient to great literature that is a little hard to explain, but once you understand it, your enjoyment of good stories will increase. It is a subversive element that surfaces as characters are developed. The writer may even try to set out the story simply: in black and white, good versus evil. But, often without realizing it, the writer will say something contradictory that adds additional layers of meaning to the text.

Let's take the simple story of Cain and Abel. Cain is the bad guy, and Abel is the good guy. God accepts Abel's sacrifice and rejects Cain's; and, in a jealous rage, Cain kills his brother. That should be enough, right? Up to that point, the story is told in a rather detached fashion. We don't have any record of the interchange between the brothers, and we don't have one recorded word from our victim, Abel. If, at that point, we were simply told that God banishes Cain, or slays him, the story would be complete.

But here is where that subversive element comes in. The story isn't simple, just like life isn't simple. Cain has done a terrible thing, but he is not just a villain. He is a man—a child of God—with all of the potential for good that his slain brother possessed. How do we know that? Because our author helps us get to know Cain by recording a conversation he has with God. It would make sense for the author to introduce us to Abel. He is the good guy. He is our role model. But instead, we are taken into the mental and spiritual world of Cain. We are not allowed to despise him; we are actually invited to empathize with him! Instead of congratulating ourselves on being good like Abel, the turn in the scriptural narrative forces us to realize that we are also like Cain, and that we need the grace of God—just like he did.

And that is what all great literature does. Just when we are comfortably thinking that we understand everything and that we are safely on one side of the fence, the fence gets knocked down and we see our own vulnerability. As Pogo said so eloquently, "We have met the enemy, and he is us."[21] Scripture opens our shut-up hearts and helps us see that the line between the villain and the hero is thin, and that we could easily cross it. We are left feeling that the only safety is not in rules, or laws, or walls, but in the grace of the Lord, who created and loves Cain and Abel, and each of us.

Noah's Dilemma: How Long Can You Tread Water?

GENESIS 6–10

Ancient mythology is flooded with flood narratives. (Sorry, I couldn't resist.) Tales of a deluge that covered the earth and destroyed the wicked can be found in almost every culture. Scholar and British Museum curator Irving Finkel writes: "The story of a flood that destroyed the world in which human and animal life was saved from extinction by a hero with a boat is almost universal in the world's treasury of traditional literature. . . . Flood Stories . . . have been documented in Mesopotamia, Egypt, Greece, Syria, Europe, India, East Asia, New Guinea, Central America, North America, Melanesia, Micronesia, Australia and South America."[22]

These legends contain some or all of these main features:

- A flood is planned by the gods
- One man is warned and spared
- An ark is built
- Animals are collected in the ark
- The ark lands on a mountain
- A series of birds are sent to find land[23]

Here is just one example: In Peru, when the first explorers went into the Andes and discovered the indigenous people there, they were amazed to find a very deep tradition about a universal flood that had covered the earth. One explorer named Cieza left this account in 1550:

These nations say that anciently, many years before there were Incas, the Earth being heavily populated with people, there came such a great storm and flood that the ocean overflowed its boundaries and natural course, and that water filled the earth in such a manner that all the people died, because the water rose enough to cover the highest peaks in all the mountain ranges. . . . Other people from the mountains and even those from the lowlands say that no one escaped drowning, except six

31

people who escaped in a small boat or bark, who gave birth to all the people who have lived and are since that time.[24]

Cieza seems to sense that we might be skeptical, so he concludes, "Don't you doubt this reader, because all of the people in general affirm this story and tell this that I have written about."[25]

The Sumerian legend of Gilgamesh is so similar to the story of Noah (right down to the dove and the raven sent out to find land) that there can be little doubt the two stories shared an influence, probably an older legend known to both cultures.[26]

There are two ways to look at this. One is to say that because these narratives exist in nearly every culture, the Hebrew scripture is neither authoritative nor historical; it is simply a copy of other tales that the Hebrews encountered in Babylon during captivity. The other way to look at is to say that the more people that report an event, the more likely it is that the event actually happened! And when two texts share similarities, both are usually referring to an older source. The latter approach seems more reasonable to me.

Knowing that the account in Genesis is written in the context of, and perhaps in response to, these other legends, gives us a new lens through which to view it. No scriptures are written in a vacuum; the authors are often in a kind of dialogue with the theological beliefs of the cultures that surrounded them. This adds an interesting layer of meaning to every scriptural interpretation. However, an even more important task is to decipher the messages that Hebrew parents were trying to teach their children through recounting the story of the Flood. And, by extension, decipher the messages that these ancient texts can pass along to us.

WHAT CAN WE LEARN FROM NOAH?

Noah, the prophet that God called to warn people of the coming flood, simply arises in Genesis. We don't have a birth narrative for him, like we do for Abraham and Moses.

Joseph Smith had this to say about Noah: "Jehovah . . . talked with him [Noah] in a familiar and friendly manner, that He continued to him the keys, the covenants, the power and the glory, with which He blessed Adam at the beginning."[27]

Here are three things we can learn from Noah's experiences:

1. Each of us is a new Adam or Eve. Noah is referred to as a "new Adam" because he is at the center of a "do-over" where God destroys all the earth's inhabitants, and then repopulates the earth through Noah's lineage. God repeats to Noah the exact command that he gave to Adam and Eve: "Be fruitful, and multiply, and replenish the earth" (Genesis 9:1). As a part of our temple worship service, we are invited to consider ourselves as if we were Adam or Eve, and the message I take from that is that the history of the world is contained in the life of each of its inhabitants. Your life is unique, your posterity is unique, and your moral choices help create the kind of life that your posterity will inherit. Like Adam and Eve—and Noah— each of us represents the beginning of an endless chain of events. Everything begins all over again with each new life.

2. When all hope is lost, there is still hope. Though Noah and his family lived through a terrible devastation, God intended for them to eventually thrive. So it is with us. When the rain stopped, Noah sent out a bird to see what was out there, but when the bird failed to find land, Noah did not give up hope. He kept sending the bird out until the bird had found land.

This is a beautiful metaphor for clinging to hope, even when the floods sweep away everything that is meaningful and dear. For example, when death, divorce, or depression threaten to destroy the life we have built, we can send out a bird to find a landfall on which we can build a new way of thinking. We may have to send the bird of hope out again and again, until a safe landing place is found. And when we find a new place, we can turn to the creator of the earth for a building plan.

The image of hope as a bird resonated with Emily Dickenson. Perhaps she had Noah and his feathered emissaries in mind when she penned these lines:

> "Hope" is the thing with feathers—
> That perches in the soul. . . .
>
> And sweetest—in the Gale—is heard—
> And sore must be the storm—
> That could abash the little Bird
> That kept so many warm—[28]

3. At some point, you will be laughed at for your faith. It's fine to be religious when it is fashionable, but when the day comes that faith is considered folly, what will you do then? Thomas Merton said, "Suddenly there is a point where religion becomes laughable. Then you decide that you are nevertheless religious."[29] Currently, for example, it has become very unpopular to believe in the literal Resurrection of Jesus, the reality of the Godhead, and the historicity of the events in the Bible. By making these things seem ridiculous, an environment is created where intelligent people are ashamed to accept the miraculous and supernatural.

Noah is our hero here. This man built a boat on dry land, and it wasn't even raining. Perhaps it comes more from the art we've seen than the actual text, but I think most of us have a visual of Noah, working away on the ark, surrounded by a crowd of laughing, mocking neighbors. Did he go to bed at night doubting his vision? We don't have any record of him doing so. He clearly believed that God had spoken to him, and he went right on building the ark in the sunshine, knowing that the rain would come. His ability to grasp his God-given vision, and then be true to it, earns him a place in biblical lore.

The artist, Flora Scovel-Shinn, said, "Every great work, every big accomplishment, has been brought into manifestation through holding to the vision, and often just before the big achievement, comes apparent failure and discouragement."[30]

Noah didn't have time to learn the lessons of revelation when it was starting to rain. Before the crisis occurred, he needed to have the certainty that he knew how God spoke to him.

CHANNELING NOAH IN OUR DAILY LIVES

Last year, I taught at BYU Education Week for the first time. and on the last day, I had an unexpected and special experience. Several people—whose lives my late father, Luman Green, had touched during his years as a bishop in Lake Arrowhead, California—experienced a miraculous reunion in my classroom. As the hour drew to a close, I knew that I felt a special spirit, but perhaps I wasn't in tune enough to know just how special. Then one of Dad's former ward members came up to me and said, with tears streaming down her cheeks, "Marilyn, your father is here." I realized that my father, from the other side of the veil, was still reaching out to help members of his flock. It was the kind of experience that you cherish, but perhaps would not share with others.

A few weeks later, I went to lunch with a friend who's not a believer in any particular faith. Her husband had recently been diagnosed with ALS, and this was a painful time for her. She told me how devastating it was that, not only had her husband been diagnosed with this terrible disease just when they were getting ready to retire, but in the last year, both her mother and a favorite aunt had died, and even her dog—a dear companion for fourteen years—had died as well. (Those of you who are dog lovers know that that's right up there on the loss scale.) So many hard things were happening in her life that it was sad to see her suffering.

So when she said, "Well, what have you been up to?" I decided to change the subject by telling her about teaching at Education Week and a little about my lessons. She shook her head sadly and said,

> I sometimes think that one of the best-kept secrets of the kingdom is that the scriptures open the door to the receipt of revelation.
> —Bruce R. McConkie[31]

"Marilyn, I'm glad you still believe in the Bible and can teach that class, because I've lost my faith. I don't believe in God anymore. What kind of God would give my husband this disease? What did we do to deserve this? And what kind of penance am I being asked to pay? Everyone close to me has died. I'm facing this all alone and it makes no sense to me. I have no faith left."

I had no idea how to reply. Her pain was so great that some cliché or platitude seemed insulting. Then suddenly it came into my mind to tell her about the last day that I taught, and how I had felt my father close to me. I felt quite uneasy about sharing something so sacred with someone who didn't share my beliefs, and I wondered if she would even understand what I meant. But I felt the prompting so strongly that I just let it pour out. I shared everything about my father, and how I felt his spirit there in the room with me that day. And then I said this: "I feel that the reason your mother and your aunt died was so that they could be close to you for this trial. Because they could never be as close to you and as supportive of you here as they could be from the other side of the veil." And then, to my complete surprise, I added, "And your mother is here, right now." And when I said it, she broke down and started to cry and threw her arms around me.

There we were, standing on the lawn in front of the restaurant, with patrons walking by and looking at us, weeping in each other's arms. My friend told me that she knew her mother's spirit was there with us. I knew that it must be so, because I hadn't even thought of it until the minute before I said it. I was so thankful that, at least that one time, God was able to send a message of love through me—just as he had used the woman in my class to let me know that my father was near during a challenging time.

Noah reminds us how important it is to learn the different ways that God speaks to us because He might have a very important message for us to relay to others, that may be essential for their spiritual survival. Depending, of course, on how long you can tread water!

One thing Joseph Smith's experience shows us is that receiving revelation requires effort on our part. There may be rare exceptions when the Lord has to urgently warn us of danger or prompt us to immediate action, but most often if we want to receive revelation we must work for it. . . .

Joseph Smith described the "serious reflection" that ultimately led him to receive the revelation he sought (JS–H 1:8). This was not casual curiosity, but something he pondered and thought about often and for some time. . . . Clearly, pondering leads to revelation. . .

[The] principle of obedience is one that is often overlooked in receiving revelation, but we can't expect God to give us what we ask of Him if we are not willing to give Him what he asks of us. Generally speaking, we will not receive revelation that we are not willing to follow and we show our willingness to follow his revelations by obeying the commandments he has already revealed. . . .

[The Spirit of revelation] comes with power and force to the feelings of our heart causing us to reflect on it again and again. This is the kind of revelation that is difficult to recognize, especially for the inexperienced. In fact, as President Boyd K. Packer once explained, recognizing the Spirit of revelation is like recognizing the taste of salt. It is difficult to describe in words and can ultimately only be known by experience.

–Mark A. Mathews[32]

The Tower of Babel and the Power of the Word

GENESIS 11

> In the beginning was the Word, and the Word was with God, and the Word was God.
>
> The same was in the beginning with God.
>
> All things were made by him; and without him was not any thing made that was made. (John 1:1–3)

These opening verses from the Gospel of John are some of the most enigmatic lines in scripture. Let's unpack them. "In the beginning was the Word, and the Word was with God." We know that Christ is known as "the Word," and that He was in the beginning with God, and that through Him the worlds were created. But in Genesis, we are also told that when God spoke, the world came to be. "And God said, Let there be light: and there was light" (Genesis 1:3), and so forth. God speaks, and creation happens. So the Word that is with God certainly refers to Christ. But it seems also to refer to the words of power that God speaks through Christ, in order to create the world.

And now that we have piled up meanings for the word, "word," we must return to its basic meaning: the medium through which we communicate. Words, as John Widtsoe tells us, are actually symbols that stand for something.

> We live in a world of symbols. We know nothing, except by symbols. We make a few marks on a sheet of paper, and we say that they form a word, which stands for love, or hate, or charity, or God or eternity. The marks may not be very beautiful to the eye. No one finds fault with the symbols on the pages of a book because they are not as mighty in their own beauty as the things which they represent. We do not quarrel with the symbol G-o-d because it is not very beautiful, yet represents the majesty of God. We are glad to have symbols, if only the meaning of the symbols is brought home to us.[33]

The story of the Tower of Babel draws our attention to the power of language. The deep reverence that the Jews have for the Word of God is directly tied to their understanding of the power of the Word, not only to create, but to guide, administer, and even destroy. When people can no longer communicate with each other, everything breaks down. When pride grows so great that people try to set the terms for their relationship with the Creator things really go south.

One of the recurring themes in Genesis is the misuse of godly powers. God forbids man to eat from the tree of knowledge of good and evil. When Adam and Eve disobey, and partake, God says,

> Behold, the man is become as one of us, to know good and evil: and now, lest he put forth his hand, and take also of the tree of life, and eat, and live forever:
>
> Therefore the Lord God sent him forth from the garden of Eden. . . ." (Genesis 3:22–23)

Unlimited knowledge without righteousness to guide it is a little like tossing the keys of the family car to the ten-year old. A child can turn on the car and push on the gas pedal, but that doesn't mean he can drive; disaster will surely result. Humankind had some growing to do before they were ready for immortality. But instead, they went looking for a shortcut!

In this last, curious chapter of what are called the primeval narratives, humankind gets the idea that they can build a tower that will reach to heaven. And God, looking down from heaven, makes this remark, "Behold, the people is one, and they have all one language; and this they begin to do: and now nothing will be restrained from them, which they have imagined to do" (Genesis 11:6).

Taking our cue from Genesis, we can assume that God is not jealous of the power or ability of the humans. Instead, He knows the power of the Word, and that when people speak with one voice they may have more power than they can safely handle.

WORDS CAN HURT MORE THAN STICKS AND STONES

One of the lessons I take from the Tower of Babel is that words are extremely powerful. We can underestimate the power that our words have. If God used words to create the world, then we should be careful how we sling them around. On the other hand, if we use words properly, they can wield tremendous power for good.

Taking the story parabolically, we might compare building a family to building a spiritual tower that—unlike the Tower of Babel—really does lead to heaven. This tower is built with loving relationships that are expressed through actions and words. When we criticize or insult one another, the construction goes into reverse—we take bricks off the tower. As a result, we'd better be sure that any comments we make to each other are constructive, and not negative. Negative, critical comments slow down the building process. So many family members tease each other and make jokes at each other's expense, feeling that such behavior is harmless. It's not. Each insult is a brick taken off the walls of our tower. We build by using words of love and encouragement, which are words of power. Criticism, teasing, and negative comments are words of destruction. Encouragement, praise, and words of faith help build a family that represents a fortress against a dangerous world. There is no stopping a family that is united in the language of love. And thus what was a negative result when people were seeking the wrong thing becomes the source of unlimited possibility. Our words can help build the world we dream of.

"Behold, the people is one, and they have all one language; and this they begin to do: and now nothing will be restrained from them, which they have imagined to do" (Genesis 11:6).

NOTES

1. Robin Sacredfire quoted in, Water of Life (@wateroflife25.12.2015), 2017, "When people talk about destiny . . . ," Facebook, May 19, 2017.
2. Levine says: "And God fashioned man from the dust of the earth," reflects a Hebrew pun: "Man" is *ha-adam*, "theadam"; "adam" derives from adamah, arable soil or, here, "ground." A better translations

would speak of an "earthling from the dust of the earth" or a "human" from the "humus," the loamy soil." Amy-Jill Levine, "Old Testament: Adam and Eve," in *The Great Courses*, course no. 653 (Chantilly, VA: The Teaching Company), DVD.

3. Bruce R. McConkie in, Robert L. Millet and Kent P. Jackson, eds., *Studies in Scripture Vol. 3: Genesis to 2 Samuel* (Salt Lake City: Deseret Book, 1985), 55.

4. Attributed to Tracey Gersten. See C. W. Nevius, "Dreaming of Norman Rockwell but having holidays with family," *SFGate*, December 24, 2006, accessed August 22, 2017, www.sfgate.com /bayarea/nevius/article/Dreaming-of-Norman-Rockwell-but -having-holidays-2464831.php.

5. Peter Kreeft, *Jesus Shock* (South Bend, IN: St. Augustine's Press, 2008).

6. Jeffrey R. Holland, *For Times of Trouble: Spiritual Solace from the Psalms* (Salt Lake City: Deseret Book, 2012).

7. US Constitution.

8. John E. Kramer, *Blythe: The Fight for Faith and Freedom* (Freedom Forge Press, 2017), 265.

9. Henry B. Eyring, "'My Peace I Leave with You,'" *Ensign*, May 2017.

10. Marion G. Romney in, L. Lionel Kendrick, "Personal Revelation" (Brigham Young University devotional, May 20, 1997), speeches.byu .edu/talks/l-lionel-kendrick_personal-revelation/.

11. *Lectures on Faith*, 1:15–16, lecturesonfaith.com/1/.

12. J. Reuben Clark, in Conference Report, April 1960, 21.

13. Claudine Bigelow, "Creativity" (Brigham Young University devotional, August 4, 2015), speeches.byu.edu/talks/claudine -bigelow_creativity/.

14. Dieter F. Uchtdorf, "Happiness, Your Heritage," *Ensign*, November 2008.

15. "Can Entrepreneurship Be Taught? Richard Branson's Mother Says Yes," Mary C. Mazzio, *Time*, May 9, 2012, accessed August 22, 2017, business.time.com/2012/05/09/can-entrepreneurship-be-taught -richard-bransons-mother-says-yes/.

16. Linda Sillitoe, "Song of Creation," *Dialogue: A Journal of Mormon Thought* 12, no. 4, (Winter 1979), www.dialoguejournal.com/wp -content/uploads/sbi/articles/Dialogue_V12N04_97.pdf.

17. Maya Angelou in, Amy F. Davis Abdallah, *The Book of Womanhood* (Eugene, OR: Cascade Books, 2015), 186.

18. Arthur Robert Peacocke, *The Palace of Glory: God's World and Science* (Hindmarsh, South Australia: ATF Press, 2005), 61.

19. Bernard Shaw, *Mrs. Warren's Profession: A Play in Four Acts* (London: Archibald Constable & Co., 1906), act II, p. 193.

20. Attributed to Victor Frankl.

21. Walt Kelly, *Pogo: We Have Met the Enemy and He Is Us* (New York: Simon and Schuster, 1972), 11.

22. Irving Finkel, *The Ark Before Noah: Decoding the Story of the Flood* (New York: Doubleday, 2014), 84.

23. Richard Neitzel Holzapfel, *Jehovah and the World of the Old Testament* (Salt Lake City: Deseret Book, 2009), 27.

24. Kirk Magleby, "'And the Waters Prevailed': Some Andean Indian Versions of the Flood," *New Era*, January 1983.

25. Ibid.

26. Richard Neitzel Holzapfel, "Flood Stories," in *Jehovah and the World of the Old Testament*, 27.

27. *Teachings of the Prophet Joseph Smith,* sel. Joseph Fielding Smith (Salt Lake City: Deseret Book, 1976), 171.

28. Emily Dickinson, "'Hope' is the thing with feathers," no. 314.

29. Thomas Merton, *The Intimate Merton: His Life from His Journals*, Patrick Hart and Jonathan Montaldo, eds. (San Francisco: HarperCollins, 1999), 373.

30. Florence Scovel Shinn, *The Game of Life and How to Play It* (New York: Simon and Schuster, 1925), 19.

31. Bruce R. McConkie, *Doctrines of the Restoration*, ed. Mark L. McConkie (Salt Lake City: Bookcraft, 1989), 243, quoted in Dallin H. Oaks, "Scripture Reading and Revelation," *Ensign*, January 1995.

32. Mark A. Mathews, "How to Receive and Recognize Revelation for Yourself," *Meridian Magazine*, March 2, 2017, ldsmag.com/how-to-receive-and-recognize-revelation-for-yourself/.

33. John A. Widtsoe, "Temple Worship," *The Utah Genealogical and Historical Magazine* 12, no. 2 (April 1921), 62.

Personal Notes

_____

_____

_____

_____

_____

_____

_____

_____

_____

_____

_____

_____

_____

_____

_____

_____

_____

_____

_____

_____

_____

_____

_____

_____

_____

_____

_____

_____

_____

_____

_____

_____

_____

_____

_____

_____

_____

_____

_____

_____

_____

_____

_____

_____

Chapter Two

PATRIARCHS AND MATRIARCHS

Three's a Crowd:
Abraham, Sarah, and Hagar

GENESIS 12–21

Abraham, at the age of seventy-five, hears the voice of God telling him to leave his native land and go into a strange country, where God will make of him a great nation (see Genesis 12:2). So he takes his family and that of his nephew Lot along, and they go into the land of Canaan (see Genesis 12:5). But, right from the start, things do not look all that promising. There is a terrible famine, so they must continue on down into Egypt, where Sarah is taken into Pharaoh's court and nearly made a concubine (see Genesis 12:10–20). Lot ends up, through a series of adventures, living in Sodom—not the best neighborhood (see Genesis 14). Later, Abraham negotiates with God for the safety of Lot and his family (see Genesis 19:27–29).

Sarah is beautiful—so much so that Abraham is in continual danger because of her beauty—but she is unable to bear children. So she decides to try for an heir by giving her maidservant, Hagar (who may have been part of the compensatory gift that Pharaoh offered to Abraham in apology for nearly marrying his wife), to Abraham. This means that Hagar is suddenly elevated from the role of a slave to that of a second wife. When Hagar gives birth to Ishmael, everything changes for both women. Hagar is elevated even further, and Sarah surely feels threatened. Soon, the very same kinds of jealousies, fears, and rivalries that have split families forever cause Sarah to deal "hardly" with Hagar, and Hagar runs away (see Genesis 16:6). An angel tracks her down and sends her back home, only for her to be banished later after Isaac's birth by her jealous mistress, Sarah. But Hagar receives the same promises that were given to Abraham, and Ishmael, her son, does indeed become the father of a great people (see Genesis 17:20). Finally, angels appear and promise Abraham that Sarah will conceive, which she finds laughable, but the miracle happens, and Isaac is born (see Genesis 18:6–12; 21:1–3).

So life works out for them like it does for many of us, and we can relate to them. We make a plan according to our vision of how events should transpire, and then we go forward. And nothing works out like we expect! All of these experiences try the faith of Abraham, Sarah, and Hagar, and these events give them an opportunity to learn more about God and how He deals with us. Abraham makes a few errors in judgment; but, on the whole, he is a kind, conciliatory, generous person whose whole aim is to follow God's commands. We cannot only relate to him, we can look to him as a role model. All of this is leading us to the great twenty-second chapter—called the *Akedah* (the binding of Isaac)—where God commands Abraham to offer his beloved son Isaac as a human sacrifice. I think that it is helpful to read this tragic, troubling, yet transcendent tale in the context of the experiences that have come before.

WHEN ALL ELSE FAILS, TRY OBEDIENCE

One common factor in the stories that precede the Akedah is that they show us how badly things work out when we try to fix them ourselves. I don't presume to say whether or not Sarah should have brought Hagar into the family, but once she did, she needed to trust God and treat Hagar properly. Hagar needed to trust God and stick to her duties. Abraham needed to trust God and follow

His will, rather than let his wife bully him into sending Hagar away. If we behave properly, things will, eventually, work to our good; we can then turn to the Lord and He'll help us fill in the gaps. Once we take the solution into our own hands, thinking that a good end will justify less than righteous means, we are on our own.

But even then, God's mercy will attend us. God honors our covenants even when we lose faith in them. Even though Sarah succumbed to jealousy and drove Hagar away, God was with her. Even though Abraham succumbed to Sarah's decision to banish Hagar, God had a backup plan, and He saved Hagar and Ishmael. Certainly those experiences contributed to the fact that Abraham had enough faith to trust God when He asked him to raise the knife and slay his own son. After the difficult things Abraham had lived through, and the miracles that he had seen, he could say, like Job, "Though he slay me, [or my son] yet will I trust in Him" (Job 13:15).

Abraham's experiences teach us that God always has a backup plan, and we are never alone—no matter how far into the wilderness of selfishness, jealousy, or sin we might have wandered. That brings me a great deal of comfort. I know that, at times, I have caused damage in other people's lives, as Sarah did in Hagar's, and I pray that God will always intervene to soothe the wounds I may inflict through my carelessness or cruelty.

There is another message here for me. Reading about Sarah and Hagar makes me wonder how many times we jump in to solve a problem without asking God what the best course might be? Sarah felt a need to act because she had not been blessed with a child. And years later, when Sarah overheard the angels saying that she would give birth to a child in her old age, she laughed. She still didn't realize that God was all-powerful, and His solution would be greater than any "fix" she could have orchestrated on her own. At the wonderful fulfillment of that prophecy, Sarah named her darling boy Isaac—referring both to her initial laughter and her eventual rejoicing.

TOOLBOX: TYPE SCENE

A type scene is a scenario that happens in different variations throughout the Bible. If one woman meets her future husband at a well, it's a romantic moment. If that scene happens a few times in different forms, then it becomes a type scene with something to teach us.

The Bible uses type scenes to help us uncover new layers of meaning. For example, Jesus meets the Samaritan woman at the same well where Rachel met Jacob (see Genesis 29:10). This comes as the culmination of many type scenes in this category. Moses meets his wife at a well (see Exodus 2:15–17). Saul, in a sad variation on the type scene, is searching for some donkeys and does not find a partner at the well, which gives us a hint that all will not bode well for his kingship (see 1 Samuel 9:3–4). By the time that Christ— the bridegroom—meets the Samaritan woman, the scene has extra layers of meaning because it is a familiar type scene to the Jews.

Once we encounter two or three of these type scenes, we can begin to look for the layers of meaning. For example, the type scene of the barren wife who miraculously conceives and bears a child has meaning in our lives when God's promises do not seem to be fulfilled. It is given to us to bring us hope when we need it most. Abraham received the promise of endless posterity, but Sarah was barren. But through faith, that promise was obtained; Abraham is now the only person in human history to be recognized as the father of three of the world's major faiths. He could hardly have visualized that future when he reached the age of one hundred years, and nothing was happening. Type scenes increase our faith in God's promises to us because the same lesson is repeated over and over.

Is Anything Too Hard for the Lord?

GENESIS 18

The motif of the weak and simple person being chosen to do great things runs consistently through the Old Testament. Hagar, an Egyptian slave, becomes the mother of a great nation, and receives essentially the same promises that Abraham receives. Sarah, old and skeptical, is miraculously blessed with a child and also becomes the matriarch of a great nation. Over and over, the younger son, or the less desirable candidate, is chosen to lead. This becomes a type scene (to learn more about type scenes, see the Toolbox on page 48) that prepares us for the birth of Jesus Christ in a stable. Since most of us feel that we are not exceptional or chosen, the implications of this recurring theme for our lives is great.

> We consider that God has created man with a mind capable of instruction, and a faculty which may be enlarged in proportion to the heed and diligence given to the light communicated from heaven to the intellect; and that the nearer man approaches perfection, the clearer are his views, and the greater his enjoyments, till he has overcome the evils of his life and lost every desire for sin; and like the ancients, arrives at that point of faith where he is wrapped in the power and glory of his Maker and is caught up to dwell with Him.
>
> –Joseph Smith[1]

And this theme extends into our day. For example, when Spencer W. Kimball was called to lead the Church in 1973, he was old, ill, and felt inadequate to the task. Cancer had taken one of his vocal chords, causing him to speak in a whisper. There just wasn't much about him that seemed "prophetic," but after the sudden death of

Harold B. Lee—a man much younger and healthier than he was—he suddenly found himself at the helm of the Church. Elder Boyd K. Packer, one of the Twelve Apostles, recalled President Kimball sitting alone in the Church President's office quietly weeping, saying: "I am such a little man for such a big responsibility!"[2]

But almost immediately, President Kimball began to reshape the vision of the Church regarding missionary work. In his great address, "When the World Will Be Converted," delivered to audiences around the globe, he challenged us to open our eyes and see what God could see.[3] In January of 1975 I watched a video of this talk at the Language Training Mission in Hawaii, where I was learning Japanese in preparation for my missionary service in Sendai, Japan. I will never forget President Kimball holding up a picture of Sarah, laughing, as the angels tell Abraham that she will bear a child. I can still hear his gravelly voice saying, "Is anything too hard for the Lord?"[4] He could see something that we could not see. Up until that time the missionary force was mostly made up of Americans, but President Kimball had a vision of young people from each nation teaching the gospel to their own countrymen. It seemed rather far-fetched, since the Church had few members in other countries, and the majority were new converts, but he traveled around the world, giving this talk over and over again.

I was newly arrived in the Japan Sendai Mission when President Kimball came to Tokyo in April of 1975 to speak at a conference there. American missionaries were not invited to the meeting; we remained in our areas because President Kimball wanted every seat to be filled with Japanese Saints. Members traveled from all over Japan to see and hear the prophet speak in a great stadium, his whisper of a voice magnified through the public-address system.

When I arrived in the Sendai Mission, there was one Japanese sister and about half a dozen Japanese elders. The rest of the almost two hundred missionaries were Americans. That day in Tokyo, thousands of young people heard a prophet's call to leave their homes and go into the mission field to teach their own countrymen and women, and they rose to the vision.

My next companion, Masako Inagaki, attended that conference with her fiancé. They were saving their money to get married, but after President Kimball's talk, they pooled their funds and turned in their papers. Both served missions. (A few years ago, I got to see Sister Inagaki again. She and her faithful husband are the parents of seven children, several of who have served missions.) From that time, all the rest of my companions were Japanese, and by the end of my mission there were twenty-eight Japanese sisters in our mission alone, and nearly fifty Japanese elders. Every one of the six Japanese missions experienced the same influx of native missionaries. Those of us who were a part of that great surge in missionary effort had the thrill of seeing prophecy fulfilled.

SEEING OURSELVES THROUGH GOD'S EYES

What if we could see what God sees about our lives? What is it now that seems just too hard to overcome, but that could be conquered with His help? Perhaps it's worth asking ourselves, when we

> Imagine yourself as a living house. God comes in to rebuild that house. At first, perhaps, you can understand what He is doing. He is getting the drains right and stopping the leaks in the roof and so on: you knew that those jobs needed doing and so you are not surprised. But presently [H]e starts knocking the house about in a way that hurts abominably and does not seem to make any sense. What on earth is He up to? The explanation is that He is building quite a different house from the one you thought of—throwing out a new wing here, putting on an extra floor there, running up towers, making courtyards. You thought you were being made into a decent little cottage: but He is building a palace. He intends to come and live in it Himself.
>
> —C. S. Lewis[5]

51

feel overwhelmed, "Is anything too hard for the Lord?" and invite Him to show us what He sees that we are missing.

Neither Sarah nor Hagar could imagine how great God's plan was for them. They could not appreciate the greatness in each other, and they could not appreciate the greatness in the man they had married. We need God's help in order to have a clearer vision of the people around us, as well as a clearer vision of ourselves. It is a vision far beyond that which the world would teach us. What might He accomplish through us, if we trusted Him more? Is anything too hard for the Lord?

Abraham and the Impossible Choice

GENESIS 22

There is a recurring motif in the Bible that concerns impossible choices. Time after time, our heroes are faced with problems that seem simply unsolvable, and they are asked to make a choice where, in short, you just can't win! Either path incurs painful consequences.

The first example is, of course, our parents in the Garden of Eden. Faced with what they perceived to be two conflicting commandments—multiply and replenish the earth and do not partake of the tree of knowledge of good and evil—Adam and Eve chose to obey one and reject the other. The consequence of that decision is known as the Fall of Adam.

One great lesson that I take from their experience is this—be careful whom you choose as an authoritative source of information. We are told in the scriptures that Eve makes the decision about what to do based on information she receives from Satan. Now, in this case, she may have really received accurate information, but it would be interesting to know if there really was "no other way" for Adam and Eve to have moved forward in their progression. If they had chosen to trust in God, would another way have opened up for them to keep both of His injunctions?

Many times it appears that there are only two choices available to us, when in fact, there might be a third option that is invisible at the time of trial.

ABRAHAM MAKES AN IMPOSSIBLE CHOICE

Abraham faces a similar dilemma when he receives God's promise that his posterity will be endless, yet his wife passes into menopause without bearing him a child. They try to fix the problem themselves, by bringing Hagar into the family, but still, there is no posterity from Sarah. It is not a complete solution by any means.

Then comes the great miracle—the birth of Isaac. This promised child, born long after it was physically possible, becomes the first in a long line of miraculous births that foreshadow the birth of our Lord. How his parents must have cherished and safeguarded him!

Sarah was so protective of him, in fact, that she perceived Hagar and Ishmael as a threat and sent them away. Isaac was everything; he was literally the hope of Israel.

So what does God do? He throws down the gauntlet, and challenges Abraham to let go of the most important thing in his life. And by so doing, He presents Abraham with an impossible choice. Do I follow God's command to sacrifice my only son (a command that seems contrary to every other thing I know about Him), or do I take matters into my own hands and try to solve this myself?

> "A religion that does not require the sacrifice of all things, never has power sufficient to produce the faith necessary unto life and salvation; for from the first existence of man, the faith necessary unto the enjoyment of life and salvation never could be obtained without the sacrifice of all earthly things.
> —Lectures on Faith[6]

Abraham, of course, had a record of how Adam and Eve took matters into their own hands and chose to disobey one of the commandments in order to keep the other. Abraham could have done the same thing, but instead he chose to obey without question. That is why he is called the father of the faithful. And at the last moment (perhaps past when Abraham had given up hope), there was a ram in the thicket and an angel at his elbow, staying his hand (see Genesis 22:10–13). The impossible had become possible. Abraham had learned what Jesus later taught, that we really only gain our lives when we learn to let them go.

WHAT TO DO WHEN YOU ARE FACED WITH AN IMPOSSIBLE CHOICE

At some point, many of us will face situations where it seems impossible for us to do what God wants with an honest heart, because what God is requiring seems unlike what we understand God to be. What we do in those moments may affect not only our futures, but also the destinies of future generations.

Michael McLean, a well-known composer and singer of LDS-themed music, understands what it means to hit the wall of conflicting commandments. He described a crisis of faith that he experienced when his son came out as gay—after years of struggling to reconcile himself with the Church's teachings on homosexuality. McLean felt that the policies of the Church regarding homosexuality were forcing him to choose between his loyalty to the Church and support of his son. It seemed like an impossible choice.

He said, "I'm singing to everyone, you're not alone." Then he describes the agony and loneliness that his son suffered, "He was hoping that if he was good enough, prayed hard enough, served faithfully as a missionary, and kept the commandments that he'd somehow experience a miracle and become straight. . . . It's tough enough to be a gay kid in a straight world, but being the son of the songwriting icon of the Mormon Church was impossible for him. The pain was so deep that he'd considered suicide."[7]

Tested to the limit by this situation, McLean needed answers in order to make the right choice, but he could not find peace. "I felt alone," he recalls. "I couldn't feel anything. I couldn't get the spirit. I felt just like these two things, they were so far apart. How could I reconcile the feelings I had for my son and wanting to support him and wanting to be a faithful member of the Church and the policy that I couldn't feel good about."[8]

For nine long years, McLean says, he hovered between what he considered to be his only two choices: either separate himself from the Church or stay. Either choice felt like a betrayal. And, no matter how hard he prayed, he felt nothing; no answer from God seemed forthcoming.

> A man that advances in spiritual and in temporal matters at the same time, minding to keep the spiritual first, will not let the temporal lead him; he will not place his heart upon his farm, his horses, or any possession that he has. He will place his desires in heaven, and will anchor his hope in that eternal soil; and his temporal affairs will come up as he advances in the knowledge of God.
> —Jedediah M. Grant[q]

Then, he read a biography of Mother Teresa, the Catholic nun renowned for her service to the poor and dying. To his surprise, he learned that for forty-nine years, Mother Teresa struggled with a crisis of faith about her church; she disagreed with certain policies that she felt were not in sync with Jesus's teachings. No matter how hard she prayed, she could not receive an answer. So she took *that* as the answer, and just kept on in faithfulness, without giving up her sense that something was amiss in the policy, or without giving up her faithful service to the church.[10] One night, McLean had a dream about Mother Teresa, in which he accompanied her on the piano as she sang the following lyrics:

> I choose to pray to one who doesn't hear me
> I choose to wait for love that He conceals
> And though God's chosen now not to be near me
> I'm keeping promises my heart no longer feels[11]

Suddenly, McLean felt that a third choice was available to him: to go on in faithful loyalty to a church that, for the present anyway, had policies that were in conflict with his heart. He chose to "keep promises my heart no longer feels." He realized that he did not have to make the choice whether to leave or to stay *right now*. He could wait on the Lord.

McLean reports that nine years after he had made that decision, he received an outpouring of inspiration that resulted in several songs, all centering on people who had felt abandoned by God, yet went on in faith. His own experience with a seemingly impossible choice filled him with compassion for those who struggle like he did, and he now devotes himself to reaching out to them through his music.[12]

Joseph Smith once said, "'It is quite as necessary for you to be tried as it was for Abraham and other men of God. . . . God will feel after you, and He will take hold of you and wrench your very heart strings, and if you cannot stand it you will not be fit for an inheritance in the Celestial Kingdom of God.'"[13]

When we feel backed into a corner spiritually, or feel that we must make a dramatic choice about our loyalty right this minute, it might be worthwhile to remember that even when it seems that there is no other way, there might be. Wait on the Lord. Keep every commandment that you can keep, but don't feel that you must deny your true feelings. If there is something that bothers you in the policies of the Church, continue to prayerfully think about it and be open to the Spirit. Think about how many people prayed for a change in the policy of the Church regarding people of color. Their prayers were answered in the affirmative, but what good would it have done if they were gone when the change came? Others have prayed for policy changes that have not occurred. In either case, our loyalty to our covenants can help us weather the storm. Abraham is the father of the faithful because he went forward in faith, not because he stopped and decided to take over for God. And we are Abraham's children. There will be a ram in the thicket and an angel at our elbow. God will not fail us; we can trust Him.

Abraham's test was beyond our capacity to understand, but the joy he experienced was commensurate with his pain. Neal Maxwell said:

> If you were to collect the agony for your own sins and I for mine, and multiply it by that number, we can only shudder at what the sensitive, divine soul of Jesus must have experienced in taking upon himself the awful arithmetic of the sins of all of us—an act which he did selflessly and voluntarily. If it is also true (in some way we don't understand) that the cavity which suffering carves into our souls will one day also be the receptacle of joy, how infinitely greater Jesus' capacity for joy, when he said, after his resurrection, "Behold, my joy is full." How very, very full, indeed, his joy must have been![14]

Carol Lynn Pearson's poem compares Abraham's test to the labor of birth. Any mother can tell you that the joy of birth is worth the pain, and, in fact, the pain is the source of joy.

> Ask the
> Almost-mother,
> Her body heaving and torn—
>
> Only from
> Exquisite pain
> Is beauty born.[15]

Isaac and Rebekah: A Celestial Rom-Com

<small>GENESIS 24</small>

What would you guess is the longest chapter in Genesis? It might surprise you to know that the longest chapter in Genesis (sixty-seven verses) is the story of Isaac and Rebekah. It's very interesting that they not only take the time to slow down and tell this romantic love story in great detail, but they tell it three times! As often happens in the Old Testament, things are repeated three times—just in case you didn't get it the first or the second time.

After Abraham has been commanded to sacrifice Isaac and they go up on Mount Moriah, Abraham reaches a turning point in his life. After that, he basically comes back and prepares for his death. In the next three chapters (see Genesis 23–25), he gets his assets in order, buries Sarah (see Genesis 23), and the most important thing he does is arrange to get Isaac married. Isaac is forty (see Genesis 25:20), and the heir, as Ishmael has been sent away. You can imagine that he was doted on so much that nobody noticed that he got to be forty and wasn't married and out on his own! This is very common today; I think this is something many of us can relate to with these young people living in our basements and garages.

GOD AS MATCHMAKER

Abraham was old, and well stricken in age: and the Lord had blessed Abraham in all things.

And Abraham said unto his eldest servant of his house, that ruled over all that he had, Put, I pray thee, thy hand under my thigh. (Genesis 24:1–2)

This is a euphemism, of course, for what my Bible as Literature professor modestly called the "organ of generation." Another translation of this line (from the VOICE translation of the Bible) reads, "The *trusted* servant took the oath, holding in his hand Abraham's power to give life" (Genesis 24:9). This is important. Abraham is requiring that his servant swear by the very seed that is the source of God's promises. The Hebrews were not shy about procreation. This way of making an oath or a covenant gave special emphasis to the importance of the seed. It must not be polluted by intermarriage with nonbelievers. What is the promise to Abraham? It's endless posterity.

> I will make thee swear by the Lord, the God of heaven, and the God of the earth, that thou shalt not take a wife unto my son of the daughters of the Canaanites, among whom I dwell:
> But thou shalt go unto my country, and to my kindred, and take a wife unto my son Isaac. (Genesis 24:3–4)

Isaac is not even going to be a part of it. The servant thinks that maybe Isaac should come along, (see Genesis 24:5), but Abraham intends to find the bride without even involving the groom!

MARRIAGES MADE IN HEAVEN

This business about how important it is whom we marry, and that God is willing to get involved in the process, is attested in the very first book of the Bible over and over. The first marriage orchestrated by God is between Adam and Eve. Then we've got Abraham and Sarah. Then we've got Rebekah and Isaac. Many of the great love stories in the Bible come in that first book. The family is the foundation of the civilization, and God intends to get these families right.

A popular Bible website says this, "It becomes obvious from the outset of this story that God is the real matchmaker in the marriage. . . . The servant . . . , her brother and her father agreed. 'The matter comes from the Lord.' . . . No matter what kinds of problems a marriage may encounter, they will be easier to solve if both husband and wife have a settled assurance that God has brought them together."[16]

THE WOMAN AT THE WELL

We may not really appreciate wells, but that is because we get our water easily from faucets. The well was the source of life in biblical times, and was visited several times a day. And the arduous task of drawing and carrying the water was a woman's job. The woman at the well becomes a pervasive type scene in the scriptures. And the motif closes out beautifully when Jesus sits down at the same well where Jacob and Rachel met, centuries later, and explains to the Samaritan woman that he is, in fact the source of living water (see John 4:6–14). He is what the well had been symbolizing throughout the centuries.

The servant took the ten camels to the well at the same time that the women went to draw water. He prays:

> . . . O Lord God of my master Abraham, I pray thee, send me good speed this day, and shew kindness unto my master Abraham.
>
> Behold, I stand here by the well of water; and the daughters of the men of the city come out to draw water:
>
> And let it come to pass that the damsel to whom I shall say, Let down thy pitcher, I pray thee, that I may drink; and she shall say, Drink, and I will give thy camels drink also: let the same be she that thou hast appointed for thy servant Isaac; and thereby shall I know that thou hast shewed kindness unto my master. (Genesis 24:12–14)

Well, of course, out comes Rebekah, and we get a glimpse into her character right from the start. She runs, she hastens, she is not afraid to speak to strangers, and she very quickly lets Abraham's servant know that her family is well-to-do and can provide for him and his caravan. She is very proactive. "She said moreover unto him, We have both straw and provender enough, and room to lodge in" (Genesis 24:25). Rebekah is not a girl who will be sitting at home, waiting for the phone to ring. She makes things happen. By contrast, Isaac, you'll recall, is passive. He is absent for this scene. He's forty years old, and he is allowing the servant to do his courting for him! Isaac and Rebekah are two very different people.

Right away, Rachel lets Abraham's servant know who she is, and he realizes that she is his master's grandniece.

> And the man bowed down his head, and worshipped the Lord.
> And he said, Blessed be the Lord God of my master Abraham, who hath not left destitute my master of his mercy and his truth: I being in the way, the Lord led me to the house of my master's brethren. (Genesis 24:26–27)

After some debate with Rebekah's brother, Laban, Rebekah went with Abraham's servant (see Genesis 24:29–51). And not long after, she and Isaac are married (see Genesis 24:67).

"I BEING IN THE WAY": GOD AS YOUR MATCHMAKER

If you are looking for a marriage partner, Genesis 24 has a great deal to teach you. We can ask for God's guidance, but we can't get His help without "being in the way." This means that you have to look, act, and make decisions like a person who wants to attract the opposite sex. You need to go places where appropriate potential spouses might be. You need to amass enough wealth to buy a ring or contribute to the household. Asking God for a miracle is important, but you, by "being in the way," will be led by God. If you are not "in the way," He can't do it all. Your willingness to sacrifice will open doors to you, through which, at some point, the hero or heroine of your story will walk.

TOOLBOX: COMEDY AND TRAGEDY

There are two classic forms of drama: comedy and tragedy. If you study classical drama, you might have been surprised to learn that comedies are not necessarily funny, and tragedies are not necessarily serious all the time. The definition of a comedy is that it ends with a happy ending, usually with a wedding. If the play ends in a wedding, it's a comedy. If it ends with everyone dying, it's a tragedy. When you look at Shakespeare, *Othello* is a tragedy because at the end, he kills his wife (Desdemona)—along with everyone else that he can get his hands on— and then he kills himself. In contrast, *Much Ado About Nothing* is a light and funny story. But if you think about it, it has a more serious underlying story; the Duke wants to kill his fiancée because he thinks she's been unfaithful. She avoids Desdemona's fate by faking her own death. But, it ends in a wedding, and they all live happily ever after, so it's a comedy. One is a comedy and one is a tragedy.

Modern drama is a bit more complex, and is more interested in displaying the messiness of life. It's also what the Hebrews are doing in the Old Testament, which is what makes the text feel almost modern. Genesis 24 is a classic romantic comedy: we're excited to see what will happen between Rebekah and Isaac, I think that's one of the reasons we love it so much. It ends in a very romantic wedding scene, and is one of the few places in the Bible where it says the groom actually loves the bride!

Jacob and Esau: Forgiveness 101

GENESIS 27–33

One of the great themes in Genesis is forgiveness and reconciliation. Adam and Eve find out that as soon as they leave the garden opposition enters the world in a variety of forms, including noxious weeds, menstrual periods, and disputations about how to follow the rules. Irritation may be the most pernicious form of opposition. I'm sure that they also discovered that as children arrived, the tension grew. My husband used to remind our teenage boys every time they went out in the car, "Remember to be patient, because basically everybody is mad." Given the nature of the world we live in, it's safe to say that, at any given moment, each of us is battling some kind of nagging irritation, and it may not take much to push one or two of us over the edge.

All of this has to do with the willingness to forgive and be reconciled with those whom we love on a daily basis. When this does not happen, resentments accumulate and trouble ensues. Cain (obviously nursing a bushel of grudges) was pushed over the edge by the one final thing that offended his pride, and ended up committing the first murder.

It is a sad irony that the first murder is committed over a disagreement about the proper way to offer sacrifice to God. Cain's jealousy over God's preference for Abel's offering is a foreshadowing of endless debates about how to properly worship God; these debates have been the cause of so much strife and bloodshed. Divisions in religious observance are still used as an excuse for terror and violence throughout our troubled world. But Adam and Eve model a different approach: after receiving forgiveness from God, they are born again and live lives of righteousness. Their example was the one to follow.

If Cain had simply forgiven Abel, or at least agreed to disagree, how would the history of the earth be different? This conflict, regarding forgiveness and reconciliation, goes on as we enter the story of Jacob and Esau—our next example of brothers that rival for

God's favor. Again, history will be shaped by a family feud. Jacob is deceitful and has his mother's support. Esau is careless and does not appreciate his birthright. Rather than learn to exist in harmony, they push matters until a rift occurs that lasts twenty years and changes their lives forever.

WHERE AM I IN THIS STORY?

These two stories challenge us to examine our own behavior. Are our family relationships enriching, or ruining our lives? How many of us have hesitated to attend a family event because we will meet someone there that we are having a disagreement with? How many of us have harbored grudges for years? Jacob had to live far from his home because of his actions and the anger those actions caused in his family. How often, like Jacob, do we exile ourselves from the garden of familial love because we can't get along with the other people who live there?

HOW DO WE GET BACK TO THE GARDEN?

Given the fact that familial disharmony causes much of the trouble on earth, we ought to think a little more about how to get over the hurt and anger that drive us away from those we love. Genesis has a lot to teach us on this subject, and it begins with an unlikely hero: Esau. Esau's remarkable response to Jacob's return

> We are not enemies, but friends. We must not be enemies. Though passion may have strained it must not break our bonds of affection. The mystic chords of memory, stretching from every battlefield and patriot grave to every living heart and hearthstone all over this broad land, will yet swell the chorus of the Union, when again touched, as surely they will be, by the better angels of our nature.
>
> –Abraham Lincoln[17]

after twenty years signals an amazing turn in the narrative of Genesis. Esau was robbed of his birthright and the blessing that went with it (see Genesis 25:30–34). His own mother actually plotted against him (see Genesis 27:5–17). We don't know much about Esau's life during the next twenty years, but we do know that Jacob got a little of his own medicine back. In his marriage arrangement, Jacob is deceived by his new family as thoroughly as he once deceived his father (see Genesis 29:18–25), and he lives with a father-in-law who tries to exploit him as much as he wished to exploit his brother (see Genesis 30:25–36).

Jacob's journey toward reconciliation with Esau took twenty years—years during which he hopefully learned some important lessons. The man he became, returning to his homeland with his wives and children, still retains elements of his former self. Looking out for number one, he sends his wives and kids ahead of himself as human shields, putting the least favorite in front, and keeping Rachel and Joseph close (see Genesis 33:1–2). But, Jacob is also sincerely penitent. He is a flawed hero, but his heart is in the right place.

As the dreaded moment of meeting his brother arrives, Jacob extends the honor that is traditionally offered by a vassal to the *suzerain*, or lord, and bows to the earth seven times before Esau (see Genesis 33:3). It is clear that Esau has also grown more world-wise because he's flanked by four hundred men when he comes to meet his brother. But he shows no desire to punish Jacob (see Genesis 33:1). Instead, he runs to meet him and embraces him, and is gracious to Jacob's wives and children (see Genesis 33:4–7). His behavior and comments offer us a few hints into the mysterious process of forgiveness. In the New International Version of the Bible, it says,

> But Esau ran to meet Jacob and embraced him; he threw his arms around his neck and kissed him. And they wept.
>
> Esau asked, "What's the meaning of all these flocks and herds I met?"
>
> "To find favor in your eyes, my lord," he said.
>
> But Esau said, "I already have plenty, my brother. Keep what you have for yourself."

"No, please!" said Jacob. "If I have found favor in your eyes, accept this gift from me. For to see your face is like seeing the face of God, now that you have received me favorably. Please accept the present that was brought to you, for God has been gracious to me and I have all I need." And because Jacob insisted, Esau accepted it.

Then Esau said, "Let us be on our way; I'll accompany you." (NIV Exodus 33:4, 8–12)

FOUR STEPS TO FORGIVENESS

As a child, I was taught the four steps of prayer along with the four steps of repentance, and I repeated those teachings as a missionary and Church instructor. It is comforting to have some steps to follow when facing a large, abstract principle, isn't it? I've noticed, however, that nobody has offered a formula for forgiveness. When I am offended or hurt, I know I must forgive, because the scriptures make it clear that forgiving others of their trespasses is essential to being forgiven by God for my own trespasses. But how do I go about turning my angry, defiant heart into a forgiving, merciful one? I need some steps to follow! So, with the help of some of the great characters in the scriptures, here's my formula for forgiveness.

Step #1: Stop Adding Up the Offenses

Most offenses don't come on their own, they come in bunches; it is tempting to continually add them up, mull over them, and repeat them to any sympathetic friend who will listen. When you are cheated by that unscrupulous person who attends the same Church that you do, lives next door, or is a member of your family, you may have trouble letting it go. It's easier to go over and over the wrongs that have been done. Esau teaches a great lesson when he is reunited with Jacob; he chooses not to discuss the individual offenses that

> " True forgiveness is not an action after the fact, it is an attitude with which you enter each moment.
> –David Ridge[18]

Jacob had committed. Instead, he firmly places the past in the past, and focuses on the present—extending courtesy to Jacob's family and just moving forward.

Step #2: Count Your Blessings—You Have Enough

No one person or event can take away all of our blessings, even if feels like your offender has done so. Job came close to losing everything, but he was still breathing, and so he used that blessing as a starting point to build a new life (see Job 27:3; 33:4). Esau neither bemoans his many losses at Jacob's hands, nor does he downplay his current abundance. He simply says, "I have enough, my brother; keep that thou hast unto thyself" (Genesis 33:9, KJV).

In the parable of the prodigal son, the father is dismayed that his faithful son is so angry with his brother. He says, "All that I have is thine" (Luke 15: 31). But that is not enough for the brother; he is angry that his wasteful brother is welcomed home with feasting and joy. The inability to forgive poisons our ability to enjoy that which we have.

Step #3: Realize That It Isn't All About You

As He writhed in agony on the cross, Jesus said of those who drove the nails into his hands and wrists, "Father, forgive them; for they know not what they do" (Luke 23:34).

Esau was a clueless youth who didn't know what he was doing; he gave away his birthright for a mess of pottage (see Genesis 25:29–34) Jacob was a young, ambitious fellow who thought the ends justified any means. He really didn't know what he was doing either. Over the years, both men were seasoned and tested by time. Though we do not share in Esau's story, the fact that he comes in a condition of obvious affluence, attended by hundreds of men, shows that there was

> Forgiveness is freeing up, and putting to better use the energy once consumed by holding grudges, harboring resentments, and nursing unhealed wounds. It is rediscovering the strengths we always had and relocating our limitless capacity to understand and accept other people and ourselves.
>
> –Dr. Sidney Simon[19]

more substance to him than we see in the early scenes. It's unlikely that either man understood the seriousness of what they did when they were young. This is true of many offenses; they are committed more in ignorance than in malice. Rather than see every offense as pointed directly at us it helps to recognize that there is usually an element of ignorance in hurtful actions, and we should make allowance for it. As Hamlet said to his friend Laertes,

> Let my disclaiming from a purposed evil
> Free me so far in your most generous thoughts,
> That I have shot mine arrow o'er the house,
> And hurt my brother.[20]

Step #4: Know That Forgiveness Is a Gift from God

The power to forgive has two halves: it requires an act of will on our part and an outpouring of grace on God's part. Both parts are essential. In a moving scene (that will later be repeated in Jesus's parable of the prodigal son) Esau runs to meet and embrace his brother. As he does so, grace pours out on them both. Jacob, who has wrestled through the night in search of God's blessing, finds that blessing here in the frank forgiveness of his elder brother (see

> "The Savior desires to save us from our inadequacies as well as from our sins. Inadequacy is not the same as sinfulness—we have far more control over the choice to sin than we may have over our innate capacity. The Lord will not save us *in* our sins, but *from* them. However, he can save us *in* our inadequacies as well as *from* them. A sense of falling short or falling down is not only natural, but essential to the mortal experience. But, after all we can do, the Atonement can fill that which is empty, straighten our bent parts, and make strong that which is weak.
>
> —Bruce R. Hafen[21]

Genesis 32–33). Jacob marvels at the mercy extended to him, as he had marveled the night before at meeting God face-to-face (see Genesis 32:30). He connects the two experiences thus: "For to see your face is like seeing the face of God, now that you have received me favorably" (NIV Genesis 33:10).

Forgiveness is a miracle, and God is the only source of miracles. Without divine help, we can no more forgive the sins of others than we can forgive our own sins. We can only step forward and begin the process of forgiveness by opening our hearts and minds to a forgiving attitude, and then asking for God's grace to provide the miracle. When we do this, we will find that to forgive is to enter into the presence of God. To fail to forgive is to forever shut ourselves out of that presence. M. Catherine Thomas observes: "Forgiveness is primarily an issue of Presence, because with forgiveness comes the restoration of the Presence of God."[22] Forgiveness is the only way back to the garden.

TOOLBOX: RESONANCE AND ALLUSION

In order to add emotional strength and meaning, biblical stories often feature a deliberate use of language that reminds us of another story or passage. This is known as resonance or allusion. Resonance and allusion are similar activities, and are far more subtle than just quoting an older text. When skillfully deployed, they cause the listener to stretch a little; they usually evoke an emotional reaction.

An example of resonance occurs in the description of Esau's reconciliation with Jacob. The scripture reads: "But Esau ran to meet him, and embraced him, and fell on his neck, and kissed him: and they wept" (Genesis 33:4, KJV).

Jesus's followers would have known this passage from the Torah, and when Jesus relates the story of the prodigal son, he references it deliberately: "But when he was yet a great way off, his father saw him, and had compassion, and ran, and fell on his neck, and kissed him" (Luke 15:20).

As Amy-Jill Levine says in her book, *Short Stories by Jesus*, many of Jesus's parables have connections to older, familiar Jewish stories that would have resonated with His listeners in a way that is hard for us to understand in our time, without a careful study of their context. Getting a sense of this resonance is important:

"If we stop with the easy lessons, good though they may be, we lose the way Jesus's first followers would have heard the parables, and we lose the genius of Jesus's teaching."[23]

NOTES

1. *Teachings of the Prophet Joseph Smith,* sel. Joseph Fielding Smith (Salt Lake City: Deseret Book, 1976), 51.

2. Edward L. Kimball, *Lengthen Your Stride: The Presidency of Spencer W. Kimball* (Salt Lake City: Deseret Book, 2005).

3. Spencer W. Kimball, "'When the World Will Be Converted," *Ensign,* October 1974.

4. Ibid.

5. C. S. Lewis, *Mere Christianity* (New York: HarperCollins, 1972), 205.

6. *Lectures on Faith,* 6:7, lecturesonfaith.com/6/.

7. Jamie Armstrong, "Michael McLean Opens Up About His 9-Year Faith Crisis and How He Found His Testimony Again," *LDSLiving,* accessed August 24, 2017, www.ldsliving.com/Michael-McLean -Opens-Up-About-His-9-Year-Faith-Crisis-and-How-He-Found -His-Testimony-Again/s/83606.

8. Ibid.

9. Jedediah M. Grant, in Journal of Discourses, 4:152.

10. See Brian Kolodiejchuk, ed., *Mother Teresa: Come Be My Light; The Private Writings of the "Saint of Calcutta"* (New York: Doubleday, 2007).

11. Armstrong, "Michael McLean Opens Up About His 9-Year Faith Crisis and How He Found His Testimony Again," www.ldsliving .com/Michael-McLean-Opens-Up-About-His-9-Year-Faith-Crisis -and-How-He-Found-His-Testimony-Again/s/83606.

12. Ibid.

13. *Teachings of Presidents of the Church: Joseph Smith* (2011), 231.

14. Neal A. Maxwell, "But for a Small Moment" (Brigham Young University devotional, September 1, 1974), speeches.byu.edu/talks /neal-a-maxwell_small-moment/.

15. Carol L. Pearson, in Melannie Svoboda, *In Steadfast Love: Letters on the Spiritual Life* (New London, CT: Twenty-Third Publications, 2007), 64.

16. "3. Talk to Me—The Story of Isaac and Rebekah," *Bible.org,* accessed September 19, 2017, /bible.org/seriespage/3-talk-me-story-isaac-and -rebekah.

17. Abraham Lincoln, First Inaugural Address, March 4, 1861.

18. David Ridge in, Glenn Smith, Jr., *The Key of Forgiveness: Unlocking the Door for a More Powerful Christian Walk* (Central Point, OR: Eagle's Wings Publishing, 2008), 75.

19. Dr. Sidney B. Simon and Suzanne Simon, Forgiveness: How to Make Peace with Your Past and Get on With Your Life (New York: Grand Central Publishing, 1990).

20. William Shakespeare, *Hamlet*, ed. C. W. Crook (London: Ralph, Holland & Co., 1908), 5.2.223–26. References are to act, scene, and line.

21. Bruce C. Hafen, "Beauty for Ashes: The Atonement of Jesus Christ," *Ensign*, (April 1980), italics in original.

22. M. Catherine Thomas, *Light in the Wilderness—Explorations in the Spiritual Life* (Salt Lake City: Digital Legend, 2010), 4.

23. Amy-Jill Levine, *Short Stories by Jesus: The Enigmatic Parables of a Controversial Rabbi* (New York: HarperCollins, 2014).

Personal Notes

_____

_____

_____

_____

_____

_____

_____

_____

_____

_____

_____

_____

_____

_____

_____

_____

_____

_____

The User-Friendly Old Testament

_____

_____

_____

_____

_____

_____

_____

_____

_____

_____

_____

_____

_____

_____

_____

_____

_____

_____

_____

_____

_____

_____

_____

_____

Chapter Three

JOSEPH: THE FIRST ACTION HERO

The Journey of the Hero

GENESIS 37–50

In his landmark work *The Hero With a Thousand Faces*, Joseph Campbell lays out an archetypal pattern that is followed by heroic figures in literature and oral legend. Some of the key milestones in the Hero's Journey are these:

1. Leaves the comfort of home
2. First resists, then accepts a divine call
3. Meets mentors and/or divine helpers
4. Is branded, marked, and/or receives a new name
5. Faces adventures and challenges
6. Endures an ultimate ordeal
7. Experiences a reward, and journeys home[1]

Joseph of Egypt is a great example of this literary trope, and he brings to the adventure two qualities that are particularly striking, and that help us identify him as a type of Christ. This transforms Joseph's story from a simple morality tale into a true Christian allegory.

First, Joseph's integrity is a key device in his story. Again and again, when Joseph is tested, he does not complain or grow bitter. He simply steps up and does the best he can, even though his best efforts often fail. He responds to each challenge by being true to his own values, regardless of the consequences. His experience in the prison is particularly heartrending. The narrator gets our hopes up by having Joseph correctly interpret the dreams of the butler and the baker, only to be crushed when he is forgotten by those ungrateful servants, and left to languish in the prison (see Genesis 40). We are invited into several scenarios where Joseph could have chosen to be selfish or sinful, for who would know what occurs in a dirty jail cell or in the private confines of Potiphar's wife's chamber? (see Genesis 39:7–21) But, no matter the circumstance, Joseph is true to his family, his employers, and his covenants. We cannot read this story without asking ourselves what we would do in the same circumstance.

> The quality of leader is reflected in the standards they set for themselves.
>
> —Ray Kroc[2]

Second, Joseph has a unique spiritual gift—kind of like a super-power in an action movie—he can interpret dreams. He uses this gift unselfishly and courageously, and it is the key to his success. His story challenges us to examine our own spiritual gifts—the tools that are available to us on our quest—and to take steps to develop them. Joseph's story reminds us that identifying and using our spiritual gifts will add crucial power to our lives when it is needed.

TEENAGERS AND THE HERO'S JOURNEY

Now, putting ourselves in the story of Joseph, let's think of the elements that can apply in a modern setting. Heading out of our respective comfort zones into the larger world happens for most of us during our teenage years. During that time, we often have the heady feeling that we are actually alone, and that no one will know if we make some bad decisions. Joseph's story is a good reminder that there are no real secrets in life.

> What I think is that a good life is one hero journey after another. Over and over again, you are called to the realm of adventure, you are called to new horizons. Each time, there is the same problem: do I dare? And then if you do dare, the dangers are there, and the help also, and the fulfillment or the fiasco. There's always the possibility of fiasco. But there's also the possibility of bliss.
>
> —Joseph Campbell[3]

A crucial stage in the teenage years is the development of integrity. The degree to which a young person embraces integrity will determine, to a large extent, the spiritual success of their life. Joseph's integrity is highlighted for us by a chapter that is placed right in middle of this narrative: Genesis 38. This chapter does not contain a story about Joseph; instead, it tells a story about his older brother, Judah—the rightful heir (see Genesis 49:8–10). Judah's son had died, but his daughter-in-law Tamar—who should have been married to the next son in order to preserve the inheritance—is cast aside (see Genesis 49:7–11). After years of neglect, she decides to take action. She dresses as a harlot and places herself in Judah's path as he travels on family business. Judah—in stark contrast to the reaction of Joseph to Potiphar's wife—has relations with Tamar and leaves her a token of payment (see Genesis 49:14–18). When she conceives, she produces the token and Judah is shamed into admitting both his sin and his mistreatment of her (see Genesis 49:26). The story of Judah and his unfortunate daughter-in-law Tamar offers a prime example of someone who thinks they can get away with something that no one else sees. The account of Judah's weakness when tested serves to highlight Joseph's integrity.

Though Joseph is a strong person, he would not have been successful without the use of his unique spiritual gifts. Each of us has unique gifts that we can use to make the world a better place. Have we identified those gifts, and are we developing them? In addition to his ability to interpret dreams, Joseph is a natural leader with great managerial skills that he puts to good use. Joseph's proactive approach to life is so inspiring; no matter where he lands, he buckles down and does his best. Then pretty soon, he is running the place—whether it is Potiphar's house or the prison or the kingdom of Egypt. Do we play the role of the victim or the hero in our life story?

WHAT ARE YOUR SUPERPOWERS?

Your spiritual gifts are your superpowers. They give you the ability to be effective in certain situations where others might fail. Now you might think that you don't have any spiritual gifts, but that is because you may be placing too narrow of a definition on the term. Marvin J. Ashton reminds us that many spiritual gifts are not flashy, or readily evident, but can be used effectively to bless others:

> Let us review some of these less-conspicuous gifts: the gift of asking; the gift of listening; the gift of hearing and using a still, small voice; the gift of being able to weep; the gift of avoiding contention; the gift of being agreeable; the gift of avoiding vain repetition; the gift of seeking that which is righteous; the gift of not passing judgment; the gift of looking to God for guidance; the gift of being a disciple; the gift of caring for others; the gift of being able to ponder; the gift of offering prayer; the gift of bearing a mighty testimony; and the gift of receiving the Holy Ghost.[4]

FORGIVENESS AND RECONCILIATION

Certainly one of the greatest spiritual gifts is the gift to be able to forgive; this is a gift that Joseph cultivates during the years when life deals him one blow after another. Regarding the gift of forgiveness, David Sorenson said:

It can feel as if the pain or the injustice is the most important thing in the world and that we have no choice but to seek vengeance. But Christ, the Prince of Peace, teaches us a better way. It can be very difficult to forgive someone the harm they've done us, but when we do, we open ourselves up to a better future. No longer does someone else's wrongdoing control our course. When we forgive others, it frees us to choose how we will live our own lives. Forgiveness means that problems of the past no longer dictate our future destinies and we can focus on the future with God's love in our hearts.[5]

When Joseph is reconciled with his brothers, he models several behaviors that are worth considering. Though he forgives them, he still protects himself from further harm at their hands. Wisely, he does not trust them completely; they haven't earned his trust. But there is no bitterness in his heart. Though his brothers tried to kill him, he chooses to take the view that God used the whole experience in order to bring about His will. In the book *The Four Agreements*, we are told: "Whatever happens around you, don't take it personally. . . . Nothing other people do is because of you. It is because of themselves."[6]

Joseph manages to see past the evil intentions of his brothers and focus instead on the many ways that God has blessed all of them through their trials. This attitude marks him as a type of Christ, and one of the truly heroic prophets in the Old Testament. I consider the scene where he has to leave the room to weep after hearing his brothers discuss his kidnapping and their father's grief to be one of the greatest moments in scripture (see Genesis 44:20–34). His cry, "I am Joseph; doth my father yet live?" goes right to my heart (Genesis 45:3). If we have ever been a part of a serious division in our own families, these words call us to repentance. No matter what happens, and no matter who started the conflict, families must learn to forgive and forget. Joseph shows us that the hero's journey must begin and end with the united family.

HOW THE CHURCH CAN HELP YOU
DISCOVER YOUR INNER HERO

Service in the Church can help you find your inner hero because it asks you to leave your comfort zone and do things you're afraid of; it causes you to be spiritually, physically, and mentally stretched. All of the elements of the hero's journey come into play when we accept callings: we have mentors, we seek and receive divine help, and we enter into unknown territory. We face terrifying adventures (like teaching seminary) and exhausting challenges (like working in the nursery). Our endurance may be pushed to the limit (years of Girls' Camp or scout outings), and we may feel overwhelmed. But for every hero, there awaits, in the end, a reward and a journey home.

The Church, like the family, is a community that gives us the chance to become the hero of our own lives, rather than just a person tossed along by events. Church service gives us an opportunity to be part of something that is bigger than ourselves, a community in which we can practice the virtues that we preach. That is the heroic approach to life, and it's a beautiful way to live. So when you're asked to do something that you're afraid of, that dismays you, or that just doesn't seem sensible, think about it in the framework of the hero's journey.

SOMETIMES THE JOURNEY
STARTS EARLY IN THE MORNING

When we had three small children and I was just a few weeks pregnant with the fourth one, our bishop called me to be an early-morning seminary teacher. He explained that we had no one from our ward enrolled in seminary, and he needed a strong teacher to get a program going. I couldn't believe he asked me! My husband traveled a lot, and I had such small children; it just seemed crazy. I kept thinking, *I just ought to say no.* But instead, I said "yes." I taught for six months—until complications with my pregnancy forced me to stop. I was blessed to teach the New Testament for those six months, and I had many sweet moments with those kids.

Still, it was a hard time, and I was exhausted. Most nights, I was up several times with the little ones, and then had to pull myself out of bed at 4:45 a.m. to be ready to teach at 6:00 a.m. As a consequence, I was so worn out by the time I had my daughter Andrea that I couldn't heal very well, and I had health problems for about a year after her birth. For many years, I wondered if I had made a mistake in accepting that call. One day, when Andrea was a grown woman with a baby of her own, we were having a conversation about that time. I said, "You know, that's an example of how, in the Church, we should know when to say 'no.' I should've said 'no' that time. I shouldn't have accepted that calling. I should've safeguarded my health because I was a mother and I had small children, and that should have come first."

Andrea's reply surprised me. She said, "Mom, I think you are wrong! I think you did the right thing when you accepted that call. I'm so glad that while you were carrying me, you were teaching about the Savior every morning. And I'm glad to have a mother who made that sacrifice because when I have to do hard things, I think about that." I didn't know at the time that the decision that I had made would impact the child I was carrying in such a positive way. We want to teach our children to live with vision, not just to take the easy road; we want them to walk the hero's journey. Perhaps the best way to do that is to try to walk it ourselves, even though, at the time, it may not seem like it makes much sense.

The gospel gives us a vision that we can be more than just people who are mired in the details of daily life. We are taught that we actually can have relationships that take hold of eternity, and that our lives can have an impact for good in the world. That's the dream the gospel gives us, and that's the dream that Joseph exemplifies.

TOOLBOX: NARRATIVE STRUCTURE

The story of Joseph is actually a small novel, or novella. Beginning to end, it offers suspense and surprises. The characters come to life through their private conversations. The resolution of the drama is beautifully crafted and deeply moving. This is no accident; it is structured with intention and inspiration in a series of dreams, descents, and ascents that are quite breathtaking. The story affects us like it does not just because of the events it describes, but because of its narrative structure.

The narrative structure of a work can be described in two parts: the story itself (for example, whether the story is a comedy or a tragedy), and the form, or the way the author chooses to present the story. Most of us realize that the Bible stories are not told in a strictly linear fashion. The author may cover several generations in one verse, and then take, for example, sixty-seven verses to tell the story of the courtship-by-proxy of Isaac and Rebekah. These choices add up to a narrative structure.

The great literary critic Northrop Frye described the entire Bible as a "divine comedy."[7] That is, the story begins at a good stage, followed by a decline and descent into various forms of danger and disaster, and ends happily. This happens in the book as a whole—beginning in Eden and ending in the heavenly visions found in Revelation. And then, within the narrative, the pattern occurs several times with a repeating theme of the apostasy and restoration of Israel.

"This gives us a narrative structure that is roughly U-shaped," Frye says. "The apostasy being followed by a descent into disaster and bondage, which in turn is followed by repentance, then by a rise through deliverance to a point more or less on the level from which the descent began."[8]

It's quite interesting to look at the various books (and the books within books) of the Bible and trace the narrative structure. We are not just given data; we are being taken on a journey. That is part of the beauty of the Bible as literature.

"And Got Him Out": Potiphar's Wife and Internet Porn

GENESIS 39

And it came to pass after these things, that his master's wife cast her eyes upon Joseph; and she said, Lie with me.

But he refused, and said unto his master's wife, Behold, my master wotteth not what is with me in the house, and he hath committed all that he hath to my hand;

There is none greater in this house than I; neither hath he kept back any thing from me but thee, because thou art his wife: how then can I do this great wickedness, and sin against God?

And it came to pass, as she spake to Joseph day by day, that he hearkened not unto her, to lie by her, or to be with her.

And it came to pass about this time, that Joseph went into the house to do his business; and there was none of the men of the house there within.

And she caught him by his garment, saying, Lie with me: and he left his garment in her hand, and fled, and got him out. (Genesis 39:7–12)

At one point or another, most of us have found ourselves in a situation like Joseph's, where we make crucial choices within the illusion of privacy. I call privacy an illusion because we are never, in fact, alone, but it may seem like we are and that our actions will affect no one but ourselves. In the age of the Internet, the temptation Joseph faced with his master's wife may happen every single night when the lights go out but the phone is still within arm's reach. The easy accessibility of pornographic material may feel like a relentless pursuer to the struggling young man or woman. The staggering statistics can be discouraging: "30% of Internet data is pornography. 136 billion pornographic videos were viewed on smartphones in 2015."[9] Pornography is a $97 billion industry.[10]

Faced with these staggering statistics, we may feel as powerless as Joseph. But Joseph's response has something to teach us about the connection between personal power and private actions.

We are fooling ourselves if we think this is just a male problem. A recent survey reports that more than a third of women watch pornography at least once a week. The research also shows how the digital age has made porn more accessible: 90 percent of the 3,000 female respondents said they watched it online and two-thirds said they watched it on their smartphones.[11]

WHO'S IN CONTROL HERE?

Though Potiphar's wife appeared to be in a position of control over him, Joseph, still had the power to choose. Though given a great deal of responsibility by his master, Joseph had no rights; he was a essentially a slave. Potiphar's wife saw Joseph, wanted him, and began to pursue him relentlessly—"day by day" (Genesis 39:10) There didn't seem to be any way for Joseph to win in that situation; no matter which way he turned, he would end up in trouble. In order to free himself from dishonor, Joseph had to actually go to prison, which is an interesting metaphor. Joseph's actions can help young people combat the plague of pornography that is waging such destruction among both men and women.

There is no doubt that our devices are starting to control us. Studies show that when people are not allowed to constantly check their mobile devices, their anxiety grows. When a device is checked, there is a release of a chemical cocktail—a little surge of satisfaction—that keeps us coming back for more. Dopamine is released when we hit the search button, and an opioid is released when we actually find something we are looking for. A combination of seeking (dopamine) and liking (opioid) chemicals can keep us at the keyboard or locked to our phones for hours. But gradually, the rush of seeking may overwhelm the more subtle satisfaction of finding. The endless scrolling through social media sites and Google searches can become addicting, even if the content is fairly benign. Researcher Susan Weinschenk states:

These two systems, the "wanting" (dopamine) and the "liking" (opioid) are complementary. The wanting system propels you to action and the liking system makes you feel satisfied and therefore pause your seeking. If your seeking isn't turned off at least for a little while, then you start to run in an endless loop. The dopamine system is stronger than the opioid system. You tend to seek more than you are satisfied.[12]

This helps us understand why many of us waste hours scrolling through social media and search engines. But when you add the electric shock of pornography to that gentle seek-and-find stimulus, you have a "killer combination," a powerful stimulant that is instantly renewed with just the click of the mouse. At this point, the user may begin to constantly seek more stimulation—triggering the same neurological results that are found with drug users.

Porn consumption follows a very predictable pattern that's eerily similar to drug use. Over time, excessive levels of "pleasure" chemicals cause the porn consumer's brain to develop tolerance, just like the brain of a drug user. In the same way that a junkie eventually requires more and more of a drug to get a buzz or even feel normal, regular porn consumers will end up turning to porn more often or seeking out more extreme versions—or both—to feel excited again. And once the porn habit is established, quitting can even lead to withdrawal symptoms similar to drugs.[13]

> A sex-saturated society cannot really feel the needs of its suffering members because, instead of developing the love that looks outward, it turns man selfishly inward. Imperviousness to the promptings of the still small voice of God will also mean that we have ears but cannot hear, not only the promptings of God, but also the pleas of men.
>
> —Neal A. Maxwell[14]

JUST GO WITH THE FLOW AND YOU MIGHT DROWN

Scientists use the term "flow" to describe the deep level of concentration that occurs when our brains are fully engaged and a sense of time disappears, such as when we are reading an engrossing novel, watching an exciting movie, or are engaged in a scintillating conversation.[15] These moments have an impact on the brain: deep neural pathways are carved that will enable the brain to easily return to that satisfying environment. In the case of the intense satisfaction that is engendered by pornography, which taps into one of our most basic urges, the constant return to the same stimulation can actually make changes in the brain that are like ruts in the road.[16]

Unfortunately, the change in neural pathways has a trade-off: the focus on intense personal stimulation found in porn erodes the ability to enjoy intimacy with a partner, in both men and women. An epidemic of erectile dysfunction in young males, and a general reduction in the ability to form a lasting, intimate connection with

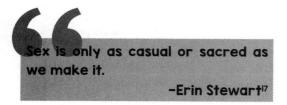

Sex is only as casual or sacred as we make it.

–Erin Stewart[17]

another person are only two of the devastating effects of pornography. Psychologist Jordan Peterson states: "[Internet pornography] is like Treasure Island in Pinocchio. It's all pleasure with no responsibility. That's deadening. It's parasitical in a sense . . . and it taps into one viciously powerful primordial motivation. These [young men] are being blasted by what biologists call "super stimuli" all the time. . . . It's not good. It's an easy out."[18] It keeps men from going out and developing a healthy relationship.[19]

PRIVATE + PROACTIVE CHOICE = POWER

Faced with the scientific research, it is easy to adopt a victim mentality toward Internet pornography; it may seem so powerful that there is no resisting it. But Joseph shows us that there is always a choice. Potiphar's wife seemed to have all the power, but Joseph still had the power to act, and he did. He "got him out" (Genesis 39:15). Today's generation may feel that they are powerless to resist the pull of pornography, but they are not. They can choose to step away; they can even choose to impose

> When faced with a challenge, happy families, like happy people, just add a new chapter to their life story that shows them overcoming the hardship. This skill is particularly important for children, whose identity tends to get locked in during adolescence.
>
> –Bruce Feiler[20]

on themselves a sort of "prison" by moving their mobile devices out of the room at night, or switching them off for periods of time during the day. The private, proactive choice to avoid the constant search for thrilling images may not be observed by anyone, but it will have positive repercussions in every area of life.

One parent and researcher, Lisa Ann Thomson, offers eight suggestions to empower young people against the inroads of Internet porn (we'll discuss five of them here):

1. Address access: Start with outer defenses. Use filters, enable parental and content controls, establish an open-book policy, and keep electronics in common areas.
2. Preach of Christ: Physical filtering can only go so far. If we help children gain a testimony of Heavenly Father's love and the Savior's atoning sacrifice, that is the greatest filter of all.
3. Teach healthy sexuality: "It is not enough to label pornography as bad; parents also need to teach their children what is good." Maintain an ongoing dialogue and make it easy for children to ask questions whenever they have them.
4. Shatter the myth of pornography: "In discussions about pornography, parents should point out that pornography is mythical on all levels. The behaviors portrayed in pornography are neither normal nor a reflection of what should be anticipated or expected in a healthy relationship."

5. Teach that there is hope: Emphasize that the Savior's power is real and that it makes change and repentance possible.[21]

The illusion of power, and the illusion of privacy, can combine to fool us into relinquishing responsibility for our actions. If we remember that real power comes from righteous living—and that our actions should be the same whether we are alone or with others—we are learning the lessons that Joseph has to teach us.

> "Nothing paralyzes our lives like the attitude that things can never change. We need to remind ourselves that God can change things. . . . Outlook determines outcome. If we see only the problems, we will be defeated; but if we see the possibilities in the problems, we can have victory.
> —Warren W Wiersbe[22]

Hard Time: The Lessons of Confinement

GENESIS 40–41

We don't talk about prison very much in polite society, but most of us know someone who has been in jail. I've have known several people (some of them relatives) who somehow just got on the wrong side of the law and ended up incarcerated for some period of time. And the likelihood of knowing someone in prison is growing, along with the number of people who go there. As of March 2017, there are 2.3 million people who are in US prisons.[23] According to the Bureau of Justice Statistics, there are just under 7 million adults in the US correctional system—as of 2015.[24] If someone is in the correction system, it means that they've been in prison, they're about to go to prison, or they're on parole. This adds up to nearly 9 million people, or 1 in 36 Americans. "The federal prison population increased by almost 800 percent between 1980 and 2013, often at a far faster rate than the Bureau of Prisons could accommodate in their own facilities."[25]

There is something very visceral about the idea of being locked up, isn't there? It's a terrifying thought. My husband and I have a close friend, who's usually an upstanding citizen, but who got into a brief altercation with his ex-wife's new husband. He felt like it wasn't very serious, but the man went home and called the police and had him arrested. Suddenly this law-abiding man was thrust into a strange new world—a world where he was treated like a criminal—and it changed his life. He said that one of the most surreal parts of the experience was being taken downtown and escorted, handcuffed, into the labyrinthine county jail. "It was just absolutely terrifying," he said. "There were no windows,

> Oh, how we wish for more honesty and less corruption, more goodness instead of so much cleverness, and more wisdom in lieu of unanchored brilliance.
>
> –Neal A Maxwell[26]

so I couldn't see out, couldn't orient myself; I had no idea where I was. There was a complete loss of personal control. I was confined, (unjustly I felt) but apart from making my phone call, I had no idea what to do next. I was frightened of the guards, and even more frightened of the other prisoners. I sat with my head in my hands, wondering how I got there and how I was going to get out!"

Our friend's experience would have been something like Joseph's. Young, pampered, and privileged, he suffered several forms of confinement. First, he was thrown into a pit, then he was sold to a passing caravan, and then he was forced into a life of slavery at Potiphar's house. After all he had gone through, we can only imagine Joseph's terror at finally being thrown into a dungeon—unjustly accused of attempted rape by Potiphar's wicked wife. Every one of us has experienced, on some level, a feeling of confinement—even if it is simply that we have ended up in a bad situation and don't know how to get out. Joseph has something to teach us about what we can learn from confinement.

DECEIT AND DISGUISE

It has been said that integrity is what we do when we think that nobody is watching. Joseph's integrity stands in stark contrast to the deceitful actions of most of the people around him. Deceit and disguise are themes that often appear together in Genesis, and there is usually quite a bit of talk about clothing that goes along with them. The "Joseph Saga" is preceded by three stories in quick succession that feature these themes and add extra emphasis to Joseph's story: Jacob disguises himself as Esau in order to deceive Isaac and steal the birthright blessing. Leah (under Laban's direction) disguises herself as Rachel in order to take her place on their wedding night. Tamar, the neglected daughter-in-law of Judah, disguises herself as a harlot in order to claim her right to bear children. In each story, clothing is crucial to the deception, and the prize that is sought has to do with birthright.

Jacob gives his favorite son, Joseph, a coat of many colors (also translated as a "ornamented robe[27]"), and this becomes a symbol of his privileged status (see Genesis 37:3–4). Later, this robe is taken to his father in order to deceive him into thinking Joseph has been slain by a beast (see Genesis 37:31–34). When Potiphar's wife accuses Joseph, she takes hold of his garment as he flees, and uses it to deceive her husband (see Genesis 39:13–18). When Joseph is finally called into Pharaoh's presence after years of waiting, he changes clothes again. "Then Pharaoh sent and called for Joseph, and hurriedly brought him out of the dungeon; and when he had shaved himself and changed his clothes, he came to Pharaoh" (see Genesis 41:14, NASB). Joseph later loads his brother Benjamin's pack with five ornamented garments, to show Benjamin's favored status (see Genesis 45:22). Again and again, Joseph's clothing (the symbol of his covenant status) keeps coming back to remind us of who he really is.

One of the identifying features of Latter-day Saints is their clothing. We dress modestly, and—if we have made temple covenants—wear a ceremonial garment under our clothing. The garment, as a symbol of the covenant, is a very powerful symbol. Though it seems strange to others, for Latter-day Saints it represents a daily commitment to God. Like Joseph's robe, our clothing reminds us that we are of royal lineage.

A REFINING FIRE AND A CHALLENGE TO US

It's interesting how many prophets, ancient and modern, end up in prison for a brief period of time because of their religious beliefs. They are often sanctified and humbled by the experience. The young Joseph, who bragged about his dreams to his brothers, becomes a mature, humble man in prison. By the time he meets Pharaoh, he is ready for the next challenge. As a more modern example, Joseph Smith spent months in the oxymoronically named Liberty Jail, and experienced the same refining fire. Many other great men and women have learned great lessons in confinement, and their stories should fill our hearts with empathy toward those we might otherwise be tempted to shun. Joseph Smith said of his experience: "Those who have not been enclosed in the walls of prison without cause or provocation, can have but little idea how sweet the voice of a friend is; one token of friendship from any source whatever awakens and calls into action every sympathetic feeling. . . . Then the voice of inspiration steals along and whispers . . . , 'Peace be unto thy soul.'"[28]

In one of Jesus's sermons about service, He talks about visiting those in prison (see Matthew 25:43–44), Thus, it might be worthwhile for us to be prayerful about ways to help those who are behind bars. One woman who was a volunteer in a women's prison described the outpouring of the Spirit that she felt in their midst: "You can see a change in their countenance. You can see emerging in them a belief that they can have a good life regardless of their past. Once they start to realize that their worth is great, they just blossom."

So perhaps the first lesson we can learn from confinement in the scriptures is to reach out to those who are imprisoned, either in actual prisons or in other ways that are equally as devastating.

"BE STILL AND KNOW THAT I AM GOD"

The second lesson that confinement teaches us comes from being forced to hold still. Most of us don't stop moving until something stops us, but the scriptures tell us that the Lord will bless us for taking moments out of our lives to "be still and know that I am God" (Psalm 46:10). A series of confinements forced Joseph into periods of contemplation, where he acquired a kind of self-knowledge that served him well (see Genesis 39:21). Perhaps because he never gets rewarded for doing the right thing, Joseph ceases to worry about the consequences of his actions; he has the confidence to face Pharaoh in what must have been a very tense interview, and simply speak the truth (see Genesis 41:15–16, 25, 38–39).

CONFINEMENT AS A BLESSING

Confinement can be a blessing. This is a lesson that many of us learn during times of illness: a time that can certainly feel like a prison. Pregnancy can create that experience for many women. In fact, pregnancy used to be called a "confinement," and it was because, up until fairly recently, women stayed home when they were pregnant. They were excluded from any public appearances.

In our modern age, pregnant mothers are just as active and busy as everyone else. One wonders if there was some wisdom in a time of rest, stillness, and contemplation preceding the birth of a child.

My last pregnancy was a time of pain and frustration for me. Because of complications, I was first confined to a wheelchair; and, then, in the sixth month, confined to bed with early labor brought on by kidney stones. It had been a big decision to have a fifth child, and I was pretty sure that God was going to bless me for being so heroic! But instead, there I was, trapped in my house with four little kids needing my care, and I was unable to walk or even lift a child into my arms. I couldn't understand it.

Without going into all the details of that experience, I'll cut to the important part. Because of all of the complications, the doctors decided to induce the baby three weeks early. While I was waiting in the hospital hallway for a bed to be available, I went into labor, and after only a few contractions, the baby's heart rate dropped dramatically. I was rushed into an operating room and an emergency Cesarean section was performed. The umbilical cord was wrapped around the baby's neck and chest, cutting off his air supply as soon as labor began.

It was little while later that I realized that if I had not had the kidney stones, I would never have been in the hospital on the monitor when the first labor pains occurred. If I had followed the normal pattern and waited until the labor was severe, it would have been too late. That confinement and the resulting kidney stones that I cursed as I suffered through that pregnancy actually saved that baby's life. That was a great lesson to me: our confinements, even our imprisonments, may be actually a life-giving blessing from God.

Hopefully we won't actually end up in prison, but most of us will experience confinement in some way. Pregnancy, depression, or serious illness may imprison us. Transgressions may cause us to be disfellowshipped or excommunicated from the Church—a very real confinement. Addictions can also create a personal prison. Perhaps we may find ourselves confined with a sick or disabled family member for whom we are the caregiver. At times when I have been in that role, I like to remember that Charlotte Bronte's period of confinement as she cared for an ailing father had a glorious result; during those months, she wrote the novel Jane Eyre.[29] So sometimes when we feel stuck, it might actually be God giving us the opportunity to hold still and have something wonderful happen. Great opportunities can come during times of confinement.

Go back over your life and examine those times when it feels like you've been confined or frustrated because there were so many things you were unable to do. When we grow discouraged, we can remember Joseph's words to his brothers: "Have no fear! . . . God intended it for good, so as to bring about the present result—

> **Many of us are in are in our own prisons that aren't made of iron bars.**
>
> **–Harper Hill[30]**

the survival of many people."[31] Isn't it wonderful to know that God intends everything that happens to us in our lives to be for our good? It's up to us—through living righteously and clinging to our covenants—to learn the lessons He wants to teach us through times of confinement.

Spiritual Adults: How Prisons, Floods, and Plagues Can Help Faith Grow

Genesis 37–50

Joseph is the first of many teenagers who end up being heroes in the Bible. Most of them fact incredible challenges, but they are up to it. The hardest and most rewarding calling that I have had in the Church was teaching early-morning seminary. Early-morning seminary is a pretty exciting challenge. Though *my* brain was never fully awake at that hour, there were some pretty sharp, inquiring minds at work in that room. I realized pretty quickly that you'd have to get up even earlier in the morning to fool this group of teenagers, and I loved that about them.

Teenagers are at the age where the brain kicks in and begins to question everything that has been loaded into it during the first stage of life. Studies on the teenage brain tell us that during the period between the ages of twelve and twenty-five, the brain, already 90 percent formed, enters a period of refinement. Unused synapses are "pruned" and the frontal areas, so crucial for making choices and controlling behavior, become more streamlined and are able to function more rapidly. Some of the more annoying qualities of adolescence (thrill-seeking, peer-clinging, defiant behaviors) are actually essential in preparing the teenage brain for the great "exodus" that will define that teenager's future—the move away from home and family.[32] A recent article in *National Geographic* makes this interesting statement about adolescence:

> The period's uniqueness rises from genes and developmental processes that . . . play an amplified role during this key transitional period: producing a creature optimally primed to leave a safe home and move into unfamiliar territory.
>
> The move outward from home is the most difficult thing that humans do, as well as the most critical—not just for individuals but for a species that has shown an unmatched ability to master challenging new environments.[33]

> "People say teenagers think they're immortal, and I agree with that. But I think there's a difference between thinking you're immortal and knowing you can survive. Thinking you're immortal leads to arrogance, thinking you deserve the best. Surviving means having the worst thrown at you and being able to continue on despite that. It means striving for what you want most, even when it seems our of your reach, even when everything is working against you.
>
> –Francesca Zappia[34]

DISASTER PRECEDES THE MIRACLE

The move from a safe home into unfamiliar territory also aptly describes the spiritual path of the teenager. As a seminary teacher, it was a fascinating experience to enter into the books of Genesis and Exodus with two dozen teenagers, and see what we could find in those pages to help them on their journey. What we found surprised us. For example, there were miracles, certainly, but not warm, fuzzy ones. In the Old Testament, we don't find gentle, heartwarming moments with health suddenly restored or blindness cured, as we find the New Testament under the ministering hands of the Savior. No, here we find a more frightening set of circumstances.

> "Never lend your car to anyone to whom you have given birth.
>
> –Erma Bombeck[35]

God sends a flood to destroy mankind, but then miraculously gathers a faithful few onto the ark. He allows poor Joseph to end up in prison for years, yet gives him a series of dreams that eventually set him free. He gets the

Egyptians' attention with famine, flood, and plague, and then sends His prophets to show His power. And in the meantime, everybody (most of the prophets included) makes big mistakes, and suffers consequences. It's pretty scary stuff, and much of it warrants an adult rating. (I'll never forget the time a sweet fourteen-year-old girl raised her hand and said, "Could you just explain to me exactly what circumcision is?" Causing the male half of the room to visibly curl up in embarrassment. Good times.) In the Old Testament, we have definitely left the safe home of simple faith and entered into "unfamiliar territory."

That's why I think the Bible is great reading for teenagers. For one thing, it's difficult, and it causes the mind to stretch and reach, which is so good for that still-growing brain. Better still, most of the great theological questions are raised in the Bible (many of them in the book of Genesis alone), but not all of them are answered. We could, for example, spend the whole year discussing the first line: "In the beginning God created the heaven and the earth" (Genesis 1:1). Generations of theologians, scientists, and Bible readers have spent centuries discussing just what that line means: Is there really a beginning? How did the Creation happen? How long did it take? Or consider the paradoxical situation where, in order to obey one commandment, Adam and Eve must choose to disobey another. This dilemma is very familiar to teenagers, who are forced every day to choose between confusing options and find the greater good. The Old Testament invites us to take the first giant step into spiritual adulthood. With its puzzling and inspiring stories, it encourages us to both think and believe.

Unfortunately, in today's society, spiritual adults are an endangered species, and, the climate is a pretty chilly one for the thinking believer. In

> Some young people don't know who they are, what they can be or even want to be. They are afraid, but they don't know of what. They are angry, but they don't know at whom. They are rejected and they don't know why. All they want is to be somebody.
> –Thomas S. Monson[36]

school, through the media, and in almost every other setting, our kids are taught that to believe in God is foolish, and that intelligent people put aside all that superstitious nonsense as they reach adulthood. It is important for believing adults to be voices in the wilderness, to assure young people that it is not necessary to give up on God, and that a basis of faith may, in fact, empower one to think more clearly and rationally. But that doesn't mean it will always be smooth sailing. The great believer and thinker Joseph Smith said, "A fanciful and flowery and heated imagination beware of; because the things of God are of deep import; and time, and experience, and careful, and ponderous and solemn thoughts can only find them out."[37]

THE DIFFERENCE BETWEEN GOD AND SANTA CLAUS

As we talk about the miracles in the Bible, we have to find a way to separate fact from fiction. Ironically, one of the best ways to do this is to read a lot of fiction. As children, we are told fairy tales and mythological stories. They are an important part of every culture; these legends and stories help children come to terms with all of the unseen dangers of existence. When we are little, we believe in Santa Claus, the tooth fairy, and the boogeyman. Other fairies work miracles: they might sprinkle dust to help us fly. Or, like Dorothy, if we click our heels three times and think, *There's no place like home*, we will miraculously get there.

From fairy tales and stories we move to novels—works of fiction and fantasy where the laws of nature apply and yet can be transcended in certain circumstances. Marvelous coincidences occur in fiction that rarely occur in real life. These coincidences move the narrative along and cause a resolution of the conflict: The poor girl learns, at the last moment, that she is an heiress. The missing grandfather turns out to be the person living next door. 'X' actually does mark the spot where the missing treasure can be found, and the poor man finds it and is saved. How do we differentiate these fictional miracles with the miracles in the Bible? One of my students posed the question this way: "We have Greek myths, and old legends, and fictional stories, and then the Bible with its Eden and ark and flood and plagues. What is the difference between the false stories and the true ones?"

A good starting point to address this issue is to consider the difference between God and Santa Claus. When we are children, we believe that Santa will bring us gifts if we are good. Now, many adults have never progressed beyond the childish view of God as Santa Claus, and grow bitter and angry if God does not, in fact, bring them the things on their list. (In fact, behind many of the cynical, sophisticated philosophies one reads about life and its lack of meaning, one can feel the hurt and anger of the child who, though they tried to be good, didn't get what they prayed for.) But, as Paul told us, there comes a time to stop thinking like a child and put away childish things (see 1 Corinthians 13:11). God isn't Santa Claus, and the Old Testament makes that point in big, bold statements. God is a loving being, but He is also great and powerful and scary; you don't want to get on the wrong side of Him. God is a far more complex being than we can understand as children, or even as adults. The Old Testament, with its floods and plagues and curses, issues a humbling challenge to us: we may not be as smart as we think we are. God's thoughts are not our thoughts (see Isaiah 55:8–9), and it takes a lifetime of solemn and ponderous thinking on our part to even begin to find Him out. God is not Santa Claus. If we are good, we may or may not get what we want, but He still loves us and wants to help us progress.

So what is the difference between the miracles of the Bible and fictional stories? The difference is in their power. Unlike the wishful thinking in the myths and fairy tales, there is an actual, moving power behind the stories in the Bible. It is like the difference between a toy model of a car and one with a real engine. When you put the key in the engine of a real car and push on the gas, it lurches forward—it has power in itself. It can take you somewhere wonderful, or it can run over you, but either way, it's real. Santa is a story, and God is really there. When God acts, things happen, though we don't always understand them. This is why missionaries don't have to "sell" the gospel. They only have to hand over the key to the car by inviting people to get on their knees and pray about the scriptures. When investigators do so in faith, the car lurches forward and begins to move, and the awed investigator hangs on for the ride. If you pray to Santa, you end up with a sweet story, and cookies and milk on a plate. If you pray to God, a new power is unleashed in your life. As Alma said, "Is this not real?" (Alma 32:35). It is.

MIRACLES HAPPEN EVERY DAY

According to the Book of Mormon, belief is the magic ingredient that actually makes miracles happen in real life (see 4 Nephi 1:5). In my experience, most people—though they may not be religious—believe in miracles. Stop any person on the street and ask if anything miraculous has ever happened to them, and you will hear a story. There is hardly a person who hasn't had something stranger than fiction happen in their real lives.

As we begin to talk about miracles, even small ones, we should mentally remove our shoes; we are on sacred ground. Unfortunately, many miracles go unappreciated, and this is a shame, because they are meant to be a source of joy in a dark world. As we read fiction and experience what J. R. R. Tolkien called the "sudden, joyous turn"[38] of the narrative that brings resolution, we are better prepared to appreciate the real miracles that happen in our own life narratives. As we recognize these miracles, express gratitude for them, and write them down and share them with our children, they will increase in our lives, and so will our faith.

In the midst of the plagues of Egypt, there fell a thick cloud of darkness over the land. For three days, the Egyptians couldn't see a thing, and they fell over each other in the dark. But the scripture tells us, "All the children of Israel had light in their dwellings" (Exodus 10:23). With the Bible stories as a starting point, a thoughtful faith can grow toward a perfect brightness. We can move from childish ideas to a state of spiritual maturity where we can recognize the hand of God. When real miracles occur, we will appreciate them for what they are—small beacons to light us on our journey back home.

> Grant me the ability to be alone; may it be my custom to go outdoors each day among the trees and grass, among all growing things, and there may I be alone, and enter into prayer, to talk to the One that I belong to.
> —Rabbi Nachman of Bratzlav[39]

NOTES

1. Joseph Campbell, *The Hero with a Thousand Faces*, 3rd ed. (Novato, CA: New World Library, 2008), 41–74.
2. Attributed to Ray Kroc.
3. Joseph Campbell, *Pathways to Bliss: Mythology and Personal Transformation* (Novato, CA: New World Library, 2004), 133.
4. Marvin J. Ashton, "'There Are Many Gifts,'" *Ensign*, November 1987.
5. David E. Sorensen, "Forgiveness Will Change Bitterness to Love," *Ensign*, May 2003.
6. Don Miguel Ruiz, *The Four Agreements: A Practical Guide to Personal Freedom* (San Rafael, CA: Amber-Allen Publishing, 1997).
7. Northrup Frye, *The Great Code: The Bible and Literature* (New York, Houghton Mifflin Harcourt Publishing, 1981), 169.
8. Ibid.
9. Lisa Ann Thomson, "Eight Strategies to Help Children Reject Pornography," *Ensign*, August 2017.
10. Ibid.
11. WITW Staff, "Study finds that 1 out of 3 women watch porn at least once a week," *The New York Times*, October 22, 2015, nytlive.nytimes .com/womenintheworld/2015/10/22/study-finds-that-1-out-of-3 -women-watch-porn-at-least-once-a-week/?mcubz=1.
12. Kent Berridge in, Susan Weinschenk, "Why We're All Addicted to Texts, Twitter and Google," *Psychology Today*, September 11, 2012, accessed August 25, 2017, www.psychologytoday.com/blog/brain -wise/201209/why-were-all-addicted-texts-twitter-and-google.
13. "How Porn Affects The Brain Like A Drug," *Fight the New Drug*, updated August 23, 2017, accessed August 25, 2017, fightthenewdrug .org/how-porn-affects-the-brain-like-a-drug/.

14. Neal A. Maxwell, *A Time to Chose* (Salt Lake City: Deseret Book, 1972).

15. Steven Pace, "Acquiring Tastes through Online Activity: Neuroplasticity and the Flow Experiences of Web Users," *M/C Journal* 17, no. 1, (2014), journal.media-culture.org.au/index.php /mcjournal/article/view/773.

16. Norman Doidge, *The Brain That Changes Itself: Stories of Personal Triumph from the Frontiers of Brain Science* (New York: Penguin Books, 2007), 108–9.

17. Erin Stewart, "Erin Stewart: Sex is only as casual or as sacred as we make it," *Deseret News*, February 21, 2017, accessed August 25, 2017, www.deseretnews.com/article/865673851/Sex-is-only-as-casual-or -as-sacred-as-we-make-it.html.

18. "Jordan Peterson—How Pornography Affects on Young Men," YouTube video, 3:52, posted by "Logic View," May 7, 2017, www .youtube.com/watch?v=oTjZvlKfNtk.

19. Ibid.

20. Bruce Feiler, "The Stories That Bind Us," *The New York Times*, March 15, 2013, www.nytimes.com/2013/03/17/fashion/the-family -stories-that-bind-us-this-life.html?mcubz=1.

21. Thomson, "Eight Strategies to Help Children Reject Pornography."

22. Warren W. Wiersbe, *The Bumps Are What You Climb On* (Grand Rapids, MI: Baker Books, 2002).

23. Peter Wagner and Bernadette Rabuy, "Mass Incarceration: The Whole Pie 2017," *Prison Policy Initiative*, March 14, 2017, www.prisonpolicy .org/reports/pie2017.html.

24. "Key Statistic: Total Correctional Population," *Bureau of Justice Statistics*, accessed August 25, 2017, www.bjs.gov/index .cfm?ty=kfdetail&iid=487.

25. "Phasing Out Our Use of Private Prisons," *The United States Department of Justice*, August 18, 2016, accessed August 25, 2017, www.justice .gov/archives/opa/blog/phasing-out-our-use-private-prisons.

26. Neal A. Maxwell, in Joseph B. Wirthlin, "Personal Integrity," *Ensign*, May 1990.

27. Genesis 37:3, footnote *d* in, Adele Berlin and Marc Zvi Brettler, eds., *The Jewish Study Bible: Featuring the Jewish Publication Society TANAKH Translation* (New York: Oxford University Press, 2004), 74.

28. Joseph Smith, in *History of the Church*, 3:293.

29. Elizabeth Gaskell, *The Life of Charlotte Bronte* (London: Penguin Books, 1997), 304–10.

30. Harper Hill, in Alisha Tillery, "Hill Harper Talks Cancer, New Book," *Ebony*, September 18, 2013, accessed August 25, 2017, www .ebony.com/entertainment-culture/hill-harper-talks-cancer-new -book#axzz4qnZ3Vmwe. Adele Berlin and Marc Zvi Brettler, eds., *The Jewish Study Bible: Featuring the Jewish Publication Society TANAKH Translation*, 2nd ed. (New York: Oxford University Press, 2014).

31. David Dobbs, "Teenage Brains," *National Geographic*, October 2011, accessed August 25, 2017, ngm.nationalgeographic.com/2011/10 /teenage-brains/dobbs-text.

32. Ibid.

33. Joseph Smith, in *History of the Church*, 3:295.

34. Francesca Zappia, *Made You Up* (New York: HarperCollins, 2015), 417.

35. Attributed to Erma Bombeck.

36. Thomas S. Monson, "Yellow Canaries with Gray on Their Wings," *Ensign*, August 1987.

37. J. R. R. Tolkien, "On Fairy-Stories," in *The Monsters and Critics and Other Essays*, ed. Christopher Tolkien (London: George Allen and Unwin, 1983), 153.

38. Nancy Dunnan, *Your First Financial Steps* (New York: HarperPerennial, 1995), 185.

39. Rabbi Nachman of Bratslav, in *The New Reform Judaism: Challenges and Reflections* (Lincoln: University of Nebraska Press, 2013), 16.

Personal Notes

———————————
———————————
———————————
———————————
———————————
———————————
———————————
———————————
———————————
———————————
———————————
———————————
———————————
———————————
———————————
———————————
———————————
———————————
———————————
———————————
———————————
———————————
———————————
———————————
———————————
———————————

Chapter Four

THE EXODUS

Exodus for the Rest of Us: An Overview

Exodus, according to the Jewish Study Bible, "Is arguably the most important book in the Bible since it presents the seminal events in Israel's history and the definitive institutions of its religion, themes that have reverberated through all subsequent Jewish and Western history."[1] The forty years of wandering in the wilderness make great drama. But what does the book of Exodus mean to us today? Here are three takeaways from Exodus:

1. God is involved in our lives, but usually in mysterious and confusing ways. Moses is another example of an obscure child that has a great destiny. Like the Savior, Moses is born into a humble home and must be hidden to save his life. Miraculous things happen that put him in the unique position to represent his people. (Without his upbringing in Pharaoh's household, could he have even gotten an audience with the great king?) The Old Testament is chock-full of these stories, where small and simple people are used to make great things happen.

2. There is a big difference between miracles and magic tricks. Moses is given the power to work miracles, and Pharaoh's magicians are able to copy several of them. However, the sorcerers are unable to do anything positive or creative; they can only make more of

the bad stuff. These days, we have our own set of sorcerers, and the Internet is the box of magic tricks. It can give you the illusion of learning, when you are only browsing. It can give you the illusion of privacy, when in reality, unseen people are watching and tracking your habits. And above all, it offers both the worst and the best that people are creating, almost effortlessly. As parents and influencers, it is important to teach our children the difference between miracles and magic. Miracles heal the soul, inspire, and give strength to do what is right. Magic tricks tend to shock and awe, which leads to a need for a greater shock and awe, and eventually, they may lead to an addiction to the rush. Pharaoh got the difference too late, and his loss was great.

3. The commandments are conditions of a covenant. The Ten Commandments are modeled after the ancient treaties that were established between overlords and their vassals. The formal style signaled to this mixed group of Israelites (and the other enslaved people who left with them) that God was serious about a relationship. He would guard and protect and bless them on condition of their obedience to certain stipulations. As the narrative unfolds, we will see how the Israelites become mired in the minutiae of the commandments and lose sight of their covenant relationship. Could this happen to us? When I asked our class to discuss the difference between covenants and commandments, one sister responded, "Commandments are open to interpretations. You can argue about them all day. A covenant is simple. You are either in or you're out." I liked that.

Would you describe yourself as a covenant person or a commandment keeper? Are you one whose relationship with God is not based on scorekeeping, but on loving promises that have been exchanged? Exodus gives us a lot to think about in our own journey, and much to apply that may save us wasted time and sorrow. As one rabbi said, "In every generation one should look upon himself as if he personally had gone out of Egypt."[2]

THE BIRTH OF A SAVIOR

For those of us raised on annual reruns of the movie *The Ten Commandments*, it is hard to separate Moses from Charlton Heston, and get a picture of the real man. A close reading of Exodus reveals a fascinating character that is both flawed and truly heroic.

The story of Moses begins with a reference to Joseph (now four hundred years in the grave) that reminds us of the reason that there is a large group of Hebrews living in Egypt (see Exodus 1:6, 8). These days, when the historicity of the events in the Bible is continually questioned, many claim that there is no real evidence that a vast number of Israelites lived in Egypt. However, there are several references in Egyptian texts to foreign pastoralists who would show up in Egypt during times of drought. The fertile Nile Delta drew them there, and many of them stayed. Historian James K. Hoffmeier notes: "Egyptian textual sources and archaeological evidence conclusively demonstrate . . . a substantial foreign presence in the Nile Delta . . . When the Hyksos ruling and military elite retreated to Canaan . . . around 1525 BC, it is generally believed, the majority of the Semitic-speaking population remained in Egypt."[3]

Though Joseph held an important place in Egypt, things changed over the centuries. As the story opens, a new ruler arises in Egypt who "knew not Joseph" (Exodus 1:8).

The author peeking out from behind a wax figure of Charlton Heston as Moses.

> And he said unto his people, Behold, the people of the children of Israel are more and mightier than we:
>
> Come on, let us deal wisely with them; lest they multiply, and it come to pass, that, when there falleth out any war, they

join also unto our enemies, and fight against us, and so get them up out of the land.

Therefore they did set over them taskmasters to afflict them with their burdens. And they built for Pharaoh treasure cities, Pithom and Raamses.

But the more they afflicted them, the more they multiplied and grew. And they were grieved because of the children of Israel. (Exodus 1:9–12)

Forced labor, also knows as corvée, has been used throughout history, and provided the manpower by which the Egyptians completed the pyramids and other massive projects. And it wasn't just the Israelites that were forced into labor camps. The Egyptians would enslave different groups that they had captured or who had emigrated to Egypt during times of famine. Later, when the Israelites departed, they took with them other people from the forced labor groups (see Exodus 12:38). Still later, we see King Solomon revive this practice and enslave his own people to complete his ambitious projects (see 1 Kings 9:20–21).

Forced labor, though a step above abject slavery, is not an easy life. There is a piece titled "Satire of the Trades" that was written during this time by an Egyptian who (just as we do now) was trying to persuade his son to go to college and qualify for a job where he didn't have to do manual labor. He says this: "I will describe to you the brick maker. His loins give him pain. Though he is out in the wind, he works without a cloak. His arms are spent from exertion, and having mixed all kinds of dirt all day, when he eats bread with his fingers, he washes them at the same time."[4]

SAVED BY WATER

Water and deliverance are connected thematically throughout the scriptures. Rivers flow through Eden, nourishing it. The earth is cleansed of evil by the Flood. Patriarchs find their matriarchs by a well. There are symbols of being saved by water all the way up to the baptism of Jesus. The birth of Moses signals another great deliverance by water.

Now a man from the house of Levi went and took as his wife a Levite woman.

> The woman conceived and bore a son, and when she saw that he was a fine child, she hid him three months.
>
> When she could hide him no longer, she took for him a basket made of bulrushes and daubed it with bitumen and pitch. She put the child in it and placed it among the reeds by the river bank (Exodus 2:1–3, English Standard Version)

This little detail about caulking the basket with bitumen and pitch is a nice example of resonance, as it conjures up an image of the ark. Just as Noah and his family were saved in an ark on the water, Moses was also saved by an ark on the water. And the Israelites—spoiler alert—will later to be saved by water. Just as Moses is hidden in the bulrushes, the Israelites will be surrounded by the Red Sea, or the Sea of Reeds.[5] Moses's Hebrew name, Mosheh, means "complete." And just as Pharaoh is commanding that all of the male children be thrown into the river to drown, a promised deliverer is saved on the water, and drawn out of the water by Pharaoh's own daughter. Moses completes the saving circle.

We are told that Moses grows up in the house of Pharaoh. He may have been one of many children in Pharaoh's house, but he certainly lives a privileged life. Though raised as an Egyptian, his Hebrew mother was his wet nurse, so we know that Moses would have been aware of his lineage (see Exodus 2:7–9, KJV). As a grown man he sees an Egyptian beating a Hebrew slave one day, and something snaps. He kills the man and must flee (see Exodus 2:11–15).

If we look at the record carefully, we see that Moses didn't kill the Egyptian taskmaster without thinking; there was definitely an element of premeditation, as well as a deliberate effort to cover up the crime. "Looking this way and that and seeing no one, he killed the Egyptian and hid him in the sand" (Exodus 2:12, NIV).

As a privileged son in the house of Pharaoh, Moses would not have been raised to think of people equally; he would have been taught to treat certain people as beneath him. So, why not dispose of an Egyptian taskmaster? But instead of thanking him, his own people treated him as if he had committed a crime, and this made him realize that he might be in trouble with Pharaoh as well. So he fled. Eventually, like all the prophets (and even Jesus himself), he ends up at a well. There, predictably, he finds a wife, and they later have a son (see Exodus 2:15–22). Moses works for his father-in-law as a shepherd (see Exodus 3:1). And so we move into the second phase of Moses's life, and his encounter with the burning bush.

The Burning Bush:
Moses and Modern Revelation

EXODUS 3; MOSES 1

There is a scriptural tradition that Moses was 40 when he went to Midian and that he lived in Midian for 40 years (see Acts 7:23). He was 80 when he had the vision at the burning bush (see Acts 7:30), and he was 120 when he died (see Deuteronomy 34:7). His life path mirrors the journey of the Israelites. Though we, as literal thinkers, tend to obsess over exact accuracy of the numbers, the Israelites recognized the numbers as a symbol that tied him to Noah once again. Jesus and His gospel chroniclers understood this, and they built on the resonance by using the number forty in regard to Jesus's fast in the wilderness. We can imagine that Moses's time in the land of Midian was an opportunity to rethink everything. His new father-in-law was a priest, and would have had many years to teach Moses a religious perspective. But it is the encounter with God at the burning bush from which Moses emerges a different man. What happened at this crucial juncture in his life path?

There is a very famous verse of scripture that I have always found intriguing. "And this is life eternal, that they might know thee the only true God, and Jesus Christ, whom thou hast sent" (John 17:3). This concept of knowing God is very important, but I'm not sure I understand why. After all, can we humans even begin to comprehend God? And what about that act of comprehension constitutes "life eternal"? Moses has something to teach us here. He begins as a man who lives for himself, and then as one devoted to his family. At the burning bush, Moses is introduced to a new way of thinking when he actually confronts God.

> Earth's crammed with heaven,
> And every common bush
> afire with God:
> But only he who sees,
> takes off his shoes,
> The rest sit round it and
> pluck blackberries.
> —Elizabeth Barrett Browning[6]

First Moses sees a burning bush that is not consumed by the fire, and then God speaks to him—telling him that he is on sacred ground. Then, in the classic pattern of the hero's journey, He issues a call to Moses, revealing His concern for the people of Israel and His intention to rescue them. Moses will be His emissary. But before that can happen, Moses has a lot to learn.

Here, we are fortunate to have the benefit of modern revelation. In the book of Moses, Joseph Smith recorded a more extensive vision that Moses had sometime after his first vision of the burning bush:

> When Moses was caught up into an exceedingly high mountain,
> And he saw God face to face, and he talked with him, and the glory of God was upon Moses; therefore Moses could endure His presence.
> And God spake unto Moses, saying: Behold, I am the Lord God Almighty, and Endless is my name. . . .
> And now, behold, this one thing I will show unto thee, Moses, my son, for thou art in the world, and now I show it unto thee. (Moses 1:1–3, 7)

EVERYTHING I NEVER WANTED

I think God has suggested something here to us by offering Moses something he really needed, but didn't know he needed. And that something was a new vision of himself and the world around him. If we need a suggestion of a good prayer to offer in times of trial, it might be this: "Heavenly Father, could you show me my world the way you see it, as opposed to the way I see it? Could you give me a larger vision of my life?" Moses looks, and he beholds the world in which he's been living, but he sees it through God's eyes, and it is life changing.

This moment in scripture stands as a good reminder to me when I get tangled up in the details of doctrine. It's good to study the doctrine, but we need to remember that our perspective is so limited that we really can't get the big picture, except in those exceptional moments when God lifts our vision to a higher level. So we should be very tolerant of the opinions of others.

When I think about doctrinal disputes, I sometimes have a mental vision of two fleas on the back of a dog, having a big argument about what breed the dog is. We little fleas know that we are on a dog because all the evidence points that way. It smells like a dog, it tastes like a dog, and occasionally we can hear it bark! But beyond that, we can't see much. We could be on a poodle, or we could be on a mastiff. Endless arguments about it won't help; we need to be lifted up to see the bigger picture. And until that happens, why argue about the details? Just hang on for the ride!

But for this transcendent moment, Moses gets to see what God sees, "Moses . . . beheld the world upon which he was created; and Moses beheld the world and the ends thereof, and all the children of men which are, and which were created; of the same he greatly marveled and wondered" (Moses 1:8). Then something even more remarkable happened:

> And the presence of God withdrew from Moses, that his glory was not upon Moses; and Moses was left unto himself. And as he was left unto himself, he fell unto the earth.
>
> And it came to pass that it was for the space of many hours before Moses did again receive his natural strength like unto man; and he said unto himself: Now, for this cause I know that man is nothing, which thing I never had supposed.
>
> But now mine own eyes have beheld God; but not my natural, but my spiritual eyes, for my natural eyes could not have beheld; for I should have withered and died in his presence; but his glory was upon me; and I beheld his face, for I was transfigured before him. (Moses 1:9–11)

"Man is nothing, which thing I never had supposed" (Moses 1:10). What does Moses mean by this? God has granted him a marvelous vision, and he has been transfigured in order to receive it. He ought to be feeling like he is of great worth. What does he mean when he says, "Man is nothing"? Well, predictably, the minute something this transcendently spiritual happens, Satan comes along to try to muddy the waters. And in his conversation with Moses, we get a greater insight into what Moses means by "nothing." "Satan came tempting him, saying" Moses, son of man, worship me" (Moses 1:12).

Well, since Moses just found out that he was nothing, you'd think that there'd be no way he could fight against Satan. But instead, Moses stands right up and says,

> Who art thou? For behold, I am a son of God, in the similitude of His Only Begotten; and where is thy glory, that I should worship thee?
>
> Get thee hence, Satan; deceive me not; for God said unto me: Thou art after the similitude of mine Only Begotten. (Moses 1:13, 16)

Then he says, "I will not cease to call upon God, I have other things to inquire of him: for his glory has been upon me, wherefore I can judge between him and thee" (Moses 1:18).

These two apparently conflicting concepts are actually complementary. Left to ourselves, we begin to see our little lives and our concerns as the center of the universe. When Moses sees all of creation through God's eyes, he realizes what a small drop of water each man is in that ocean of creation. But each drop, each man and woman, is created in God's image. The whole ocean is contained in each precious drop, making each drop infinitely precious.

> "A person will worship something, have no doubt about that. We may think our tribute is paid in secret in the dark recesses of our hearts, but it will out. That which dominates our imaginations and our thoughts will determine our lives, and our character. Therefore, it behooves us to be careful what we worship, for what we are worshipping we are becoming.
>
> —Ralph Waldo Emerson[7]

Regarding the size of the "ocean" of God's creations, I like the story about the naturalist, William Beebe.

> [William] made a visit to another naturalist whose name was Theodore Roosevelt. In describing the visit, William Beebe said that each evening, after a talk in Roosevelt's home at Sagamore Hill, the two men would go out on the lawn and gaze up at the sky to see who could first detect that faint spot of light-mist beyond the lower left-hand corner of the Great Square of Pegasus. Then one or the other would recite: "That is the Spiral Galaxy of Andromeda. It is as large as our Milky Way. It is one of a hundred million galaxies. It is 750,000 light-years away. It consists of one hundred billion suns, each larger than our sun." After an interval Beebe reported that Mr. Roosevelt would grin at him and say, "Now I think we are small enough. Let's go to bed."[8]

GOD KNOWS YOUR NAME

Though we may not encounter any burning shrubbery, most of us have had experiences where we have received a very direct, clear answer to prayer, or felt the love of God. In those moments, we feel at once both our own nothingness and our divine worth. God is everything. I am nothing on my own, but because I am enfolded in His grace, the adversary has no power over me. We have a sense that God knows who we are, and cares about what happens to us.

Eugene England, in his beautiful book, *Why the Church Is As True As the Gospel*, related a story about an early pioneer named Joseph Millett that illustrates this point. Brother Millett's life of service and sacrifice was recorded in his journal, and during a time of hunger and privation in a place called Spring Valley, we find this simple entry.

> One of my children came in, said that Brother Newton Hall's folks were out of bread. Had none that day. I put . . . our flour in sack to send up to Brother Hall's. Just then Brother Hall came in. Says I, "Brother Hall, how are you [fixed] for flour." "Brother Millett, we have none." "Well, Brother Hall, there is some in that sack. I have divided [it] and was going to send it to you. Your

children told mine that you were out." Brother Hall began to cry. Said he had tried others. Could not get any. Went to the cedars and prayed to the Lord and the Lord told him to go to Joseph Millett. "Well, Brother Hall, you needn't bring this back if the Lord sent you for it. You don't owe me for it." You can't tell how good it made me feel to know that the Lord knew that there was such a person as Joseph Millett.[9]

Perhaps the most startling, and life-changing thing about coming to know God, is to realize how fully and intimately He knows us. He knows our names, our needs, and—small as we are— we matter to him. That is one great lesson that Moses can teach us.

> "I can see how it might be possible for a man to look down upon the earth and be an atheist, but I cannot conceive how he could look up into the heavens and say there is no God.
> —Abraham Lincoln[10]

Miracles for Dummies: Pharaoh's Hard Heart

EXODUS 4–14

One question that usually arises as we read Exodus is why the Pharaoh persists in resisting God, even when so many devastating plagues occur to convince him of God's power. The Bible repeats over twenty times that "God hardened Pharaoh's heart," but we know through Joseph Smith's revision of those passages that this was actually Pharaoh's choice—he hardened his own heart: "And the Lord said unto Moses, When thou goest to return into Egypt, see that thou do all those wonders before Pharaoh, which I have put in thine hand, and I will prosper thee; but Pharaoh will harden his heart, and he will not let the people go" (Joseph Smith Translation, Exodus 4:21 [in Exodus 4:21, footnote c]).[11]

It's easy to grow impatient with Pharaoh as he experiences one plague after another, and then, as soon as the threat is removed revokes his promise to let the Israelites go. But are we any different? If we were, there wouldn't be a multi-billion-dollar industry for diet products! Every time we suffer from overeating or struggle to get last year's bathing suit on this year's body, we may vow to change our behavior. But when the summer is over, we may simply forget what we promised to do.

And in the area of miracles, do we do any better than Pharaoh at recognizing the hand of God in our lives? If we did, churches would be full, and the people in the pews would be worshipping rather than scrolling through emails on their phones during the service. When we read the story of Pharaoh—stubbornly chasing the Israelites right down into the Red Sea, assuring his own destruction and that of his army—can we see ourselves, stubbornly chasing wealth, or social approval, or selfish gratification, even though we are in imminent danger of drowning in a sea of insignificance?

It's hard not to get seriously irritated with the children of Israel, as they carp and complain to Moses every time anything goes wrong. How could they complain to him about the way things were going, when God had shown so many miracles? How much proof did they need? And how could they immediately turn to worshipping a golden calf, just because Moses didn't come down off the mountain right when they thought he would? What is wrong with these people?

If you have ever had to run a youth conference, or a youth camp, or tried to plan a ward party, you've met some of the children of Israel. There will always be people who will complain no matter how hard you try. Ask any youth leader what the biggest problem in their organization is, and the answer will often be, "The youth are great; it is the adults that are giving us trouble!" And all of us take a turn being that person at times, don't we? When one of our own children is neglected by a leader, or a spouse is treated unfairly, or we ourselves suffer some sort of indignity in a Church setting, how quick we are to lash out, and how slow we are to be appreciative.

All of this has something to do with knowing God. As we edge closer to His greatness and glory and as we take off our shoes and stand on holy ground, we begin to discern the difference between God and ourselves. We are small. We get caught up in small concerns, and make a fuss over very little things. God is big. He sees the big picture, and He deals with the big issues. The closer we get to knowing Him, the easier it is to feel what He might feel about the daily dilemmas that we face. Reacting to small situations with big vision is part of what it means to know God.

WHAT'S IN A NAME? I AM THAT I AM

Names are a pervasive theme in the scriptures; they signal power and dominion. Adam names the animals and his wife. Names are changed to signal a covenant, or a new life mission: Abram to Abraham (see Genesis 17:5), Sariah to Sarah (see Genesis 17:15), Jacob to Israel (see Genesis 32:28). All of this finds its culmination in the conversation at the burning bush, when Moses asks God what his name is.

> And Moses said unto God, Behold, when I come unto the children of Israel, and shall say unto them, The God of your

fathers hath sent me unto you; and they shall say to me, What is his name? what shall I say unto them?

And God said unto Moses, I am that I am: and he said, Thus shalt thou say unto the children of Israel, I am hath sent me unto you. (Exodus 3:13–14)

Orthodox Jews do not say the name of God because it is too holy. (Tradition says that, anciently, the only time they would ever say the Lord's name was on the annual Day of Atonement when the priest went into the Holy of Holies. And at the moment, the chanting of the choir would swell so that no one else could hear it but God.[12]) Today, when Jews read the Bible aloud, they say *Adonai*, which means "my Lord," instead of pronouncing the four consonants for God's name, YHWH, also called the Tetragrammaton.[13] Thus, they avoid saying the sacred name.

> I have an old edition of the New Testament in the Latin, Hebrew, German and Greek languages. . . . I thank God that I have got this old book; but I thank him more for the gift of the Holy Ghost. I have got the oldest book in the world; but I [also] have the oldest book in my heart, even the gift of the Holy Ghost. . . . The Holy Ghost . . . is within me, and comprehends more than all the world; and I will associate myself with him.
>
> —Joseph Smith[14]

As an interesting side note: The Germans took these three vowels—*A*, *O*, and *I*—and put them in between the consonants that make up the name of God in Hebrew: YHWH. And it came out "Yahovah," or in English, "Jehovah." So, we get "Jehovah" from the Germans, "Adonai" from the Jews, and "Yahweh" from the written texts.[15] These days, it has become popular for Christian sects to use the word "Yahweh" in reference to God. Our local Jewish rabbi assures me that you would never hear a devout Jew say that word out loud, and finds it odd that it has been appropriated by Christians!

IT'S A GOOD THING WE'RE NOT LIKE THAT!

The elaborate measures taken to avoid saying the name of God are an example of an even more elaborate set of restrictions that were instituted by the Jewish fathers in order to ensure that an actual law would never be broken. These laws are known as the *gezeirah*, or "fence laws."[16] "The gezeirah are laws instituted by the rabbis to prevent people from accidentally transgressing Torah mitzvah. These laws are generally referred to as putting up a fence around the Torah. An example of such a 'fence' is the prohibition of hanging a writing instrument on Shabbat so one would not accidentally violate the mitzvah to rest on Shabbat."[17]

Jesus repeatedly reproved the Pharisees and scribes for an obsession with regulations and rules. This should warn us that it is easy for this to become a problem in our observance of the commandments. For example, if you were raised in the LDS Church, you were taught the four steps of prayer when you were very young. If you came from another faith culture, you might have been taught to recite the Rosary or the Lord's Prayer in a certain way. Children in the LDS Church are carefully taught to use formal language, such as "thee" and "thou," when addressing God. We are taught first to express thanks, then ask for what we needed, and close in the name of Jesus Christ. As children we were cautioned, "Don't talk *to* Jesus, talk to Heavenly Father in Jesus's name. Don't be too casual. Show proper respect." And so forth. All of these guidelines are good. I'm glad I learned them, and I taught them to my children because it is important to learn how to pray in an attitude of reverence and respect. But I had an experience on my mission that has stayed with me, making me wonder if we spend too much time on the form and forget the real function of prayer.

A FIRST CONVERSATION WITH GOD

Forty years ago in Japan, there were very few families in the Church, and the branches were small, so my companion and I were thrilled when we found a whole family that wanted to learn more about the gospel. It wasn't just the mother and children; the father was very interested as well. We offered to do a family home evening with them, and when that night arrived, we gathered on the tatami mats around the table for dinner. I asked Mr. Suzuki if he would offer a prayer. He felt a little hesitant, and said that he had never prayed aloud, except to recite a Buddhist chant. It seemed inappropriate to go through the steps of prayer right then, so I just invited him to say whatever he felt in his heart to God, and that would be sufficient. The next few moments are frozen in my memory forever.

This good man simply looked up into heaven and said (as near as I can remember), "Father, these women have come to us like angels from God, with a message for our family. Thank you for sending them to us. Will you help us understand what they have to teach us?" Then he looked back at us, with full expectation that we would then deliver God's message. I count this as one of the most beautiful prayers I have ever heard.

We taught several lessons to the Suzuki family. One day after we had been teaching them for a while, I again asked the father to offer the prayer. By that time, we had taught our prayer lesson, and everyone knew all of the steps. I noticed that the father didn't look up anymore, he bowed his head, and addressed the Lord reverently. He used the right prayer language; he said thanks in the right spot and asked for blessings at the right time and

> Speaking about praying to our Father in heaven, I once heard Joseph Smith remark, "Be plain and simple and ask for what you want, just like you would go to a neighbor and say, I want to borrow your horse to go to [the] mill."
> —Henry W. Bigler[18]

closed the prayer properly. But there was something different, even impersonal, about that prayer. The family did not join the Church, and soon lost interest in our message. Somewhere between that first, direct address to God, and all of our careful teaching, the fire went out.

When we feel critical of the children of Israel for missing the point of the miracles, or when we laugh at Pharaoh for being so stubborn, we might be missing the message that Exodus has for us. The children of Israel were not saved by the law—the law came later. When the angel of death crept into the villages and took the firstborn babies, those that had the blood of the lamb guarding their homes were safe. Hanging the Ten Commandments on the door would not have saved them. It is only through Christ's grace that we can find the critical point of balance between the law and the Spirit, between bondage and freedom. Just knowing about God isn't enough, you have to know Him to enter into life eternal. And if, as Joseph Smith said, eternal life is by definition the kind of life that God lives,[19] then it makes sense that knowing Him is the gateway to that loving, creative, eternally elevating existence. That is the message of the burning bush: I am that I am. The law is not God. The rules are not God. God is God, and only He is mighty to save.

TOOLBOX: DRAMATIC IRONY

Dramatic irony is a literary device in which the full significance of a character's words or actions are clear to the audience or reader but are unknown to the character. This device is so common that we may not notice it; great stories give us a God's eye view of the actions of the characters. Knowing what some or all of the characters do not know makes us a little nervous and engages our emotions; we get a little rush of excitement each time they are faced with choices, even when we already know the how the story will resolve itself.

Uses of dramatic irony in the Bible are almost too numerous to mention, but a supreme example is found in the story of Moses and the ten plagues, which is retold each year at the Feast of the Passover. Each time the story is retold, the tension builds with each plague, and we catch ourselves thinking, "Oh, the Pharaoh will let the people go now, won't he? He won't get to the place where all the kids get killed, will he?" Yes, he will. The phrase "[Pharaoh] hardened his heart" is repeated over twenty times. This is intentional; it builds the dramatic tension so that it never gets old. When we read it in that light, we get a sense of the masterful construction of this story.

There's an old joke that the reason the movie *Titanic* made so many billions of dollars, is that fourteen-year-old girls kept going back to see it again, hoping that it would end better this time! That is dramatic irony. Knowing the end from the beginning, or knowing even part of what the characters don't know, doesn't make a great story less interesting, it makes it timeless. The Bible stories are the pinnacle of this artistic form.

The Passover, Thanksgiving, and the Sacrament: The Gospel and the Sacred Feast

EXODUS 12

And it shall come to pass, when ye be come to the land which the Lord will give you, according as he hath promised, that ye shall keep this service.

And it shall come to pass, when your children shall say unto you, What mean ye by this service?

That ye shall say, It is the sacrifice of the Lord's passover, who passed over the houses of the children of Israel in Egypt, when he smote the Egyptians, and delivered our houses. And the people bowed the head and worshipped. (Exodus 12:25–27)

Since Moses is obviously a type for Christ, the Passover as a prefiguration of the sacrament is part of that symbolic package. In fact, the concept of the sacred feast is worth thinking about because feasts are a part of religious observance in every culture. Our own uniquely American feast, Thanksgiving, has its roots in the Passover as well. The Pilgrims were a deeply religious group, and they saw their journey to North America as a modern-day Exodus. Historian Bruce Feiler writes:

"When the band of Protestant breakaways left England in 1620, they described themselves as the chosen people fleeing their pharaoh, King James. On the Atlantic [their leader, William Bradford], proclaimed their journey to be as vital as 'Moses and the Israelites when they went out of Egypt.' And when they got to Cape Cod, they thanked God for letting them pass through their fiery Red Sea."[20]

Feiler goes on to explain that the great feast that was given was modeled on the Jewish feast of the Sukkot, which was instituted for Israel to thank God for saving them from bondage.[21] At the first Thanksgiving feast, an edict was read that compared William Bradford to Moses.[22] And when Thanksgiving was officially made a national holiday, this proclamation was read by the President of the United States.

> Whereas it is the duty of all Nations to acknowledge the providence of Almighty God, to obey his will, to be grateful for his benefits, and humbly to implore his protection and favor—and whereas both Houses Of Congress have by their joint Committee requested me "to recommend to the People of the United States a day of public thanksgiving and prayer to be observed by acknowledging with grateful hearts the many signal favors of Almighty God especially by affording them an opportunity to peaceably establish a form of government for their safety and happiness.[23]

Though it has become secular in nature, Thanksgiving, like the Passover, was originated as a religious holiday—a festival sacrament where God's people offer thanks. As Christians, we have the sacred feast of the sacrament every Sunday. I like thinking of the sacrament as a little Thanksgiving feast. I know, we are missing the sweet potatoes and the turkey, but the element of thanksgiving is a very important part of the sacrament. Rather than always just thinking about our sins, I think it's a wonderful thing to think of the sacrament as a time where we can just sit and be grateful for all of our many blessings.

ARE WE FEASTING OR FASTING?

This brings up the idea that we may be skimping a bit on the gospel feast. Though I've never been able to document it, I think that it was Jedediah M. Grant who said, "In the church, we know the difference between the history of the feast, and the feast itself." I find this quote very challenging. Whenever I am teaching a lesson, or even just talking about the gospel with someone, I ask myself, "Am I talking about the history of the feast, or am I actually feeding this person?" There is a big difference. Jesus didn't talk to the five thousand about how important it is to have a nourishing lunch; He made five thousand fish sandwiches and passed them around. He warned His disciples not to send people away hungry (see Matthew 14:13–21).

When we consider that we have the gift of the Holy Ghost, and the priesthood, and the power of the Redeemer in our church, it stands to reason that we ought to be making something happen every time we gather together. We ought to be feeling the Spirit! We ought to be filled at the end of a meeting. Jesus told His disciples not to send people away hungry, and I believe He means us to be feasting every time two or three or more are gathered in His name.

Every month on the first Sunday, Latter-day Saints fast for two meals, and donate the money they would have used for those meals to feed the hungry. On this day, we hold a special meeting where we "bear our testimony" about the ways God has poured out His grace on us. This phrase, to "bear" a testimony, is a revealing one. A testimony is more than an assurance; it is a burden as well. Once we know that God lives and that Jesus is the Christ, we are invited to help bear His cross by sharing that message with the world.

Many people are shy about standing up and sharing in this way. They hesitate to do so, and hope someone else will do it instead. Thus, many of our testimony meetings have long spaces where no one speaks. I find this remarkable. I can look around our congregation and see dozens and dozens of amazing people with testimonies that are strong and vibrant. Yet they sit and remain silent. So instead of enjoying a gospel feast, the congregation is left fasting spiritually as well.

Our testimonies are based on the times when we feel God's presence, His love for us, and His concern for our individual lives. Our testimonies are based on the times when we have felt, in a way that was undeniable, that spiritual things were real, and not just an emotion or a wishful thought. Yet, because they cannot be proven empirically, a testimony is, in the words of Harold B. Lee, "fragile . . . as hard to hold as a moonbeam."[24] If those feelings go unexpressed and unappreciated, they can fade. These "fragile" feelings are the fabric from which we fashion a way of living and a belief system. Sharing those feelings in a sacred setting comprises the moments of feasting in the Church that nourish everyone. Are we offering those moments to our children, to our students, to those in the Church community with whom we interact? If not, why not?

The gospel itself is a feast; we partake of the feast when we feel the Holy Spirit. Otherwise, we're just talking about rules, regulations, good ideas, and helpful thoughts. Those do not offer real strength when things get really hard. Inspiring slogans are not going to keep the angel of death from coming into your house. Only the blood over the door will do that, and that protection comes from the Lord Himself.

BRINGING THE FEAST HOME

Next time you sit down to Sunday dinner as a family, think about the sacred feast and what it represents. When the faithful young warriors said to Helaman, "We do not doubt our mothers knew it" (Alma 56:48), they were not talking about how well the dinner rolls turned out, or how smooth the gravy was at Sunday dinner. They were not talking about how carefully the lessons were prepared at church or how great the handouts were. Those young men had the faith to defy death because they had no doubt in their minds that their mothers knew the Savior. They had been taught this in their homes.

Moses taught his people,

> Therefore shall ye lay up these my words in your heart and in your soul. . . .
>
> And ye shall teach them your children, speaking of them when thou sittest in thine house, and when thou walkest by the way, when thou liest down, and when thou risest up. (Deuteronomy 11:18–19)

Just as the Passover and Thanksgiving feasts offer a time to talk about deliverance, the weekly sacrament feast offers an opportunity to thank our Savior for our deliverance from death and sin through His Atonement. In our homes, His grace should be a frequent topic of discussion. And once a month, when we have the opportunity to express those thanks in a sacred setting, we should be the first in line. Let's make sure that all of the people we know, know what we know.

> "We must come ... to the sacrament table hungry. If we should repair to a banquet where the finest of earth's providing may be had, without hunger, without appetite, the food would not be tempting, nor do us any good. If we repair to the sacrament table, we must come hungering and thirsting for righteousness, for spiritual growth. ...
>
> Perhaps some of us are ashamed to come to the sacrament table because we feel unworthy, and are afraid lest we eat and drink of these sacred emblems to our own condemnation. ... We want every Latter-day Saint to come to the sacrament table because it is the place for self-investigation, for self-inspection, where we may learn to rectify our course and to make right our own lives, bringing them into harmony with the teachings of the Church and with our brethren and sisters. It is the place where we become our own judges. ...
>
> No man goes away from this Church and becomes an apostate in a week, nor in a month. It is a slow process. The one thing that would make for the safety of every man and woman would be to appear at the sacrament table every Sabbath day."
>
> –Melvin J. Ballard[25]

NOTES

1. Adele Berlin and Marc Zvi Brettler, eds., *The Jewish Study Bible: Featuring the Jewish Publication Society TANAKH Translation* (New York: Oxford University Press, 2004), 102.
2. Ibid., 132.
3. Bill T. Arnold and Richard S. Hess, eds., *Ancient Israel's History: An Introduction to Issues and Sources* (Grand Rapids, MI: Baker Academic, 2014).
4. Richard Neitzel Holzapfel, Dana M. Pike, and David Rolph Seely, *Jehovah and the World of the Old Testament* (Salt Lake City: Deseret Book, 2009), 81.
5. Terence E. Fretheim, *Interpretation: A Bible Commentary for Teaching and Preaching—Exodus*, 113.
6. Elizabeth Barrett Browning, *Aurora Leigh*, bk. 7, lines 61–64.
7. Attributed to Ralph Waldo Emerson.
8. John H. Vandenberg, "'Turn Heavenward Our Eyes,'" *Ensign*, December 1971.
9. Joseph Millet quoted in, Thomas S. Monson, "Gifts," *Ensign*, May 1993.
10. Abraham Lincoln quoted in, John Phillips, *Exploring Romans: An Expository Commentary* (Grand Rapids, MI: Kregel Publications, 1969), 26.
11. Compare Exodus 4:21; 7:3, 13; 9:12; 10:1, 20, 27; 11:10; 14:4, 8, 17; Deuteronomy 2:30.
12. Amy-Jill Levine, "Old Testament: Moses and Exodus," in *The Great Courses*, course no. 653 (Chantilly, VA: The Teaching Company), DVD. See also *Jewish Encyclopedia*, s.v "Atonement, Day of," accessed August 28, 2017, www.jewishencyclopedia.com/articles/2093-atonement-day-of.
13. *Merriam-Webster Dictionary*, s.v "tetragrammaton," accessed August 30, 2017, www.merriam-webster.com/dictionary/tetragrammaton.
14. *Teachings of the Prophet Joseph Smith,* sel. Joseph Fielding Smith (Salt Lake City: Deseret Book, 1976), 349–50.
15. Levine, "Old Testament: Moses and Exodus," in *The Great Courses.*
16. Isadore Singer, Cyrus Adler, *The Jewish Encyclopedia: A Descriptive Record of the History, Religion, Literature, and Customs of the Jewish People from the Earliest Times to the Present Day*, vol. 5 (New York: Funk and Wagnalls Company, 1912), 648–49.

17. Becomingjewish.org, site discontinued.
18. *Teachings of Presidents of the Church: Joseph Smith* (2011), 221.
19. Ibid., 132.
20. Bruce Feiler, "About the Book," in *America's Prophet: How the Story of Moses Shaped America* (New York: Harper Perennial, 2009), 6.
21. Bruce Feiler, *America's Prophet: How the Story of Moses Shaped America.* See also John J. Parsons, "Thanksgiving and Sukkot: What's the Connection?," accessed August 30, 2017.
22. Morris Epstein, *All about Jewish Holidays and Customs,* rev. ed. (Brooklyn, NY: KTAV Publishing, 1970), 29.
23. George Washington, "Thanksgiving Proclamation, 3 October 1789," *Founders Online,* accessed August 30, 2017, founders.archives.gov /documents/Washington/05-04-02-0091.
24. Harold B. Lee, *Church News,* July 15, 1972, 4.
25. Melvin J. Ballard, "The Sacramental Covenant," *Improvement Era,* October 1919, 1027–28.

Personal Notes

_____

_____

_____

_____

_____

_____

_____

_____

_____

_____

_____

_____

_____

_____

_____

_____

_____

_____

_____

_____

_____

_____

_____

_____

_____

_____

_____

_____

_____

_____

_____

_____

_____

_____

_____

_____

_____

_____

_____

_____

_____

_____

_____

Chapter Five

THE LAW

From Taskmaster to Schoolmaster: The Mosaic Law

LEVITICUS–DEUTERONOMY

It's easy to be critical of the Mosaic law. Jesus made lots of comments about it, so we might feel comfortable just discarding it as something appropriate only for those Israelites, the "kindergarteners of civilization," as one of my teachers once described them. But it is important to remember that Jesus was not critical of the law *per se*. He was critical of people that were worshipping the law rather than the God who gave it. The Mosaic law was something more than a set of restrictions; it was a whole new way of viewing the world. Paul described it as "a schoolmaster to bring us unto Christ" (Galatians 3:24). I don't think I really understood this concept until I tried to learn Japanese, and discovered how our minds are shaped by the language we speak.

> Some people regard discipline as a chore. For me, it is a kind of order that sets me free to fly.
> —Julie Andrews[1]

Learning the language of the law can be viewed as a training ground to understand the workings of the Spirit.

We all have little formulas for how to do things, from doing the dishes to organizing our emails. The Japanese word *yarikata* actually works better for me than the word "formula," because it simply means "way of doing,"[2] instead of sounding like a chemistry experiment. A *yarikata* is a progression of steps, done in a certain order, that you take to complete one of the tasks of everyday life. The Japanese are obsessed with the concept of *yarikata*, and personally, I think it all begins with the Japanese language.

The Japanese language is so much harder to learn than English that the average Japanese child is in high school before they are really proficient. Just to read a newspaper requires working knowledge of about 1,500 Chinese characters, called *kanji*. And each one of these characters has a "stroke order" that must be also be memorized in order to write it properly. This means you can't just reproduce each character as you would copy a picture. You must draw each line, or stroke, of the character in the proper sequence. If you don't, as you begin to combine it with other characters, an improper stroke order will quickly become obvious. So instead of twenty-six letters that an English speaker easily learns to recognize and write, a Japanese child must learn to recognize several hundred characters, and then memorize as many as two dozen strokes per character, in order.

Let me show you one example. Here is the character that means "tree."

This is a simple, four-stroke character, and it really shouldn't matter whether you draw the part that looks like a lowercase *t* first or the part that looks like an inverted *v*, right? But look what happens when you combine this character with the one for "cherry" in order to write "cherry tree."

In this character, (now twenty-four strokes instead of four) you can see that the character for "tree" is morphing; it is less symmetrical. In order to get this right, you must start with the long vertical line, then draw the little *t* cross, then make the stroke down to the left and finish with the right half of the inverted *v*. If you don't go in this order, a practiced Japanese eye will catch it in an instant.

However, it still will be intelligible. But the Japanese written language, like Japanese gardens and even the pouring of tea, has an artistic element that is essential. Characters can also be rendered as works of art. And when writing a character grows into the creation of calligraphy, you get something like this.

So you see that the stroke order, though seemingly unimportant at first, becomes essential as the sophistication of the character increases.

The tremendous effort involved in just learning the nearly two thousand characters required to be considered literate has an effect on the Japanese brain. In fact, Dr. Tadanobu Tsunoda discovered that people who learn Japanese as their first language actually process information differently. On a visit to Cuba, he was distracted by the sounds of insects outside the conference room that made it hard for him to hear the lecture properly. In later conversations, he was surprised to learn that the other attendees did not even notice the insect noise. This led to years of research where the doctor discovered that a native Japanese speaker processes the sounds of insects as if they were words, in the left hemisphere. A Western language speaker will process those sounds as random noise.[3] Language is processed in the left hemisphere of the brain and abstract sounds, like music, are processed in the right. The Japanese language itself prioritizes certain sounds so that they are processed in the left hemisphere of the brain. This process is so well documented now that neurosurgeons are learning to operate on Japanese brains differently than Western brains.[4]

A NEW LANGUAGE FOR LIVING

Now, what does this have to do with the Mosaic law? Other than the fact that, as a person whose brain nearly exploded in the struggle to learn Japanese, I find this whole business of brain and language processing fascinating, it also helps me understand why the Mosaic law needed to be so incredibly detailed and rigid. Moses was working with a people who had been in a strange culture for four hundred years, and a good deal of that time was spent as forced laborers. They had to relearn the language of moral behavior.

It is well documented that when people are taken out of their traditional culture and forced into an alien situation, especially one where their family structures are dissolved, they may lose their basis for making moral choices. Dr. Victor Frankl, the famed psychotherapist who spent years in a series of concentration camps, contended that morality was not a basic drive; it was in each instance a conscious choice. In order to make moral choices, he says, the brain must be taken out of a state of "latency" and brought back into an active state.

"Man is never driven to moral behavior; in each instance, he decides to behave morally. . . . Thus it can be seen that mental health is based on a certain degree of tension, the tension between what one has already achieved and what one still ought to accomplish, or the gap between what one is and what one should become. Such a tension is inherent in the human being and therefore is indispensable to mental well-being. We should not, then, be hesitant about challenging man with a potential meaning for him to fulfill. It is only thus that we evoke his will to meaning from its state of latency."[5]

The law of Moses was a new language for living; it offered a whole new mindset for the children of Israel. Learning to think in a new way involved a long and difficult training process, as complex as the Japanese language is for the Japanese mind. Perhaps this complicated system of rules and regulations caused the minds of subsequent generations to develop differently. It jolted them, and pulled them out of the dormant moral state into which they had fallen. This is a helpful way to think about the law of Moses. And I do love a good *yarikata*.

> What do you do with an entire year's worth of minutes [525,600] given us each year? Doing some quick math, I spent, give or take, 62,400 minutes watching television; 174,720 minutes sleeping; 18,720 minutes doing repetitive household chores; 15,600 minutes sitting in church meetings; 65,520 minutes doing family-related activities; and 93,600 minutes doing work-related tasks for a total of about 430,560 minutes. What did I do with the remaining 95,040 minutes or, roughly 66 days last year that are unaccounted for? I have absolutely no idea! Would I have spent my time differently if I'd known I only had a year left to live? Absolutely!"
>
> —Mark Albright[6]

Putting the Power of Covenants into our Parenting

DEUTERONOMY

For you are a holy people to the Lord your God; the Lord your God has chosen you to be a people for His own possession out of all the peoples who are on the face of the earth (Deuteronomy 7:6, NASB).

We are told in Deuteronomy that the purpose of the law of Moses is to make Israel a holy people. The laws were meant to differentiate them from other cultures, and to help them see themselves as children of God. To this end, the people renewed their covenants: first in the tabernacle, and later in the temple. They were instructed to keep these covenants uppermost in their minds, and teach them to their children. "And ye shall teach them your children, speaking of them when thou sittest in thine house, and when thou walkest by the way, when thou liest down, and when thou risest up" (Deuteronomy 11:19, KJV). How shall we go about this task? How do we, as parents, teach our children what it means to be a covenant person? One of the great characters to arise from the havoc wreaked by the Nazis in World War II was an unassuming woman named Corrie Ten Boom. Her family helped shelter Jews during the Nazi occupation. Eventually, her parents were killed and she and her sister were sent to a concentration camp, where her sister died. Corrie's story is deeply inspiring, and you get a glimpse into why she grew to be such a formidable woman when she shares some of the teaching moments she had with her father when she was young.

On one occasion, as most children do, Corrie became interested in how babies are created. Her friends were talking about it, and it seemed to be a forbidden subject, making it all the more intriguing. She decided to ask her father about it.

> He turned to look at me, as he always did when answering a question, but to my surprise he said nothing. At last he stood up, lifted his traveling case from the rack and set it on the floor.

"Will you carry it off the train, Corrie?" he said. I stood up and tugged at it.

It was crammed with the watches and spare parts he had purchased that morning.

"It's too heavy," I said.

"Yes," he said, "And it would be a pretty poor father who would ask his little girl to carry such a load. It's the same way, Corrie, with knowledge. Some knowledge is too heavy for children. When you are older and stronger, you can bear it. For now you must trust me to carry it for you."[7]

THE WEIGHTIER MATTERS OF THE KINGDOM

For active Latter-day Saints, the center of our covenant process is the temple. Through the temple endowment we have an opportunity to promise the Lord that we will live in a certain way, and renew those promises each time we go back to the temple. Though we constantly encourage our members to attend the temple and testify of its central importance in our salvation, information about what transpires within the temple is a subject about which we are mostly quiet. Because it is a sacred ceremony, and because a few components of it are not to be discussed outside the temple, we may feel uncomfortable talking about the temple to our children. Unfortunately, as a result, many people assume that there is something strange or forbidden that goes on there. This is not the case. The temple offers an uplifting session of worship, and nothing that occurs there is less than wonderful and pure.

Ezra Taft Benson related an experience from his youth that illustrates the importance of talking about the temple with our children:

I am grateful to the Lord that my temple memories extend back—even to young boyhood. I remember so well, as a little boy, coming in from the field and approaching the old farm house in Whitney, Idaho. I could hear my mother singing "Have I Done Any Good in the World Today?" (*Hymns*, no. 58.)

I can still see her in my mind's eye bending over the ironing board with newspapers on the floor, ironing long strips of white cloth, with beads of perspiration on her forehead. When I asked her what she was doing, she said, "These are temple robes, my son. Your father and I are going to the temple at Logan."

Then she put the old flatiron on the stove, drew a chair close to mine, and told me about temple work—how important it is to be able to go to the temple and participate in the sacred ordinances performed there. She also expressed her fervent hope that some day her children and grandchildren and great-grandchildren would have the opportunity to enjoy these priceless blessings.[8]

DRESSED IN WHITE

I had a similar experience of being exposed to the temple "culture" before I went through on my own. When I was eighteen, my parents had my adopted sister, Kimberly, sealed to our family, so I was invited to participate in that sealing in the temple. We children dressed in white and were escorted up to one of the sealing rooms. When my parents entered dressed in their temple robes, I thought they looked very royal; they were almost shining. I instinctively understood that there was symbolic significance to the clothing they wore, though I wasn't sure what it might be. This helped prepare me for my first visit to the temple at the age of twenty-one. The clothing did not seem strange to me, as it did not seem strange to President Benson when he watched his mother iron her temple robes at home.

Each thing we can do to make the temple more familiar to our children will help them appreciate the experience more fully. We can talk with them about the covenants we make, we can share our own experiences, we can help prepare their clothing, and we can talk about why it is important.

MY LIFE IS IN GOD'S HANDS

Above all, when we talk to our children about the temple, we can share with them our faith that being covenant Christians adds power and peace to our lives. Once we are endowed, our lives are in God's hands. We are promised that God will protect us through the power of our covenants until we have finished our work on the earth. Recently, this came into play in a very personal way when my husband was diagnosed with an incurable form of blood cancer. The first reports were devastating, and we were still reeling in shock when the stake president came to visit.

> Let me suggest that the reason why temple building and temple worship have been found in every age, on every hand, and among every people, is because the gospel in its fullness was revealed to Adam, and that all religions and religious practices are therefore derived from the remnants of the truth given to Adam and transmitted by him to the patriarchs. The ordinances of the temple in so far as then necessary, were given, no doubt, in those early days, and very naturally corruptions of them have been handed down the ages. Those who understand the eternal nature of the gospel—planned before the foundation of the earth—understand clearly why all history seems to revolve about the building and use of temples.
> —John A. Widtsoe[q]

Though we were not well acquainted with him, he offered to give each of us a blessing as we faced this frightening new challenge. As President Clark laid his hands on Craig's head, he promised him that he would "live *to the nanosecond* that God intended him to be on this earth," and that "miracles will occur to bring that to pass." In the months since that blessing, Craig has felt complete peace about his condition. Each time he meets with a doctor, he responds to their questions about his state of mind with something like this, "I know that I am in the Lord's hands, and I am at peace with it. So you tell me what I need to do to prolong my life as long as possible, and I will do it." Miracles have happened that have given us the confidence that his life is, indeed, completely in God's hands.

It is a remarkable thing to feel that your life is not governed by random chance, but that God's protecting hand is on you. You may not live as long as you hoped, but you will live as long as it is part of God's plan. And you will have peace that those you leave behind are tied to you by the sacred sealing power. The blessings of temple covenants are real, and long before our children attend, they can experience its power as we share that spirit with them.

Elder John A. Widtsoe said: "We live in a world of symbols. No man or woman can come out of the temple endowed as he should be, unless he has seen, beyond the symbol, the mighty realities for which the symbols stand."[10] The "mighty realities" of the temple include the eternal nature of families, the personal nature of the Savior's love and sacrifice, and the potential for each individual to become all that the Lord envisions in us. What greater, more comforting truths could there be?

"Then Shall Ye Shout":
The Parable of Jericho's Walls

JOSHUA 6

The book of Joshua has two beautiful themes, one of God as protector and one of God as a provider. Both come together in a particular moment in the book of Joshua that has become a parable for me.

The story of the battle of Jericho is memorable because it is so dramatic. The part we remember is the great moment when the priests of Israel blow the trumpets and all the people shout, and the walls fall down. But looking at the story again, I am struck by what comes before. As you remember, the city of Jericho was under siege, and the people inside its walls were holding out against the Israelites. God instructed Joshua to have all of the clergy, in their various ranks, line up and march around the city every day, blowing *shofar*, or ram's horns. (A *shofar* is given as a traditional gift to a young man or woman at the bar/bat mitzvah). God directs the people to march behind the priests, but to remain absolutely quiet: "And Joshua had commanded the people, saying, Ye shall not shout, nor make any noise with your voice, neither shall any word proceed out of your mouth, until the day I bid you shout; then shall ye shout" (Joshua 6:10).

"NEITHER SHALL ANY WORD PROCEED OUT OF YOUR MOUTH"

This is where the parable strikes home for me. For six long days, the people were asked to march around the city, time after time. The priests got to do something; they blew the horns. Joshua got to direct everyone. But the people—the moms and dads and siblings—just had to march quietly and try to have faith.

It was Joshua who said, "Choose you this day whom ye will serve . . . but as for me and my house, we will serve the Lord" (Joshua 24:15). We try to create faithful, believing homes, and teach our children to accept the gospel teachings; we hope that, when they are grown, they will choose the same things that we have chosen. But in most of our families, there are one or more family members who choose different paths. What should we do? Well, most of us try a number of approaches. We try reasoning, preaching, cajoling, and inspiring pep talks. When those methods don't work, we may resort to manipulating, threatening, and even coercion. At that point, our children will find a way to escape and disappear. We may be forced to realize that when we said, "Choose for yourself," we really meant, "Choose what I choose, or I'm going to make your life miserable until you do!"

The lesson of Jericho for me is a lesson in trusting in the power of God and having the humility to recognize our place in the plan. It may be that what God is asking you to do is not to blow the trumpet or storm the walls. What God may be asking you to do is to be quiet and just march forward, keeping your family close, living the gospel, and loving your child, spouse, or friend unconditionally. This doesn't mean that nothing is happening. In fact, God has a plan for every one of His children—to bring them home in His way and in His time. If you are making a lot of noise when you are supposed to be quiet, you may actually be messing up the plan.

A friend of mine has a son who has been away from both his family and his faith for many years. My friend and his wife went through the long process of learning to love their son unconditionally, and to stop making all of the little comments that make it painful to be an unbeliever in a believing family. After several painful experiences, they learned to be quiet about those points on which they differed, and just try to set an example. After many years, some life experiences caused this son to come home for a period of time. Then they noticed that occasionally he would bring up a gospel subject and ask a question. They answered, but didn't preach. Time passed, and other changes slowly

> Oh Love, that will not let me go,
> I rest my weary soul in Thee;
> I give Thee back this life I owe,
> That in Thine ocean depths its flow
> May richer, fuller be.[11]

occurred. There was a growing feeling of openness; the defensiveness seemed to soften. Then the young man began to date someone who was active in the Church, which caused him to think more deeply about spiritual things.

One day, this young man was walking with his dad, and they were having a discussion about some of his feelings and questions. Suddenly, my friend says that he had a feeling go through him like electricity, and he clapped his son and the shoulder and said, "Son, maybe it's time to come back." And when he said it, his son broke down. The wall fell down, in just as tangible a way as the wall of Jericho crumbled at the shout of the people. The Lord had done His work, and because this good father learned to march along in silence until the time came to speak up, the miracle occurred.

I'm embarrassed to say how many times, in answer to a prayer about what I ought to do or say in order to fix some situation, I feel impressed that I should shut up and wait on the Lord. The trumpets are important and the marching is vital, but sometimes the most important part is to be quiet and wait for the Lord's command to shout. Rather than trying to control the dialogue, we, in essence, lend the torch to the Lord, and let Him guide the battle.

The Covenant as an Act of Grace

DEUTERONOMY 29–34

"But ye are a chosen generation, a royal priesthood, an holy nation, a peculiar people; that ye should shew forth the praises of him who hath called you out of darkness into his marvelous light (1 Peter 2:9). The covenant that God makes with Abraham is repeated to every one of the Patriarchs, along with the injunction to bless the nations of the earth by spreading God's word.[12] Finally, Moses acts as God's mouthpiece to renew this covenant with the children of Israel as they finally prepare to enter the promised land:

> Keep therefore the words of this covenant, and do them, that ye may prosper in all that ye do.
>
> Ye stand this day all of you before the Lord your God; your captains of your tribes, your elders, and your officers, with all the men of Israel.
>
> Your little ones, your wives, and thy stranger that is in thy camp, from the hewer of thy wood unto the drawer of thy water:
>
> That thou shouldest enter into covenant with the Lord thy God, and into his oath, which the Lord thy God maketh with thee this day:
>
> That he may establish thee to day for a people unto himself, and that he may be unto thee a God, as he hath said unto thee, and as he hath sworn unto thy fathers, to Abraham, to Isaac, and to Jacob. (Deuteronomy 29:9–13)

The Abrahamic covenant reverses, in a beautiful way, the curses that were laid upon Adam. In contrast to Adam and Eve's curse of noxious weeds and sorrow in childbirth (see Genesis 3:16, 18), Abraham is promised a fruitful, welcoming land and posterity as numberless as the sand. Through the covenant, men and women are brought back into the grace of God, and promised great blessings in this world as well as in the next. From that moment on, the possession of a fruitful homeland and the blessing of endless posterity are the major themes of the Old Testament.

A covenant is defined as an agreement between to parties, usually signed or written, to do or not to do some specified action.[13] During the times in which the Bible takes place, most people lived under the protection of a lord, or governor, who promised protection in return for certain acts of fealty. Several ancient treaties between the suzerain (lord) and his vassals (subjects), survive from Near Eastern nations of the time. These covenants were taken seriously. If subjects obeyed the provisions of the covenant, they could depend upon the lord to adhere to his side of the agreement. Abraham enters into a covenant with God that is very much like these treaties, and it is repeated to Isaac, Jacob, and Moses. The Ten Commandments are also written in a form very similar to the treaties of that time, with clear injunctions about what the vassals must do or not do.[14]

> Above all else, God wants our hearts. Imperfect performance can be corrected, sins can be remitted, mistakes can be erased— but God can do nothing with an unwilling and rebellious heart until it repents. However, all those who really want and work for the kingdom of God with all their strength, however great or little their strength may be, will inherit that kingdom.
>
> —Stephen Robinson[15]

One way to make sense of the passages in the Old Testament that seem to portray God as a vengeful being wreaking havoc on His people is to understand the context of covenant living. Just about everything that goes wrong with the Israelites is interpreted to be evidence that they have, in some way, violated the terms of the covenant. This type of historical interpretation is called the Deuteronomic History, and it involves a very literal interpretation of the agreement between Israel and God, based upon the context of the legal treaties that existed between suzerain and their vassals.

But the entire Bible does not support this view of history. In fact, the brilliance of the book of Job is that it flatly rejects this approach. Job's "comforters" (see Job 16:2) assure him that he must be at fault in all of his misfortunes, because if he were truly righteous, God would be blessing him. Job staunchly defends his innocence, and actually indicts God as the one who is failing to uphold the agreement. Job is also viewing the covenant in the same way that he would view a legal treaty. If he is keeping his end of the bargain, why isn't God? What has happened to the Abrahamic covenant? If God does not bless us when we do right, has the covenant ceased to be binding?

WE DON'T EARN OUR WAY TO HEAVEN

The covenant between God and Abraham, though written in the style of the legal covenants of the day, was and is different. The two parties are in different spheres—one is divine, and one is not. In addition, this treaty and its promised blessings were never based on merit. As the Jewish Bible notes, God's covenant to Abraham came "like a bolt from the blue; an act of God's grace alone."[16] The covenant preceded the law, and nobody earned God's favor—He just chose them. Over time, as commandments were given and laws of behavior were instated, the Israelites began to believe that it was their obedience that caused them to merit the blessings of God. But the actual events show otherwise. In many cases, God offers His

> "I have faith that if we caught hold of God's living candle on that truth and went out into the world—I don't care [what vocation]—just out in the world being true to the vision, we would not need to defend the cause of Jesus Christ. People would come and ask, 'Where have you found the radiance that I sense in your eyes and in your face? How come you don't get carried away with the world?' And we would answer that the work of salvation is the glorious work of Jesus Christ. But it is also the glorious work of the uncovering and recovering of your own latent divinity.
> —Truman G. Madsen[17]

promises, His blessings, and His deliverance to those who have not yet shown their obedience. As John says so succinctly, "We love him, because he first loved us" (1 John 4:19).

When Jesus begins to teach this perspective on the law to the Jews, He appears to be a heretic. When He claims He has come, not to destroy the law, but to fulfill it, He means that He is trying to take the people back to the original purpose of the law: to make people better, to help them live together in love and peace, and to open their hearts to God's way of thinking and doing. The law, according to Jesus, was never going to get anyone into heaven. The law was a gift to help them grow. Focusing on the law, instead of its giver, caused an imbalance in the attitude of the Jewish leaders toward others. As modern covenant people, we too must find the balance between obedience to our values and tolerance of others. Author Michael Wilcox states: "As recipients of Abraham's covenant today, we have the delicate challenge of blessing all the families of all the nations of the world without assimilating their values, traditions, beliefs, standards, or behaviors. . . ."[18] Earlier in his article, he states, "Today a self-righteous attitude of superiority will also prevent Abraham's modern seed from fulfilling our covenant responsibility. We are to radiate to the world a spirit of love in order to bring others to the truths of the gospel. Sometimes, if we are not careful, our neighbors and friends who are not of the Church may think we are aloof or feel superior. Wisdom and love will help us avoid repeating the mistake made by Abraham's seed during New Testament times."[19]

A GIFT OF GRACE

Over time, faith in the covenant with God deteriorated into faith in the commandments and the law. In Genesis, the patriarchs and matriarchs show faith in a personal God who is deeply involved in their lives. The commentator in the Jewish Bible explains: "In the Tanakh, faith does not mean believing in spite of the evidence. It means trusting profoundly in . . . the personal God who has reiterated His promise."[20]

Thus, when Job contends that bad things happen to the undeserving, he is correct. The law is meant to save and strengthen men and women, and disobedience to it does have consequences. But obedience or disobedience to the law is not the cause of all of the events in our lives, and the covenant is greater than our obedience or disobedience. The covenant came to us before we "earned" it, and the covenant remains even when we fail to honor it. The covenant binds our children to us, it acts in our hearts, and works on our behalf—even when we stray. Like the invisible thread that Father Brown—a fictional, twentieth-century Roman Catholic priest and detective—describes, God reaches out through His covenant "'with an unseen hook and an invisible line which is long enough to let him wander to the ends of the world and still to bring him back with a twitch upon the thread.'"[21]

When we try to come to terms with the events of the Old Testament, I think it is useful to remember that Jesus interpreted them differently than did the people who wrote them down. If we measure God's actions through the cloudy lens of those who lived hundreds of years before Jesus's coming, it can be quite disturbing. Instead, when we view the covenant between God and Israel as an act of grace, and the commandments as a guide to help them become a "holy people," we are more in line with the way that Jesus described the commandments—not as a ticket to heaven, but as a conduit through which His light could shine into the world.

"Let your light so shine before men, that they may see your good works, and glorify your Father which is in heaven" (Matthew 5:16).

NOTES

1. Attributed to Julie Andrews.
2. *Jisho*, s.v. "yarikata," accessed August 30, 2017, jisho.org/search /yarikata%20.
3. Masaomi Ise, "The Japanese Language Brain," in *Japan Close-Up*, August 2002, www2s.biglobe.ne.jp/nippon/file/jog240e.html.
4. Fabian Cremaschi and Eial Dujovny, "The Japanese language and brain localization," *Neurological Research: A Journal of Progress*

in Neurosurgery, Neurology and Neurosciences 18, no. 3 (1996), DOI: 10.1080/01616412.1996.11740406.

5. Victor E. Frankl, *Man's Search for Meaning* (Boston, MA: Beacon Press, 2006).

6. Mark Albright, "Missionary Moment: How Do You Measure a Year," *Meridian Magazine*, February 19, 2017, accessed August 30, 2017, ldsmag.com/missionary-moment-how-do-you-measure-a-year/.

7. Corrie ten Boom, John Sherrill, and Elizabeth Sherrill, *The Hiding Place: The Triumphant True Story of Corrie Ten Boom* (New York: Bantam Books, 1974), 26–27.

8. Ezra Taft Benson, "What I Hope You Will Teach Your Children about the Temple," *Ensign*, August 1985.

9. John A. Widtsoe, "Temple Worship," *The Utah Genealogical and Historical Magazine* 12, (April 1921), 62.

10. Ibid., 53–54.

11. "O Love, that wilt not let me go," *hymnal.net*, accessed August 30, 2017, www.hymnal.net/en/hymn/h/432.

12. See Genesis 12:3; 18:18; 22:18; 26:4–5; 28:14.

13. See *Merriam-Webster*, s.v. "covenant," accessed August 30, 2017, www .merriam-webster.com/dictionary/covenant.

14. Richard Neitzel Holzapfel, Dana M. Pike, and David Rolph Seely, *Jehovah and the World of the Old Testament* (Salt Lake City: Deseret Book, 2009), 111.

15. Stephen E. Robinson, *Believing Christ: The Parable of the Bicycle and Other Good News* (Salt Lake City: Deseret Book, 2002).

16. Adele Berlin and Marc Zvi Brettler, eds., *The Jewish Study Bible: Featuring the Jewish Publication Society TANAKH Translation* (New York: Oxford University Press, 2004), 30.

17. Attributed to Truman G. Madsen.

18. S. Michael Wilcox, "The Abrahamic Covenant," *Ensign*, January 1998.

19. Ibid.

20. Berlin and Brettler, eds., *The Jewish Study Bible: Featuring the Jewish Publication Society TANAKH Translation*, 35.

21. G. K. Chesteron, *The Annotated Innocence of Father Brown*, ed. Martin Gardner (Mineola, NY: Dover Publications, 1998), 79.

Personal Notes

Chapter Six

Revelation or Ranting and Raving?
Eli Learns to Discern

1 SAMUEL 1–3

Belief in the divine, or even in the supernatural, is tough to defend, because the evidence is totally subjective. People who say they have heard God's voice or seen a vision can't reproduce it for us, and even if we actually have such an experience, it is easy to doubt its veracity as time goes on. Did we really see or hear what we thought we saw or heard? As Scrooge tells his ghostly visitor Jacob Marley, "You may be an undigested bit of beef, a blot of mustard, a crumb of cheese, a fragment of underdone potato. There's more of gravy than of grave about you, whatever you are!"[1]

In other words, it's hard to trust our senses when it comes to spiritual manifestations, because our organ of discernment is the very faulty, fallible human body. Understanding this, the writers and redactors of the scriptural record take us into the whole experience of receiving a divine message—from the stages of disbelief that precede the final acceptance of the revelation, to the stages of doubt that may follow it. Here are two important lessons we learn from the Hannah and her son, Samuel, about revelation.

157

LESSON ONE: BE CAREFUL WHAT YOU PRAY FOR

With Hannah and the high priest Eli, we have an interesting new take on the iconic type scene of the barren woman being promised a child through God's messenger. Instead of a saintly woman visited by an angel, we have an almost comic scene where the woman is in such distress that the priest thinks she is drunk and rebukes her (see 1 Samuel 9–15). (It's hard to imagine an interchange like this between Gabriel and Mary, for instance.) And in this version, God's messenger is not an angel, but the weak, obese Eli—the unworthy priest who allows his sons to defile the temple. Again, the type scene is turned a bit sideways, just to keep it relatable to fallible mortals like ourselves.

We all pray for the things we want, but sometimes those things are not the best for us. Learning to pray for the right thing is the first lesson in receiving revelation. Take Hannah, for instance. Barren, and made even more miserable by the taunts of her husband's fertile wife, Hannah prays for a son. As Mother Teresa said, "A baby is always a blessing," so it's a pretty good bet that a baby is a good thing to ask for. Each year, before Samuel was born, when Hannah and her family go to Shiloh to offer sacrifice, she weeps and prays. One day, when Eli, the temple priest, rebukes her for drunkenness, Hannah refutes his accusation with an explanation of her miserable state. He rises to the occasion, and, acting as God's emissary, blesses her to be granted her wish through God's grace (see 1 Samuel 1:15–18). Hannah's desire is a righteous one and it brings out the best in an otherwise disappointing priest.

> Hope is definitely not the same thing as optimism. It is not the conviction that something will turn out well, but the certainty that something makes sense, regardless of how it turns out.
>
> –Vaclav Havel[2]

LESSON TWO: BE CAREFUL WHAT YOU PROMISE

When we are desperate, it is our natural tendency to try to make deals with deity. At a time like that, it's easy to promise something in return for something that we desperately want, but it's important to be cautious about those vows. Apparently God takes them seriously! There is a tragic example of a "rash vow" in the book of Judges. Jephthah, in a pathetic attempt to appear as tough as the other soldiers, vows to sacrifice the first thing he sees after the battle if God will just grant him the victory (see Judges 11:30–31). This does not work out well for him, because his daughter is the first thing he sees, and she is actually offered as a sacrifice (see Judges 11:34–40).

The type scene of the rash vow recurs often in the scriptures, but so does the type scene of the righteous vow. Hannah offers us an example of a righteous vow, even an inspired one, as she promises to "lend" her son to the Lord's service, if she is granted one. And so, when Samuel is born, she waits until he is weaned—about three years of age—and takes him back to Shiloh. Then, reminding the old priest about her vow and his blessing, she leaves Samuel there to be raised in the temple service:

> For this child I prayed; and the Lord hath given me my petition. . . .
> Therefore also I have lent him to the Lord; as long as he liveth he shall be lent to the Lord. (1 Samuel 1:27–28)

Most of us try to negotiate with God at some point in our lives, even Jesus begged that His bitter cup be taken away (see Luke 22:42), but that negotiation must be conditioned by a total willingness to do God's will. If you want God to bless you, go ahead and negotiate, but make sure to promise to do something that He would want—like temple service perhaps—as Hannah did, rather than something too dramatic. Though none of us would sacrifice our own children, we might be tempted to go over-the-top with excessive fasting or self-abnegation. Every Bible story challenges us to ask ourselves, where am I in this story? And what would Jesus do in the same situation? What are you praying for right now, and what are you bringing to the table in the negotiation? It's worth considering.

Hannah is here in the Old Testament as an example, but also as an archetype. A miraculous birth narrative, promises from the temple priest, and the sacrifice of her beloved son to God's service, mark her as the forerunner of Mary, the mother of Jesus. Mary's prayer, known as the Magnificat, following the Annunciation, is modeled on Hannah's prayer of thanksgiving in 1 Samuel 2. I love these lines:

> The Lord maketh poor, and maketh rich: he bringeth low, and lifteth up.
>
> He raiseth up the poor out of the dust, and lifteth up the beggar from the dunghill, to set them among princes, and to make them inherit the throne of glory: for the pillars of the earth are the Lord's, and he hath set the world upon them. (1 Samuel 2:7–8)

Jesus's primary mission was to serve the poor and the downtrodden, and this mission is predicted in the prophetic words of these two mighty women. Mary echoes Hannah's words,

> He hath shewed strength with his arm; he hath scattered the proud in the imagination of their hearts.
>
> He hath put down the mighty from their seats, and exalted them of low degree.
>
> He hath filled the hungry with good things; and the rich he hath sent empty away. (Luke 1:51–53)

We don't always know what is best to pray for, or even what to promise God in return for granting our petition, but Hannah shows us that a generous heart—willing to give even the most precious gift to God—may qualify us to be used in ways that are far greater than we can imagine. Hannah prayed for a son, and, because of her unselfish willingness to sacrifice, she became the mother of a great prophet, and the model for the mother of the Son of God.

We are assured . . . that the purposes of God
cannot fail, 'neither are there any who can stay
his hand.' Thus we know that what God begins
he will finish. There will never be a time when
he will scratch his head and say, 'My goodness!.
[sic] I really thought that was going to work.'
Or, 'I had no idea that was going to happen.'
He does not have a plan 'B.' . . . We can take
comfort and find peace in the oft-repeated
truth that God is the same 'yesterday, today,
and forever.' . . . The divine purpose in making
this declaration so many times must be an intent
to reassure his people that they can trust him.
. . . But filtered through that reassuring reality
is the certainty that often we will have no idea
of what he is doing. . . . One of the results of
this truth is that we will often be participants in
the purposes of the Lord without our knowledge.
How often have you read stories of people that
found themselves in a place or situation where
they were needed, or where prayers needed
to be answered, but who arrived without any
premonitions or preparations. . . . All of this is
a preparation for me to make this declaration:
God often works with us, directs us, or inspires
us without our knowledge.

—Ted Gibbons[3]

The Triumph of the Underdog: David and Goliath

1 SAMUEL 17

The Valley of Elah is a flat, triangle-shaped valley, located on the western edge of the Judean low hills. In ancient days, it formed an important corridor from the coastal cities up to the Judean cities of Hebron, Bethlehem, and Jerusalem. Its location ensured that it would be a crucial strategic stronghold, and over the long and tumultuous history of the Middle East, the valley has been the scene of several important battles.[4]

Just as the Iron Age was dawning (sometime around 1000 BCE), the army of the Philistines gathered on the west side of the valley and faced their archenemies, the Israelites, who were encamped on the other side. The Philistines were a seagoing people that ranged up and down the coast of the Mediterranean, pillaging cities and basically making a nuisance of themselves; the Israelites were continually at war with them. Saul, the first king of Israel, had spent his entire life fighting them.

The greatest warrior among the Philistines was a giant of a man named Goliath. He hailed from Gath, one of their five city-states, and (though accounts of his height grew with succeeding translations) stood at least "six cubits and a span" (1 Samuel 17:4), or 9'9" tall. Dressed in elaborate armor, he descended into the ravine that separated the armies twice each day for forty days, shouting out a challenge for any Israelite to meet him in single combat, and thus determine the victory (see 1 Samuel 17:5–9).

THE ACTION HERO EMERGES

The Israelites had a king who might have met the challenge, for Saul himself stood "head and shoulders" above any man in Israel (see 1 Samuel 9:2, NLT), and, in his younger days, might have been the man to combat such a foe as Goliath. But now, Saul was largely useless, possessed by dark moods that caused him to grow alternately morose and then violent, but totally unfit for combat (see

1 Samuel 16:14–15, KJV). But as Saul sat cowering in his tent, he was entertained by the young son of a sheep farmer. David, the youngest of Jesse's eight sons, had been hired to play and sing for Saul when his dark moods overtook him (see 1 Samuel 16:19, 23; 17:12, 14).

David's father had sent him down to the Valley of Elah with provisions for his older brothers, several of whom were enlisted in the king's forces (see 1 Samuel 17:17–18). There David made himself useful to the king with his musical skills, but also had the opportunity to observe the Israelites in a holding pattern as Goliath sallied forth with his daily challenge. David, outraged by the Philistine's audacity, immediately volunteers to meet the giant in single combat (see 1 Samuel 17:32). Here our brilliant narrator takes us directly into the action and makes us privy to the conversations that reveal the giant spirit of David: "And David said to Saul, Let no man's heart fail because of him; thy servant will go and fight with this Philistine" (1 Samuel 17:32).

Though no one takes his challenge seriously, no one else is willing to fight the giant, so David is given the chance. While his brothers laugh at him and Saul tries to pile heavy armor on him (see 1 Samuel 17:38–39), David makes his own preparations (see 1 Samuel 17:40). He does not consider himself to be powerless against a stronger opponent. He knows that his strength lies in his unusual mode of fighting, for he is a slinger of stones. Rejecting Saul's armor and weapons, he declares:

> . . . I cannot go with these; for I have not proved them. And David put them off him.
> And he took his staff in his hand, and chose him five smooth stones out of the brook . . . and his sling was in his hand. (1 Samuel 17: 39–40)

The biblical narrative has already taught us that David is a hero, by relating the stories of him slaying both a bear and a lion to protect his flocks (see 1 Samuel 34–35). (This fierce bravery, combined with his skill on the lyre and his poetic ability, would have made him the perfect Renaissance man—if we were anywhere near the

Renaissance!) David's Herculean feats raised him above the normal man, and inspired a mythical reverence for him in the hearts of his people.

SMALL BUT DEADLY

Ancient armies had three types of fighters: the infantry, the cavalry, and the artillery, which included both archers and slingers. Slingers carried pouches with lengths of rope attached on two sides. Stones or lead balls were placed in the pouch, and the pouch was swung in increasingly fast circles, then let go on one side—releasing the projectile with a stopping power equal to that of a modern handgun. Ancient records show that slingers could take a bird down in flight with deadly accuracy. The Romans even invented a special set of tongs designed to extract a stone or ball embedded in the flesh of an unfortunate soldier struck by a slinger. Expert slingers were able to hit a target from as far away as two hundred yards.[5]

The slinger was a powerful foe against the infantry, who were weighed down by heavy armor and shields. Though the infantry could be deadly at close range, the slingers had the advantage at a distance. If the projectile found an unprotected spot, the infantryman was a "sitting duck" for the skilled slinger.[6] As Goliath made his way down into the valley, his shield bearer going before him, he anticipated an easy contest with a smaller opponent (see 1 Samuel 17:41). He was in for a surprise. In fact, historian Robert Dohrenwend writes, "Goliath had as much chance against David as any Bronze Age warrior with a sword would have had against an [opponent] armed with a .45 automatic pistol."[7]

As they move toward each other, Goliath mocks David; he considers David hardly worth fighting, with only with a shepherd's staff in his hands. "Thou comest to me with staves?" he asks in disdain (1 Samuel 17:43). And here we see the faith, the courage, and even the poetic artistry of this remarkable young man, as he tosses back the giant's own phrase, substituting "sword," "spear," and "shield" for "sticks" to show that he is not only unafraid, but has as much disdain for Goliath's weapons as Goliath does for his.

Thou comest to me with a sword, and with a spear, and with a shield: but I come to thee in the name of the Lord of hosts, the God of the armies of Israel, whom thou hast defied. . . .

And all this assembly shall know that the Lord saveth not with the sword and spear: for the battle is the Lord's, and he will give you into our hands. (1 Samuel 17:45, 47)

Now the action begins to move very quickly. David runs toward the giant with his loaded sling, begins the rapid circular motion (taking no more than a second or two) and releases the stone, "and smote the Philistine in his forehead, that the stone sunk into his forehead; and he fell upon his face to the earth" (1 Samuel 17:49).

Goliath was down, and David seized the giant's sword and took off his head. With that stroke, the battle was decided, and the stunned Philistines quickly fled the field (see 1 Samuel 17:51). From there, David moves quickly into prominence and eventually takes the kingdom from the weaker, unstable King Saul (see 1 Samuel 18:5; 2 Samuel 2:7, 11).

THE FALL FROM GRACE

A few chapters later, the masterful author of the book of Samuel begins the story of David's fall with a hint to us that the warrior king has lost his focus. "And it came to pass, after the year was expired, *at the time when kings go forth to battle*, that David sent Joab, and his servants with him, and all Israel; and they destroyed the children of Ammon, and besieged Rabbah. But David tarried still at Jerusalem" (2 Samuel 11:1; italics added).

David's strength is as a warrior; yet, instead of leading his armies to battle, he entrusts the task to Joab. (This has ramifications later when Joab begins to wield power over the king because he knows his dirty secrets.) David remains behind in the city he has founded.

And to let us know that the king has a little too much time on his hands, our narrator informs us that, instead of fighting in the field, David is taking a nap! The contrast between this laconic, snoozing monarch and the energetic young David running to defend Israel against the Philistine army is rather striking and does not bode well.

Finally up from his nap, lounging around on the roof of the palace, David sees a beautiful woman undergoing the ritual bath required of Hebrew women at the end of their menstrual cycle. (A detail skillfully inserted by the author so that we will know that the child soon to be conceived cannot be Uriah's.) David sees her, sends men to find out who she is, and learns that she is the wife of one of his chief captains, Uriah the Hittite (see 2 Samuel 11:2–3).

> [David] sent messengers, and took her; and she came in unto him, and he lay with her. . . .
> And the woman conceived, and sent and told David, and said, I am with child. (2 Samuel 11:4–5)

WARTS AND ALL

It was not the custom for ancient Near Eastern authors to write about the errors of their kings. In Greek and Egyptian texts from the same time, kingly triumphs were embellished and mistakes were glossed over. In this, the Hebrew authors differed from their neighbors. The Hebrew authors of scripture did not hesitate to expose the follies, and even grievous sins, of their prophets and leaders. As the *Jewish Study Bible* notes, "The way David's behavior is depicted and condemned in the Bible shows the overriding importance it assigns to moral values."[8] In one of the most moving scenes in scripture, God sends Nathan the prophet to call David to repentance.

When we see Jesus teaching in parables, we can trace the practice back to moments like these, when Nathan relates a parable about a rich man who, rather than select one of his great flocks to feed a stranger, takes the one ewe lamb, the beloved pet of a faithful servant, and butchers it instead (see 2 Samuel 12:1–4). David (characteristically phlegmatic) flies into a rage at the story and condemns the selfish man to death, only to be told by Nathan, "Thou art the man (2 Samuel 12:7)." Cornered by conscience, David admits his sin and spends the rest of his life trying to repent for this crime. Nathan prophesies that David's sin will rebound back upon him: The "sword shall never depart," and the Lord "will raise up evil . . . out of thine own house" (2 Samuel 12:10, 11). David's three sons fulfill these prophecies in a terrible manner, for as a civil war erupts, they kill each other and try to kill their own father. One of his sons actually has sexual relations with David's wives and concubines on the very roof where David's tragic fall began.

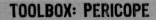

TOOLBOX: PERICOPE

A pericope (pronounced pah-ri-ko-pee) is a little 'nugget of narrative' that stands alone. Chapters are divided the way they are for different reasons and may contain several pericopes. A great example of this occurs in the story of David's rise and fall.

In an artful stroke of storytelling, our narrator condenses the three most important episodes of David's young life into concise pericopes of just four verses each. The triumph of David over Goliath and the Philistines—from the moment he begins to run toward the giant to the moment that the armies turn and flee after his defeat—is given to us in only four verses (see I Samuel 17:48–51). Then the tragic fall of David—from the moment that he sees the woman on the roof to the moment that she notifies him of her conception—is given in four succinct verses (see 2 Samuel 11:2–5). Finally, after calling Uriah home from the battle and trying twice to get him to go home and sleep with his wife so that the pregnancy could be attributed to him, David makes a willful, premeditated decision to commit murder. And this vile deed—from the moment David sits down to pen Uriah's death sentence and send it to Joab at the battlefront to the death of the faithful young man—is given to us in four verses (see 2 Samuel 11:14–17). Each recitation is a small masterpiece of understatement, which adds to the impact of the narrative.

Five Smooth Stones:
David Helps Us Fight Our Goliaths

1 SAMUEL 17

What does David's story mean to us? All of us face Goliath-size challenges in our lives—whether it be a relationship that has gone awry, something that we are afraid to face, or obstacles of ill health, financial disaster, or physical disability. Whatever challenge we may be facing, we can learn something from the young David. He had the courage and the insight to choose the right weapons; weapons that worked far better for him than the traditional weapons offered to him by the world. These weapons, or tools, looked insignificant to the untrained eye, but David knew how to unleash their power.

What are the tools that Jesus would have us use? In the Sermon on the Mount, Jesus offers us some qualities that might act like smooth stones—tools that may seem small and insignificant to the world at large, but, when used in the skilled hands of the master slinger, can be powerful against the evil forces that we encounter every day. What if, rather than burdening ourselves with cumbersome weapons like revenge, anger, manipulation, and retaliation, we instead filled our sling with less obvious, but more powerful stones, such as prayer, faith, service, forgiveness and love?

SMOOTH STONE #1: PRAYER

Jesus offered an exact pattern for prayer, instructing us to pray "in this way."

Our Father in heaven, hallowed be your name.
Your kingdom come. Your will be done, on earth as it is in heaven.
Give us this day our daily bread.
And forgive us our debts, as we also have forgiven our debtors.
And do not bring us to the time of trial, but rescue us from the evil one. (Matthew 6:9–13, NRSV)

Jesus's model of prayer is centered on God's kingdom, His will, and His protection. We ask for just enough to sustain us, and for forgiveness only in so far as we forgive others. Knowing that God can be quite unpredictable, we beg Him not to lead us into situations that we cannot handle. Do our prayers really sound like this?

It's amazing how much time we spend worrying about things, and how little time we actually spend praying about them. One woman recounted a time when she and her husband faced a serious challenge. Her mother-in-law advised them to pray together about it for seven nights in a row and then make a decision. The woman realized that she had almost never prayed about anything for seven nights in succession. When is the last time we did that?

Years ago, we moved to a new city just after I became pregnant. Within a few weeks of arriving, I began to have trouble and was bedridden for a week or two before I finally miscarried. A woman named Pat was assigned by the Church to visit me, and I will never forget our first meeting. I noticed that Pat carried a manila folder in her hand, with my name on the tab. When I asked about it, she smiled and said, in a matter-of-fact way, "Oh, this is your folder. When I pray about you, I will write down any thoughts that come into my mind and keep them here. And when I come to visit, I'll take notes of any concerns you have so I can remember to pray about them later." I was dumbfounded that she took prayer so seriously, just like Jesus did. Pat became a trusted friend and mentor, and what a wonderful thing it was to have such a friend in a time of need. I've still never made a folder about anyone, but I learned from Pat to that prayer can be a far more powerful tool than we realize.

SMOOTH STONE #2: BELIEF

Jesus's definition of belief is not static; it is active. To believe is to seek, to ask, and to trust that God will act toward us with at least the decency of the average parent.

> Ask, and it shall be given you; seek, and ye shall find: knock, and it shall be opened unto you:

For every one that asketh receiveth; and he that seeketh findeth; and to him that knocketh it shall be opened. . . .

If ye then, being evil, know how to give good gifts unto your children, how much more shall your Father which is in heaven give good things to them that ask him? (Matthew 7: 7–8, 11 KJV)

Rather than being something that is just lower than knowledge, Jesus described faith and belief as the very power behind all creation. In addition, faith is the key to salvation. Yet, rather than condemn us for our weakness in this area, Christ simply asks us to take the first step and desire to believe. I love the moment when He tells the father of a young son in need of healing that if he can only believe, anything could be possible.

"And straightway the father of the child cried out, and said with tears, Lord, I believe; help thou mine unbelief" (Mark 9:24). Jesus did help, and the child was healed, and so will we be, as we ask for His help with our unbelief.

SMOOTH STONE #3: SERVICE

Righteous works are encouraged in the Sermon on the Mount, not because they advance us in some kind of heavenly point system, but because they identify us as followers of Christ and give glory to God.

Let your light so shine before men, that they may see your good works, and glorify your Father which is in heaven. (Matthew 5:16)

Wherefore by their fruits ye shall know them. (Matthew 7:20)

No man can serve two masters: for either he will hate the one, and love the other; or else he will hold to the one, and despise the other. Ye cannot serve God and mammon. . . .

But seek ye first the kingdom of God, and his righteousness; and all these things shall be added unto you. (Matthew 6:24, 33)

When we view our acts of service as some kind of ticket to heaven, we completely miss the point. We serve because it is what God does, and this kind of selfless service becomes the greatest tool against evil that we can wield.

SMOOTH STONE #4: FORGIVENESS

The power of forgiveness is so great that it acts almost like a magic talisman, investing our lives with power and peace.

> And why beholdest thou the mote that is in thy brother's eye, but considerest not the beam that is in thine own eye? (Matthew 7:3)

> Therefore if thou bring thy gift to the altar, and there rememberest that they brother hath ought against thee;
>   Leave there thy gift before the altar, and go thy way; first be reconciled to they brother, and then come and offer thy gift. (Matthew 5:23–24)

> Blessed are the merciful: for they shall obtain mercy. (Matthew 5:7)

If you live long enough, you will have a collection of things that are hard for you to let go of, and people that you will find it hard to forgive. If you can forgive and forget, your life will be peaceful. If you can't, it won't. That's easy to say, and so hard to do, especially for those who have suffered innocently. The remarkable story of Corrie ten Boom meeting a former prison guard from the concentration camp where she and her sister had suffered (and her sister had died) reminds us that once again, all Christ asks of us is the first step. He does the rest.

Years after her incarceration and torture in the camp, Corrie spoke at a church gathering, and was afterward approached by the very guard who had been one of the worst of her guards in the camp.

> And that's when I saw him, working his way forward against the others. One moment I saw the overcoat and the brown hat; the next, a blue uniform and a visored cap with its skull and crossbones. It came back with a rush: the huge room with its

harsh overhead lights, the pathetic pile of dresses and shoes in the center of the floor, the shame of walking naked past this man. I could see my sister's frail form ahead of me, ribs sharp beneath the parchment skin. *Betsie, how thin you were!* . . .

Now he was in front of me, hand thrust out.

"A fine message, Fräulein! How good it is to know that, as you say, all our sins are at the bottom of the sea!" . . .

But I remembered him and the leather crop swinging from his belt. I was face-to-face with one of my captors and my blood seemed to freeze.

"You mentioned Ravensbruck in your talk," he was saying. "I was a guard there." No, he did not remember me.

"But since that time," he went on, "I have become a Christian. I know that God has forgiven me for the cruel things I did there, but I would like to hear it from your lips as well. Fräulein,"— again the hand came out—"will you forgive me?"

And I stood there—I whose sins had again and again to be forgiven—and could not forgive. Betsie had died in that place— could he erase her slow terrible death simply for the asking? It could not have been many seconds that he stood there—hand held out—but to me it seemed hours as I wrestled with the most difficult thing I had ever had to do. . . .

But forgiveness is not an emotion, I knew that too. Forgiveness is an act of the will, and the will can function regardless of the temperature of the heart. " . . . help me!" I prayed silently. "I can lift my hand. I can do that much. You supply the feeling."

And so woodenly, mechanically, I thrust my hand into the one stretched out to me. And as I did, an incredible thing took place. The current started in my shoulder, raced down my arm, sprang into our joined hands. And then this healing warmth seemed to flood my whole being, bringing tears to my eyes.

"I forgive you, brother!" I cried. "With all my heart!"

For a long moment we grasped each other's hands, the former guard and the former prisoner, I had never known God's love so intensely, as I did then.[9]

SMOOTH STONE #5: LOVE

Jesus commands us to love like He does. This teaching of Jesus is perhaps the most difficult. But here it is anyway:

> Ye have heard that it hath been said, Thou shalt love thy neighbour, and hate thine enemy.
>
> But I say unto you, Love your enemies, bless them that curse you, do good to them that hate you, and pray for them which despitefully use you, and persecute you.
>
> That ye may be the children of your Father which is in heaven: for he maketh his sun to rise on the evil and on the good, and sendeth rain on the just and on the unjust. (Matthew 5:43–45)

Love is an active verb, not a passive emotion. Jesus's definition of loving someone—either enemy or friend—includes blessing them, praying for them, and doing good to them. If we have trouble loving someone, we are encouraged to do these three things, and love will grow.

Diane Pace—wife of the beloved BYU religion professor George W. Pace—taught a class that I attended many years ago, and shared a story from her early days of marriage. Her husband was a farmer and also worked as a teacher, so he was very busy. It seemed that every day George just ran into the house to eat, change, and rush out to the next obligation. He seemed preoccupied and didn't pay much attention to her, and she began to grow sullen and discontented with their relationship. One day, she happened upon the scripture in 1 Corinthians 12 about spiritual gifts, and noticed the final verse where Paul promises to show us a "more excellent way" (1 Corinthians 12:31). What follows is the famous chapter on charity, or the pure love of Christ. *Could charity also be a gift of the Spirit?* she wondered. And, if so, would praying for that gift help her feel better about her husband?

So Diane decided to pray for her husband every day. At first, she sent up a general request or two for his well-being, but soon ran out of things to say. She began to be aware that in her need to be heard by her husband, she had stopped listening. Diane realized that she needed a little more "intel" on her husband so that she would have something to pray about. So when he came home, she began to ask him about his day, his concerns, the farm, and his students. And, since she was really listening and not just waiting for her turn to talk, he began to tell her more about everything. She would then pray about those things, and often had something insightful to say about them in subsequent conversations. George began asking for her opinion more, and slowly, depth and meaning crept back into conversations that had become banal and superficial. A deep bond began to form.

One day George burst into the house, explaining that he had only a few minutes to shower and change clothes before he was due at a meeting. "Come and talk to me while I get ready!" he said, and Diane felt a rush of disappointment as she told him that she must spend the time getting his shirt ironed if he was to be on time. A moment later, she heard some crashing and banging upstairs and ran up to investigate. There was George, trying to wrestle the ironing board into their little bathroom, so that they could share the few minutes that they had together. Diane's eyes filled with tears as she realized that her prayers had been answered. She had more love in her life because she had learned to love more—from the source of all love.

THE LORD SAVETH NOT WITH SPEAR AND SHIELD

The "weapons" that Christ advocates are unusual and completely counterintuitive. Every time I read the Sermon on the Mount, I am struck by how different Jesus's admonitions are from how I normally want to behave. And I'm not alone there. When wronged, we naturally want to retaliate, get revenge, or at least obtain justice. When hurt, we want to hurt in return—"an eye for an eye" (Matthew 5:38). Our natural tendency is to hang on to what is ours and be cautious about sharing, especially with those who don't seem to deserve it. We worry about our daily needs more than we worry about anything else. We love ourselves and have trouble loving others. It is human nature to act this way. However, Jesus advocates something other than human nature. He seems to believe that we actually can "be . . . perfect, even as your Father which is in Heaven is perfect" (Matthew 5:48).

It does not seem reasonable that the best way to fight the battles life brings us would be to shed our heavy armor, be more open, more loving, more forgiving, and less defensive, but Jesus contends that these small stones can actually bring down a giant. From the early life of David, we see how seemingly small things can be packed with power. From the later life of David, we also see how trusting in our own strength is the beginning of a fall.

David inspires me—not only with his triumphs, but in the way he faces his failures. He never gives up. He spends the rest of his life trying to make things right, and never abandons his faith. His is an example to everyone who feels that their mistakes disqualify them from grace. In one of the Psalms attributed to him, he says, "Create in me a clean heart, O God, and renew a right spirit in me" (Psalm 51:10). With David, I pray that God will fill my sling with the small, secret weapons that will truly give me victory. David believes it can happen, even for him. Jesus believes it can happen for all of us. We just need to have faith, load our slings with the right weapons, and run toward the battle. We won't be alone.

TOOLBOX: ACTION VERBS FOR ACTION HEROES

Every element in the story of David and Goliath exudes energy. David is always moving forward and his response to every challenge is positive. He does not fear the giant, nor does he fear the king. He steps up when everybody else steps back. He "ran toward the army to meet the Philistine" (1 Samuel 17:48). Though everyone else views David as small, weak, and vulnerable, he views himself as invincible, because he comes "in the name of the Lord of hosts" (1 Samuel 17:45).

This triumph marks the beginning of a steady rise to power that eventually places David on Saul's throne; he marries Saul's daughter, and in the end, possesses more power than is good for him or for the nation. Ironically, the slinger of stones becomes a Goliath, and will be brought down because, like Goliath, he trusts in his own strength and forgets to call upon the Lord. And it all starts with action verbs: signals that alert us that something is in motion.

Later, an examination of the action words relating to David's fall shows us something about the direction he was headed. In 2 Samuel 11, everyone was going to war but David "tarried" (2 amuel 11:1). He naps, saunters around on the roof, "looks" where he shouldn't be looking, and "sends" messengers to find out things that are not his business (see 2 Samuel 11:2–3). He doesn't even go himself. Only when his lust takes over do the action verbs kick in again. He "takes" the woman (who obviously has no say in the matter), "[lies] with her," and she "conceives" (see 2 Samuel 11:4–5). Though full of energy, these self-serving and sinful verbs show that we have come a long way from the young warrior—bringing food to his brothers, serving the king, volunteering for the mission, running toward his adversary, and stopping only to testify of the God that he serves.

Another great example of action verbs can be found in the story of Isaac and Rebekah. Take a look at the scene with Abraham's servant at the well, and examine the verbs used in relation to Rebekah: she is all action. She runs, she hastens, and she makes it happen! It is an interesting and illuminating exercise to list the verbs used in relation to the various characters, and then—if you have the courage—to imagine what verbs a biblical author would use to describe you!

A Firm Mind: King Solomon Shows Us Why We Can't Think Straight

I KINGS 1–3

King Solomon's story begins with a troubling account of how he came to power. He didn't exactly play by the rules! However, this is followed by a beautiful vision where he is offered any gift he desires; when he asks for wisdom, he is blessed by God with all of his other desires as well. Again, the Bible authors do not want us to be comfortable. They show us the seeds of Solomon's fall even before they show us his greatness.

Actually, I like the scriptures to be a little confusing, because it makes me feel better about the fact that the events of my life do not seem to be clearly delineated in black and white. I get confused; I can't always tell exactly what I ought to be doing next and exactly why things are happening the way they're happening. The characters in the scriptures are presented to us as they face some of these confusing situations, and we get to have an opinion about what our heroes should do. We might ask ourselves, how can Solomon be a great man if he welcomed all those foreign gods into the culture? It's a nice warning to us—a reminder that it's possible to be a really good person and still get way off track.

Solomon gets off track with the best of intentions. He is a great diplomat and he intends to build a great kingdom, so he starts aligning himself through marriages to a startling number of women. The numbers may be exaggerated for effect, but we are told he has seven hundred wives and three hundred concubines. (The sheer logistics of that number of wives is overwhelming!) In 1 Kings 3, Solomon allies himself by marriage with Pharaoh the king of Egypt. He marries the Pharaoh's daughter and brings her to the city of David—Jerusalem—to live there until he finishes building his palace (see 1 Kings 3:1). I don't think it is a coincidence that our author mentions the Pharaoh here. We are meant to think about this and to remember how dangerous an alliance with Egypt can be, and what the Israelites went through to get out of there the last time! The theme of "going down into Egypt" runs through the Old Testament.[10] The Nile Delta means that there will always be food and abundance there, but there is always a danger of becoming corrupted there as well. It's a little like stopping in Las Vegas while crossing the desert. You may need to fill up your car with gas and get something to eat, but be careful about those slot machines; Vegas makes it easy to get sucked in!

I also find it interesting that Solomon spent thirteen years building his palace (see 1 Kings 7:1) and seven years building the temple (see 1 Kings 6:38). The people however, continued to offer sacrifices in open shrines because, at that time, no house had been built for the Lord. Solomon, though he loved the Lord and followed the practices of his father David, also sacrificed and offered at the shrines.

What does it mean that Solomon acknowledged all of these other gods? When God says in the Ten Commandments, "Thou shalt have no other gods before me" (Exodus 20:3), and when Joshua says, "Choose [the Lord over] the gods of the Amorites, in whose land ye dwell" (Joshua 24:15), they help us understand the context of Solomon's behavior. The Israelites believed in the reality of other gods; they just chose to worship the Lord. These other deities were more legitimate and real to them than, say, Hindu gods are to Christians. Their cultures were closer, more tied together, and these other gods had a big influence on their daily lives. We hear about them all the way through the Bible. Hebrew prophets challenged their reality, but Solomon, in an effort to placate the alliances he made through marriage, offered them a higher place than perhaps God permitted.

WHAT DO YOU WANT?

It's hard to know what we really want, isn't it? Abraham Maslow said, "It isn't normal to know what we want. It is a rare and difficult psychological achievement."[11] Solomon started out wanting the right things. "In Gibeon, the Lord appeared to Solomon in a dream by night: and God said, Ask what I shall give thee" (1 Kings 3:4). In other words, the Lord is asking him, "What do you want?"

That's a good question, isn't it? What do you want? "Here I am," says God, in effect. What do you want?" In reply, Solomon says this:

"Thou hast made thy servant king . . . and I am but a little child: I know not how to go out or come in.

And thy servant is in the midst of thy people which thou hast chosen, a great people, that cannot be numbered nor counted for multitude.

Give therefore thy servant an understanding heart to judge thy people, that I may discern between good and bad: for who is able to judge this thy so great a people? (1 Kings 3:5–7)

A Bible commentator explains the significance of the term, "understanding heart:"

Binat HaLev translates as "an understanding of the heart." The word *binat* comes from the Hebrew root *bet-yod-nun* meaning "to understand or discern," and *lev* means "heart."

In Jewish tradition the heart is also the seat of all emotions. There is a midrash that lists over 60 emotions of the heart. Among these emotions: "the heart sees, hears, speaks, falls, stands, rejoices, weeps, comforts, sorrows. . ." (Ecclesiastes *Rabbah* 1:16). In Judaism, our hearts are the vessels of both our feelings and our wisdom."[10]

The Lord was very pleased with Solomon's wish. He said, in effect, "You know, you could've asked for wealth. You could've asked for a long life. You could've asked for all these things, and so what I'm going to do is I'm going to give you not only great wisdom, but I'm going to give you a long life and wealth too" (see 1 Kings 3:11–14). Whether this was a blessing or not remains to be seen. So, Solomon becomes famous, and tales are told about his wisdom. Most famously, the Queen of Sheba

> What we want speaks volumes about who we are, and our entire identity, every name by which we are known, seems to be called forth with the question, "What do you want?
>
> —Wendy Ulrich[13]

comes from Egypt to meet him, hear of his wisdom, and see his great wealth (see 1 Kings 10:1–13). Once again, he has an alliance with Egypt.

Under Solomon, Israel begins to be a great nation. Solomon builds a temple and a palace and a great wall around Jerusalem. But in order to accomplish this, he reintroduced the system called corvée, or forced labor. Traditionally, this had been imposed on alien cultures by the ruling country, as was done to the Israelites in Egypt. But Solomon imposes this terrible system on his own people. So though he raises Israel to a new level as a nation, he does so at the cost of his principles. He wants something good, but forsakes some important principles in order to achieve it. He loses track of what he really wants.

IT TAKES A FIRM MIND

Solomon reminds us that what we really want in life will eventually determine what we do. He shifted from having wisdom and understanding as his main desires, to wanting the power and prestige that comes from being a great nation. And that shift changed his actions. Solomon knew what he wanted, then lost sight of it. This is a very common phenomenon. It usually involves a dangerous dose of self-deception. If our behavior slides in response to selfish desires, it is much easier to explain that bad behavior by saying that our priorities have shifted, rather than we simply succumbed to temptation.

Here are just a few reasons why it is so hard to stay focused on what we really want:

- The human brain wants to be stimulated and also to experience pleasure and happiness.
- It is easy to confuse stimulation with happiness, because similar chemicals are triggered.
- Modern culture with its fire hose of information (internet) and constant multitasking, can turn us into stimulation junkies with divided attention.

- The ability to focus on what brings happiness, rather than just stimulation, requires training the brain muscle to focus attention—a firm mind.

In order to keep our focus, it is also necessary to learn to distinguish between desires, appetites, and passions, which feel at the time, can feel like real happiness and joy. Here are some more definitions:

Desire: "A longing or craving, as for something that brings satisfaction or enjoyment."[14]

Appetite: Desire for food, drink, bodily craving of any kind, or a special liking.[15]

Passion: A "powerful or compelling emotion or feeling" Lust, sexual desire.[16]

Notice the difference between the definitions of those urgent cravings and the definitions of happiness:

Happiness: "Bliss, contentment, felicity; an active or passive state of pleasurable satisfaction."[17]

Joy: "The emotion of great delight or happiness caused by something exceptionally good or satisfying; keen pleasure; elation."[18]

Stimulation is a good thing. Desires, appetites, and passions represent much of the fun and excitement of life. But when these things spiral out of control, we begin to be less happy. The scriptures encourage us to "bridle" our passions (see Alma 38:12). Anyone who has ridden a horse knows that a bridle will actually help a horse run faster and farther by controlling the energy expended. We learn that a firm mind is essential in order to understand truth.

> "You will know as much of God, and only as much of God, as you are willing to put into practice.
> —Eric Liddell[19]

Jacob says, "Oh all ye that are pure in heart, lift up your heads and receive the pleasing word of God, and feast upon his love; for ye may, *if your minds are firm*, forever" (Jacob 3:2; italics added). We also learn that a firm mind is a prerequisite for receiving miracles. Moroni says,

> Have miracles ceased? . . .
>
> Nay; neither have angels ceased to minister unto the children of men. For behold, they . . . minister according to the word of [Christ's] command, showing themselves unto them of *strong faith* and *a firm mind* in every form of godliness. (Moroni 7:29–30; italics added.)

And finally, a firm mind is the foundation of faith. Helaman describes the young warriors whose faith was so great that they didn't fear death: "Now this was the faith of these of whom I have spoken; they are young, and their *minds are firm*, and they do put their trust in God continually" (Alma 57:27; italics added).

A FIRM MIND: HOW DO I GET ONE OF THOSE?

So how do we develop a firm mind? In a world of distraction and overstimulation, it takes a concerted effort. Here are a few suggestions that have worked for me, and if you put your (firm) mind to it, I am sure you will be able to come up with some of your own.

- Shut off the stimuli (phone, computer, TV) for some time each day.
- Practice being still—breathing, observing—try guided meditations.
- Read and ponder—make a place where you retreat from the world.
- Develop a prayer process—make a structure for spiritual growth.
- Remember all stimulus is transitory, constantly shifting, and really not worth chasing, so when you are chasing stimulation, question it.

As Victor Frankl said, "Between stimulus and response there is a space. In that space lies our freedom and power to choose our response. In those choices lie our growth and our happiness."[20] If only Solomon could have remembered that, things might have turned out better.

NOTES

1. Charles Dickens, *A Christmas Carol* (North Chelmsford, MA: Courier Corporation, 2014), 12.
2. Vaclav Havel, *Disturbing the Peace* (New York: First Vintage Books, 1991), 181.
3. Ted Gibbons, "His Purposes Fail Not," *Meridian Magazine*, January 9, 2017.
4. "The Valley of Elah," *BibleWalks.com*, accessed September 1, 2017, www.biblewalks.com/Sites/ElahValley.html.
5. Malcolm Gladwell, *David and Goliath: Underdogs, Misfits, and the Art of Battling Giants* (New York: Little, Brown and Company, 2013), 9–11.
6. Ibid., 10.
7. Ibid., 11.
8. Adele Berlin and Marc Zvi Brettler, eds., *The Jewish Study Bible: Featuring the Jewish Publication Society TANAKH Translation* (New York: Oxford University Press, 2004), 636.
9. Corrie ten Boom, John Sherrill, and Elizabeth Sherrill, *The Hiding Place: The Triumphant True Story of Corrie Ten Boom* (New York: Bantam Books, 1974); italics in original.
10. See Genesis 37:35; 46:3–4; Deuteromony 26:5; 10:22; Numbers 20:15; Joshua 24:4; Isaiah 30:2; 52:4.
11. Attributed to Abraham Maslow.
12. Barbara Binder Kadden, "An Understanding of the Heart—Middah Binat HaLev," *ReformJuadism.org*, accessed September 1, 2017, reformjudaism.org/understanding-heart-middah-binat-halev.
13. Attributed to Wendy Ulrich.
14. *Dictionary.com*, s.v. "desire," accessed September 1, 2017, www.dictionary.com/browse/desire.
15. *Dictionary.com*, s.v. "appetite," accessed September 1, 2017, www.dictionary.com/browse/appetite?s=t.
16. *Dictionary.com*, s.v. "passion," accessed September 1, 2017, www.dictionary.com/browse/passion?s=t.
17. *Dictionary.com*, s.v. "happiness," accessed September 1, 2017, www.dictionary.com/browse/happiness?s=t.
18. *Dictionary.com*, s.v. "joy," accessed September 1, 2017, www.dictionary.com/browse/joy?s=t.

19. Eric Liddell, *The Disciplines of the Christian Life* (Excondido, CA: eChristian, 1985).
20. Victor E. Frankl, *Man's Search for Meaning* (Boston, MA: Beacon Press, 2006).

Personal Notes

_____
_____
_____
_____
_____
_____
_____
_____
_____
_____
_____
_____
_____
_____
_____
_____

Chapter Seven

POETS AND PROPHETS

Ready to Rumble: Proverbs and Ecclesiastes vs. the Psalms

"Where shall wisdom be found?" (Job 28:12). Job, in his deepest distress, asked this question, and the answer is less simple than it may seem. The old saying goes, "Another year older, and another year wiser." But I beg to differ on this one. In my experience, everybody gets older, but not everybody gets wiser! Proverbs and Ecclesiastes offer us an opportunity to examine the accumulated wisdom of the ages, and evaluate that wisdom in light of revealed scripture. We might well ask ourselves, how do we grow wiser as we grow older, and avoid the narrow cynicism that often comes along with aging?

PROVERBS: THE ORIGINAL SELF-HELP BOOK

Wisdom literature was a popular genre in the regions where the Hebrews lived. Though the proverbs are attributed to Solomon, the Hebrew that they were written in comes from a later date, so they are more likely a collection of wise sayings that are connected to him because of his legendary wisdom.

The premise of the Proverbs is this: the world is basically a level playing field, and through effort and righteous living we will be blessed with prosperity and happiness. This is the premise of most self-help literature, and the reason for its perennial popularity. Just look at the stats on this multi-billion dollar industry:

> Self-improvement represents a $10 billion per year industry in the U.S. alone. In addition to high revenues, self-help also has a high recidivism rate, with the most likely purchaser of a self-help book being the same person who purchased one already in the last 18 months. . . .
>
> Self-help books are frequently followed by a train of formulaic subsequent manuals for happiness, weight loss, success, money, or spirituality by the very same authors, fueling the 6.1% average annual growth rate projected by *Marketdata Enterprise Inc.* The *New Statesman*'s Barbara Gunnell forecasts a secure future for positive psychology, noting that "never has an age been so certain that it deserves not just freedom from distress, but positive well-being" and that "the worried well with a belief in their right to feel good are a lucrative market."[1]

The article reports that the top self-help gurus, like Tony Robbins, bring in as much as $80 million in one year from his self-help products.[2] They are, perhaps, the most trusted prophets of this generation.

IS THERE ANYTHING WRONG WITH SELF-HELP?

Proverbs represent a type of teaching that is important, both in families and in the larger civic community. Guidelines about what constitutes right social behavior matter. Strong families and strong social groups tend to have a kind of coded language that expresses their priorities. Here are some examples from the text:

- "The fear of the Lord is the beginning of knowledge: But fools despise wisdom and instruction" (Proverbs 1:7).
- A wise son maketh a glad father: but a foolish man despiseth his mother (Proverbs 15:20).
- Avoid all perverse talk; stay away from corrupt speech. Look straight ahead, and fix your eyes on what lies before you.

- A beautiful woman who lacks discretion is like a gold ring on a pig's snout (see Proverbs 11:22).
- Wealth from get-rich-quick schemes quickly disappears, but wealth from hard work grows over time (see Proverbs 13:11).

This is great stuff, and there is plenty of advice about parenting (turns out the child won't die if you spank it), romance (avoid those loose women), and career planning (whatever you do, work hard.) This would be all we need, if life was fair and good, and hard-working people got all the breaks and the bad, selfish, lazy people didn't prosper in spite of themselves. But as we know, the world doesn't always work the way it should, and so we have Ecclesiastes.

THE TEACHER SAYS, "EVERYTHING IS MEANINGLESS"

In the King James Version, the book of Ecclesiastes begins with the words, "Vanity of vanities, saith the Preacher" (Ecclesiastes 1:2). The preacher, or teacher, is *Koheleth* in Hebrew. And vanity is better translated as "fleeting," or "unsubstantial" (see Ecclesiastes 1:2, footnote *b*) The entire book is very grim. Here are some perky samples from the New Living Translation of the Bible:

- "Everything is meaningless," says the Teacher, "completely meaningless!" (Ecclesiastes 1:2).
- "The more you have, the more people come to help you spend it. So what good is wealth—except perhaps to watch it slip though your fingers!" (Ecclesiastes 5:11).
- "This, too, I carefully explored: Even though the actions of godly and wise people are in God's hands, no one knows whether God will show them favor" (Ecclesiastes 9:1).
- "When people live to be very old, let them rejoice in every day of life. But let them also remember there will be many dark days. Everything still to come is meaningless" (Ecclesiastes 11:8).

Really, if the philosophy of Ecclesiastes is all we have to cling to, we are in pretty dire shape! But at the same time, there is something beautiful about the sheer, stark, honesty of these aphorisms.

Everyone at some time reaches this dark place where we question the meaning of every truth we have been taught, and wonder if it is all just "meaningless."

Harold Bloom, the patriarch of literary critics, claims Ecclesiastes as his favorite book in the Bible, and finds it more poignant as he grows older. He quotes the marvelous lines about the seasons, and rather than pulling from it a tidy moral lesson about things being done in their right time, he feels instead the inescapable passage of time.[3]

> To every thing there is a season, and a time to every purpose under the heaven:
> A time to be born, and a time to die; a time to plant, and a time to pluck up that which is planted;
> A time to kill, and a time to heal; a time to break down, and a time to build up;
> A time to weep, and a time to laugh; a time to mourn, and a time to dance;
> A time to cast away stones, and a time to gather stones together; a time to embrace, and a time to refrain from embracing;
> A time to get, and a time to lose; a time to keep, and a time to cast away;
> A time to rend, and a time to sew; a time to keep silence, and a time to speak;
> A time to love, and a time to hate; a time of war, and a time of peace. (Ecclesiastes 3:1–8)

"Few can come into their seventies without a chill at these repetitive rhythms," writes Bloom. "Koheleth['s] genius shows us that beneath every deep, a lower deep opens."[4]

WAIT A MINUTE, IS THIS STILL THE BIBLE?

If we think of the Bible as a repository of God's word, and a record of His dealings with the faithful and faithless, where shall we put Ecclesiastes? Where is God in this book?

Personally, I rejoice that Ecclesiastes exists along with those dark, thorny chapters in Job where God's fairness is questioned. After all, these difficult questions are, at some point, asked by every thoughtful soul: What kind of God allows suffering? Why can't we trust God to take good care of us if we do our part? What good is righteousness if it is not rewarded? These questions are hurled into the void in these books, and God may choose to answer, or He may not. But the questions are important, and well worth asking. The fact that we ask them shows that we are divine in nature. Our hearts long for justice, even if we can't see it in the world around us.

PSALMS: SONGS OF THE HEART

Well then, where is the hope that God brings us? For that, we turn to the book that balances Proverbs and Ecclesiastes: the poetry of the Psalms. In sublime language, the poets that composed Psalms praise, exhort, lament, and rejoice—all in the framework of faith.

There are a few good reasons why about one third of the Bible is written in poetry. Poetry is where music and language meet. There is rhythm to it—though not always a rhyme—that echoes the beat of the heart, and that helps us remember it. It has an emotive content, and causes our minds and hearts to react together. Poetry is the highest form of human speech. Since God is the highest being, our highest speech should be offered to Him.

Poets use a series of tools, or poetic devices, as a part of their craft. Hebrew poetry does not rhyme, but instead uses puns, metaphors, similes, and rhythms that may not come across in translation. Our King James translators used every poetic device available in English to translate these poems. Many of the translators were contemporaries of Shakespeare and were part of the Golden Age of English drama.[5] In the King James Version of the Bible, we have some of the most beautiful poetry ever written. Here are just a few of the tools they used, and some examples to illustrate them.

NUTS AND BOLTS: THE POETRY OF PSALMS

Psalms, as a literary form, were an important part of Hebrew worship. . . . It was a form also used by several other religious cultures living in the region, including the Egyptians and the Syro-Palestinian peoples. Along with being expressions of praise, lament, or faith, psalms also had a definite liturgical purpose as part of temple worship. . . . John Gabel stated: "The prevalent theory now is that most (if not all) of the poems in the psalmbook were used in ceremonies at the Second Temple—sung or changed with musical accompaniment at various points in the ritual."

Psalms feature a formal "envelope" structure that usually opens with a theme that is repeated at the end. The internal structure of the Psalm may feature several types of parallelism. . . . The Psalm opens with a statement, adds a variation of that statement, and perhaps, even another variation after that. Then it retreats back to the second point, and then back to the first.[6]

Instead of rhyming successive lines of a poem, Hebrew poetry matches the thought in successive lines. This feature of Hebrew poetry is called *parallelism*.

The following are three different types of parallelism used in the Psalms:

- Synonymous Parallelism—This is a feature where the second line repeats the thought of the first line but in different words [see Psalm 2:1–3]. . . .
- Antithetic Parallelism—In this feature the second line is the opposite of the first. This type of construction [is] the least common of the different types [see Psalm 1:6]. . . .
- Synthetic Parallelism—In this poetic style the second line advances the thought of the first. Each line is synonymous but each additional line adds to the thought of the first making it more specific [see Psalm 1:1–3]. . . .

Like many of our hymns, Hebrew poetry often uses old-fashioned words and unusual expressions. The Psalms also make use of literary devices such as:

- Simile—Comparison using the words *like* or *as* [see Psalm 1:3, 4]. . . .
- Metaphor—Comparison made not using *like* or *as* [see Psalm 22:12, 16]. . . .
- Synecdoche—A part of something stands for the whole [see Psalm 51:8]. . . .

- Personification—Inanimate things are given characteristics of living things [see Psalm 85:10].[7]

What is the purpose of a psalm? Why go to all of the trouble to say something in such a formal, repetitive manner, rather than just saying what you mean, without all the flowery language? "There is something very powerful in poetic form that might be compared to compressing molecules into a small space; it unleashes power."[8] The thought and effort that go into a poetic expression increases its impact. It's a little like packing a suitcase. As I stated in *The User-Friendly Book of Mormon*, writing a poem is a little like packing a suitcase. "Each year, I go to England for a couple of weeks of literary study, and I consider it a fun challenge to try to pack for the whole trip in one carry-on bag. To do this, each article of clothing has to perform several functions—a dress or a jacket must be versatile enough to be worn a few different ways."[9]

The same is true of poetry; in a good poem, each word will have several layers of meaning and will call to mind other poetic expressions as well as increase the depth of the reading experience. Each word has an expanded impact as a result.

HOW TO CHANNEL YOUR INNER POET

In my book, *The User-Friendly Book of Mormon*, we do an exercise that is sort of like a scriptural *Mad Lib*, where we learn to write a psalm. If you'd like to try it, I invite you to take a look at that.[10] You don't have to be a great poet, however, to gain a great appreciation for the poetry of the scriptures. Simply read them aloud, and you will be halfway there. Beautiful language must be spoken aloud and heard in order to be fully appreciated.

Another way to gain a greater appreciation for the poetry of the scriptures is to sing and memorize the hymns. Most of our hymns have a scriptural basis, and many come directly from Psalms. When it is time to sing the hymn in church, sit up and sing. Don't mumble! Even if you are not a great singer, you will feel the beauty of the words if you articulate them clearly and sincerely. Sing the hymn as if Jesus were sitting on the stand. Singing is an act of praise and worship.

Finally, memorize some scriptures and hymns, and say or sing them to yourself. Doing so will help you become a more eloquent speaker because you will be memorizing beautiful patterns of speech. Your brain will be stronger and your spirit will be purer as a result.

Poetry is for everyone. The Bible tells us so!

FIND YOUR FAVORITE PSALM

I'm sure everyone has a favorite psalm. If you don't, I'd encourage you to take another look at these beautiful poems and find some that resonate with you. Mine starts with four words that make my heart sit up and smile. "I love the Lord, because he hath heard my voice and my supplications" (Psalm 116:1).

Though I don't know Hebrew, I imagine that the translators are capturing the rhythm of the original in these lines: "For thou hast delivered my soul from death, mine eyes from tears, and my feet from falling" (Psalm 116:8).

One of the hallmarks of great literature is its subversive quality. It will take you to the dark side, and then bring you back into the light. Here we go:

> The sorrows of death compassed me, and the pains of hell gat hold upon me: I found trouble and sorrow.
> . . . I was greatly afflicted:
> I said in my haste, All men are liars. (Psalm 116:3, 10–11)

Then comes the rescue:

> Then called I upon the name of the Lord; O Lord, I beseech thee, deliver my soul.
> Gracious is the Lord, and righteous; yea, our God is merciful.
> The Lord preserveth the simple: I was brought low, and he helped me. (Psalm 116:4–6)

Another bit of structural brilliance: Notice how after saying that the Lord preserves the simple, the next phrase is all one syllable words. "I was brought low, and he helped me." It doesn't get any simpler than that. When you are low, God will help you.

The conclusion of the psalm is just a series of expressions of gratitude, wondering how we could ever thank him enough. "What shall I render unto the Lord for all his benefits toward me?" (Psalm 116:12).

WHAT SHALL I GIVE HIM? GIVE MY HEART

Finally, Psalm 116 ends with this beautiful but curious phrase: "I will offer to thee the sacrifice of thanksgiving" (Psalm 116:17). A sacrifice is anything that is hard to do, something that hurts us to give away. There may be times when we are wrapped up in ourselves and caught up in our own trials and problems, and the greatest sacrifice we can give is simply to be grateful to the Lord for what we do have, and not expect any more than that. Just to be thankful for all that He has given and promise Him that we will call upon Him forever.

I love the poetry of the scriptures. From a very early age, I have felt moved by words, by their beauty and depth and sound. I'm thankful that my parents read the scriptures to me and sang the hymns in our home. I will forever cherish watching my ninety-three-year-old mother listening intently to a favorite hymn as my brothers sang it to her shortly before she died. Too weak to sing, she mouthed the words along with them, her face a picture of perfect praise as she whispered, "Brightly beams our Father's mercy."[11] I hope I go out the same way—praising the Lord in song.

EARS TO HEAR: WHY WE SHOULD MEMORIZE SCRIPTURES

"And your ears shall hear a word behind you saying, 'This is the way, walk in it,' when you turn to the right or when you turn to the left" (Isaiah 30:21, ESV).

I was called as a missionary to Japan, and in those days, the Asian languages were taught at the Language Training Mission in Hawaii. We lived in the dorms there and studied Japanese ten hours a day for eight weeks. We studied eight formal discussions that were written out for us, and that we were encouraged to memorize over the course of our missions. It amounted to dozens of pages of formal Japanese.

Sort of on a dare, three of us missionaries set out to memorize all eight discussions and "pass them off" by the end of our eight weeks in the Language Training Mission. This was an arduous task, but it turned out to be one of the most valuable things I did. Without realizing it, I was memorizing sentence patterns that my mind used in order to learn the language, just the way a child does. A child does not construct new sentences using the rules of grammar, but instead uses the sentences that she has heard as patterns to make new sentences. Memorizing all of that formal, perfect Japanese created templates in my mind so that I could make new sentences. I consider it to be the most important thing I did in order to learn the language.

> Your problem and mine is not to get God to speak to us; few of us have reached the point where he has been compelled to turn away from us. Our problem is to hear.
>
> –Henry B. Eyring[12]

Reading and memorizing scripture has the same effect on our spiritual vocabulary. The more of God's word that you know and can bring to mind, the more easily you will recognize God's voice when it comes into your mind. Even now, forty years after my missionary experience, I can "hear" when I construct an incorrect sentence in Japanese. My vocabulary is so rusty that I may not know how to correct it, but I know that it is wrong. If you want to become more skilled at knowing the voice of God, get as many of His words stuffed into your brain as you can. Memorize scriptures. Familiarize yourself with the way He talks in the scriptures. Then when you receive an inspiration, you will have an innate ability to tell if it's off track.

From Elijah to Isaiah: What Does a Prophet Do?

1–2 Kings

One of the unique things about the LDS faith is that we have prophets in our midst. We sustain the fifteen highest leaders in our Church as "prophets, seers, and revelators." What does this mean? In *The Old Testament: A Very Short Introduction*, author Michael Coogan describes a prophet as someone who foretells the future.[13] Our definition of a prophet in the Church is much wider, deeper, and bigger, and it seems to me it's that way in the scriptures too. If you really read your Old Testament, you will see that foretelling the future is only a portion of the prophet's job description.

Revelation 19:10 says that "the testimony of Jesus is the spirit of prophecy." Just think about that: if we all have the testimony of Jesus, then we are all prophets. What does it mean to be a prophet? That represents quite a lofty view of ourselves—the idea that we can be prophets in our own home. As we look at the Old Testament to see what prophets do, we can examine the lives of our modern-day prophets, to see if they are doing the same kinds of things. Then, perhaps we can look in our own homes, and see if we are acting in a prophetic manner there.

> Prophets speak not only to the people of their time, but they also speak to people throughout all time. Their voices echo through the centuries as a testament of God's will to His children.
> —Dieter F. Uchtdorf[14]

#1 A PROPHET CRIES REPENTANCE

In 1 Kings, we have the conflict between Elijah and the wicked couple Jezebel and Ahab. Elijah was talking openly about their corruption as rulers, so of course they wanted to get rid of him. Elijah is in hiding (see 1 Kings 17:3–5), but then he agrees to meet them and all of their wicked priests (see 1 Kings 18:17–21). It's one thing to read about it, but imagine if you were invited to stand in front of four hundred people who wanted to see you dead, and the rulers who had the power to do it. Wouldn't you want to avoid that situation? Elijah stepped up, and they met.

> It came to pass, when Ahab saw Elijah, that Ahab said unto him, Art thou he that troubleth Israel?
>
> And [Elijah] answered, I have not troubled Israel; but thou, and thy father's house, in that you have forsaken the commandments of the Lord, and thou hast followed Balaam. (1 Kings 18:17–18)

Elijah berates the people for vacillating between gods, and says, "How long halt ye between two opinions? if the Lord be God, follow him: but if Baal, then follow him. And the people answered him not a word" (1 Kings 18:21). Then he says, "Even I only, remain a prophet of the Lord, but Baal's prophets are four hundred and fifty men" (1 Kings 18:22).

I want you to ask yourself in your life, as the prophet or prophetess in your home, are there times when you're afraid to say what you need to say? Or are there times when you're afraid to say it to the youth that you teach, or afraid to say it to your siblings, or whoever, for fear that you will be rejected and not be liked? Perhaps you're afraid to talk about the gospel to your neighbor, for fear that you'll ruin this nice relationship you're building. Fear never stops the prophet. The prophet steps forward and courageously cries repentance when it's needed.

For an example of a modern-day prophet who courageously cried repentance, we can look to Joseph Smith. Joseph and his friends were being held on some charge, as they often were. This account, by Parley P. Pratt, shows us Joseph's character.

> [One night] when confined in a dungeon, . . . [Joseph] and his brethren were trying to get a little sleep, but were kept awake by the awful blasphemies and obscene jests of their jailers, who were recounting the dreadful deeds of robbery and murder they had committed among the Mormons. These were no idle boasts, for these awful atrocities had actually been committed. Suddenly, Joseph rose to his feet, and in a voice that seemed to shake the very building, cried out,

"Silence, ye fiends of the infernal pit! In the name of Jesus Christ I rebuke you, and command you to be still; I will not live another minute and hear such language. Cease such talk, or you or I shall die this instant."

The effect must have been electric in its suddenness. Some begged his pardon, while others slunk into the dark corners of the jail to hide their shame. The power of Jesus Christ, whose name he had invoked in his rebuke, was upon him. His hands and feet were in chains, but these the guards did not see. They saw only the righteous anger in his shining face, and felt the divine power in his voice as he rebuked them.

But if Joseph's voice was terrible as the roaring lion in his rebuke of the wicked, it was soothing as a mother's voice in comfort to the righteous. In that same name, and by the same authority with which he silenced the blasphemies of the guards, he had blessed little children, baptized repentant sinners, conferred the Holy Ghost, healed the sick, and spoken words of comfort and consolation to thousands.[15]

#2 A PROPHET BRINGS FAITH AND HOPE IN TIMES OF TRIAL

Sometimes prophets are characterized as doomsayers, and they are when they need to be. But for the most part, prophets are a positive force for good, and bless the lives of people who are struggling with illness or sin or other kinds of suffering. As an example of this, we have the interaction of Elijah with the widow in a time of famine. He blesses her and her son with a miracle, so that her cruse of oil never gives out. (see 1 Kings 17:8–16).

The following is a testimony about Gordon B. Hinckley—one of our modern prophets—by his son, Richard Hinckley. Richard is a man who understands what a prophet does because he was raised by one!

All of our modern prophets have been optimists. That certainly is true of President Hinckley. Virtually every time he speaks, he leaves us with a sense that the future is bright, and we feel optimism, hope, and the desire to do a little better. He manages to do so even while warning of the dangers and pitfalls that beset us, and even while at times chastising us.

Everything we do in this Church requires optimism. The building of temples is a sign of great optimism. The creation of new stakes and new missions; the opening of new areas to missionary work; the building of hundreds of meeting houses every year, year after year; the tremendous humanitarian effort we carry forth; the continued support of this great educational institution—all are signs of great optimism.

What is the role of a prophet? It is to warn the people. It is to preach and teach of the Savior; it is to proclaim the restored gospel to the world; and yes, it is to continue to lead, build, promote, and encourage personal growth among of all of God's children and to establish the Church in all the world in an optimistic way, in spite of and in the face of terrorists, doomsayers, economic ups and downs, wars, and rumors of wars.[16]

#3 A PROPHET WORKS MIRACLES, AS JESUS DID

This is a more sacred part of the calling of a prophet, but all of them partake of the grace of Christ to heal and bless the people. There are many examples in the Bible of the Savior and His prophets giving healing blessings, and even raising the dead. Elijah raised the widow's son, with whom I'm sure he had a close relationship.

And it came to pass . . . after these things, that the son of the woman, the mistress of the house, fell sick; and his sickness was so sore, that there was no breath left in him.

And she said unto Elijah, What have I to do with thee, O thou man of God? art thou come unto me to call my sin to remembrance, and to slay my son?

And he said unto her, Give me thy son. And he took him out of her bosom, and carried him up into a loft, where he abode, and he laid him upon his own bed.

And he cried unto the Lord and said, O Lord my God, hast thou also brought evil upon the widow with whom I sojourn by slaying her son?

And he stretched himself upon the child three times, and cried unto the Lord, and said, O Lord my God, I pray thee, let this child's soul come into him again.

And the Lord heard the voice of Elijah; and the soul of the child came into him again, and he revived.

And Elijah took the child, and brought him down out of the chamber into the house, and delivered him unto his mother: and Elijah said, See? Thy son liveth.

And the woman said to Elijah, Now by this I know that thou art a man of God, and that the word of the Lord is in thy mouth is truth. (1 Kings 17:17–24)

Almost every one of our modern-day prophets have had experiences like this. They don't brag about them, but if you get into the stories of their lives, these experiences come out. There is one in particular from the life of Lorenzo Snow that I find very moving.

> Today is not different from ages past. The Lord does not love the people of our day any less than in past times. One of the glorious messages of the Restoration of the Church of Jesus Christ is that God continues to speak to His children! He is not hidden in the heavens but speaks today as He did in ancient days.
>
> Much of what the Lord reveals to His prophets is intended to prevent sorrow for us as individuals and as societies. When God speaks, He does so to teach, inspire, refine, and warn His children. When individuals and societies ignore their Heavenly Father's instructions, they do so at the risk of trial, torment, and toil.
>
> –Dieter F. Uchtdorf[17]

When Lorenzo Snow received his patriarchal blessing from Joseph Smith Senior, he was promised, "Thou has a great work to perform in thy day and generation. . . . Thou shalt have faith even like that of the brother of Jared. . . . There shall not be a mightier man on earth than thou. . . . If expedient the dead shall rise and come forth at thy bidding."[18] This blessing came true for Lorenzo Snow.

While conducting a Church conference, he was handed a note that said a young girl who lived nearby had died. The note asked him if he would announce her funeral. Instead, Elder Snow immediately excused himself from the meeting and went to the girl's home, where her family was mourning her death.

After praying to the Lord for help, Elder Snow asked the father of the family if there was any consecrated oil in the house. The father was surprised to hear him ask for this, since his daughter had already died, but he got Elder Snow the oil. Lorenzo then anointed the girl and blessed her to come back to life and be healed, because she had not finished her work here on the earth. Elder Snow then told the parents not to feel sad anymore. Their daughter would soon come back to life. Within an hour, the daughter opened her eyes, sat up in bed, and asked, "Where is he? Where is he?" The mother said, "Where is who?" The daughter replied, "Where is Brother Snow? He called me back to the earth." Ella Jensen, the girl who was healed, lived a long life and became the mother of eight children.[19]

I asked a woman to read this story to my Bible class, and when she finished she shared this personal experience:

> This is a really touching story, and as a young child, I had a similar experience. I didn't die, but I was sent home from the hospital when I was two, and my parents were told that I needed to be at home to die there. Through a priesthood blessing, you can see I've lived a very long life. This is a very touching story to me. I'm thankful for a prophet we have on the earth. Because we have a prophet, we have priesthood power, and the priesthood power has the ability to heal us, and to save our lives, and to make us whole. I've been the recipient of not just this one time as a small child, but many times in my life, being healed through priesthood power.

Prophets are on the earth today, and we need them as much as the ancient people of Israel did. Why not take advantage of the blessings that are here for us through the prophet? In a dark and confusing world, they bring a message of repentance, hope, and healing.

NOTES

1. Lindsay Myers, "The Self-Help Industry Helps Itself to Billions of Dollars," *BrainBlogger*, May 23, 2014, accessed September 1, 2017, brainblogger.com/2014/05/23/the-self-help-industry-helps-itself-to-billions-of-dollars/.
2. Ibid.
3. Harold Bloom, *Where Shall Wisdom Be Found?* (New York: Riverhead Books, 2004), 25.
4. Ibid., 26.
5. David Teems, *Majestie: The King Behind the King James Bible* (Nashville, TN: Thomas Nelson, 2010), 190.
6. Marilyn Green Faulkner, *The User-Friendly Book of Mormon* (Springville, UT: Cedar Fort, 2016), 48.
7. "The Poetry of the Psalms," Pastor Nathanael Mayhew, *Zion Ev. Lutheran Church*, accessed September 14, 2017, atlanta.clclutheran.org/bibleclass/booksofbibleoverview/ot/psalmpoetry.html.
8. Marilyn Green Faulkner, *The User-Friendly Book of Mormon*, 49.
9. Ibid.
10. Marilyn Green Faulkner, *The User-Friendly Book of Mormon*, 50–51.
11. "Brightly Beams Our Father's Mercy," *Hymns*, no. 335.
12. Henry B. Eyring, *To Draw Closer to God* (Salt Lake City: Deseret Book, 1997), 29.
13. Michael Coogan, *The Old Testament: A Very Short Introduction* (New York: Oxford University Press, 2008), 74.
14. Dieter F. Uchtdorf, "Why Do We Need Prophets?," *Ensign*, March 2012.
15. David B. Haight, "Joseph Smith, the Prophet," *Ensign*, December 2001.
16. Richard G. Hinckley, "'Prophetic Priorities,'" (Brigham Young University devotional, May 15, 2007), speeches.byu.edu/talks/richard-g-hinckley_prophetic-priorities/.

17. Dieter F. Uchtdorf, "Why Do We Need Prophets?," March 2012.

18. Arthur R. Bassett, "The Prophet of the Lord," *New Era*, January 1972.

19. Thomas Cottam Romney, *The Life of Lorenzo Snow: Fifth President of the Church of Jesus Christ of Latter-day Saints* (S.U.P. Memorial Foundation, 1955).

Personal Notes

_____

_____

_____

_____

_____

_____

_____

_____

_____

_____

_____

_____

_____

_____

_____

_____

_____

_____

_____

_____

_____

_____

_____

_____

_____

_____

_____

_____

_____

_____

_____

_____

_____

_____

_____

_____

_____

_____

_____

Chapter Eight

MISSIONARIES

What Happens in the Diaspora, Stays in the Diaspora. Or Does It?

DANIEL 1–6

The book of Daniel is the only apocalypse in the Old Testament. An apocalypse is a book that is about the "end times," and includes hidden knowledge that is revealed. The interesting thing about the book of Daniel is that it is really two books. The first six chapters of the book Daniel are court tales, or traditional tales about the Jew living in the court of the king. Like Joseph, Moses, and some of the other characters who end up in the court of a foreign king, Daniel shows us how a Jew ought to behave in a foreign court.

Daniel is also written in two languages—Hebrew and Aramaic—a fact that made it a little challenging for translators.[1] In Daniel 2:1, it says, "And in the second year of the reign, Nebuchadnezzar dreamed dreams, wherewith his spirit was troubled, and his sleep brake from him." The king ordered the magicians, astrologers, sorcerers, and Chaldeans (courtiers), to be summoned and ordered to tell the king what he had dreamed (see Daniel 2:2). They came in and stood before the king, and the king said to them, "I have dreamed a dream, and my spirit was troubled to know the dream" (Daniel 2:3). The courtiers, or Chaldeans, spoke to the King in Aramaic, "O, king" (Daniel 2:4). From the words, "O, King," the book of Daniel switches to Aramaic all the way through Daniel 8.

To me, the most interesting thing about the book of Daniel is the picture it paints of life in the Diaspora ("the settling of scattered colonies of Jews outside ancient Palestine after the Babylonian exile"[2]) for these young Israelites. We know that after the destruction of Jerusalem in 587 BCE, the best and brightest were taken to Babylon, and Daniel and his companions were among them (see Daniel 1:1, 6–7). They could have chosen to simply blend in, but they chose instead to live their dietary laws and strictly observe their religious duties. This brought them under scrutiny when they were in the court of the king, who had gathered young men from several cultures together. Though all were given a specific diet, they refused to drink the king's wine or eat meat. They preferred to eat a nice, healthy vegan diet! And as a result they were so strong, bright-eyed, and bushy-tailed, that the king was impressed (see Daniel 1:8–19). This sets the scene.

REVELATION VS. DIVINATION

So when the King has a troubling dream, Daniel steps up and offers to interpret it. At this point, the king has set an impossible challenge to his advisors, because he cannot remember the dream, so they must discern what the dream was and then interpret it. When Daniel hears this, he gathers his companions and they pray for help. God reveals the dream and its interpretation to Daniel in a night vision, and he uses this opportunity to bear witness of the reality of his God (see Daniel 2:16–23).

> Daniel answered in the presence of the king, and said, The secret which the king hath demanded cannot the wise men, the astrologers, the magicians, the soothsayers, shew unto the king;
>
> But there is a God in heaven that revealeth secrets, and maketh known to the king Nebuchadnezzar what shall be in the latter days. Thy dream, and the visions of thy head upon thy bed, are these;

As for thee, O king, thy thoughts came into thy mind upon thy bed, what should come to pass hereafter: and he that revealeth secrets maketh known to thee what shall come to pass.

But as for me, this secret is not revealed to me for any wisdom that I have more than any living, but for their sakes that shall make known the interpretation to the king, and that thou mightest know the thoughts of thy heart. (Daniel 2:27–30)

In the pagan religions of the time, one of the traditional roles of the priest was divination. The word simply refers to foretelling the future, but its use is generally connected to the occult. Using various devices, Tarot cards, tea leaves, crystal balls, the diviner foretells the future, usually for money. Jeremiah spoke of the type of divination that was practiced: "Hearken not unto the words of the prophets that prophesy unto you: they make you vain: they speak a vision of their own heart, and not out of the mouth of the Lord (Jeremiah 23:16).

Rather than parlor tricks, Daniel turns to prayer, with the help of his faithful friends. The lesson is obvious, but the king is a long way from understanding it. At first, for him, Daniel is just the most skillful diviner. But Daniel's example, though faced with one frightening trial after another, eventually carves a place for himself that is like Joseph's in Egypt—in a position of power and trust with the king and also in a position to be able to help his fellow captives.

NO FEAR: THE FIERY FURNACE

Daniel and his friends are continually getting into trouble with the jealous advisors that have been shamed by his prophetic powers. The king keeps making rash vows, and Daniel and his friends get caught in the middle. The point of these stories is to have us ask ourselves how we are behaving in our own Diaspora. Do we choose to keep our heads down and just blend in? Or do we stand up courageously and unapologetically for our beliefs? The answer in my case is "yes." I do both. But Daniel is telling me that I can do better.

In Daniel 3, when Shadrach, Meshach and Abed-nego are consigned to a deadly, fiery furnace for refusing to worship a false idol, the king asks them why they cannot simply recant and avoid such a terrible fate. They reply:

> O, Nebuchadnezzar, we have no need to answer you in this matter.
>
> If this be so, our God whom we serve is able to deliver us from the burning fiery furnace, and he will deliver us out of your hand, O king.
>
> But if not, be it known to you O king, that we will not serve your gods or worship the golden image that you have set up. (Daniel 3:16–18, ESV)

There's the lesson, the golden nugget of truth embedded in the middle of everything else. This comment, to paraphrase it, says: "Our God can save us from the fire, but if he doesn't save us from the fire, we're still not going to serve your God." So in other words, we're not going into the fire because we think He's going to save us, we're going into the fire because we just have faith in God and even if He doesn't save us, we're going to be obedient to Him. The young men are not obedient because they know God will save them; they are obedient because they love God.

You can feel the tension growing, as the furnace is heated to seven times its usual strength (see Daniel 3:19, KJV). The use of the number seven alerts us that the number is hyperbole: it is just really hot! The story is supposed to scare you with the danger that the young men face, and then it's suppose to thrill you when God saves them. We get to live through the fear, the courage, and the rescue with them. We can see what our lives will be like when God really gets into the picture. The young men are quite polite to the king, but they're also pretty direct with him.

There is a beautiful talk titled, "But If Not," by Elder Lance Wickman, that refers to this incident in the Bible. Elder Wickman tells a story about their second child, Adam, who was born when Lance was in Vietnam on active duty and in great danger. This child was particularly precious to them. But at the age of five, he became ill.

A common childhood illness blanketed our southern California community, and Adam contracted the disease. Aside from a concern for his comfort, we were not worried. He even seemed to have a light case. Suddenly one morning he did not arise from his bed; he was in a deep coma. We rushed him to the hospital, where he was placed in intensive care. A constant cadre of devoted doctors and nurses attended him. His mother and I maintained a ceaseless vigil.[3]

When it finally became obvious that Adam was not going to recover, Elder Wickman called their stake president, and the two of them gave him a blessing.

As the familiar and comforting words of a priesthood blessing were spoken in faith and earnest pleading, I was overcome by a profound sense that Someone else was present. I was overwhelmed by the thought that if I should open my eyes I would see the Savior standing there! I was not the only one in that room who felt that Spirit. We learned quite by chance some months later that one of the nurses who was present that day was so touched that she sought out the missionaries and was baptized.

But notwithstanding, Adam made no improvement. He lingered between this life and the next for several more days as we pleaded with the Lord to return him to us. Finally, one morning after a fitful night, I walked alone down a deserted hospital corridor. I spoke to the Lord and told Him that we wanted our little boy to return so very much, but nevertheless what we wanted most was for His will to be done and that we— Pat and I—would accept that. Adam crossed the threshold into the eternities a short time later.[4]

THE LORD IS STANDING THERE TOO

Though this wonderful couple prayed in faith, no heavenly hand reached out to save Adam from death. But they were not alone in their trial; they felt a heavenly presence.

When Shadrach, Meshach, and Abed-nego were thrown into the furnace, something unexpected happened.

Then Nebuchadnezzar the king was astonied, and rose up in haste, and spake and said unto his counselors, Did not we cast three men bound into the midst of the fire? They answered and said unto the king, True, O king.

He answered and said, Lo, I see four men loose, walking in the midst of the fire, and they have no hurt; and the form of the fourth is like the Son of God.

Then Nebuchadnezzar came near to the mouth of the burning fiery furnace, and spake, and said, Shadrach, Meshach, and Abed-nego, ye servants of the most high God, come forth, and come hither. Then Shadrach, Meshach and Abd-nego, came forth of the midst of the fire.

And the princes, governors, and captains, and the king's counselors, being gathered together, saw these men, upon whose bodies the fire had no power, nor was an hair of their head singed, neither were their coats changed, nor the smell of fire had passed on them.

Then Nebuchadnezzar spake, and said, Blessed be the God of Shadrach, Meshach, and Abed-nego, who hath sent his angel, and delivered his servants that trusted in him, and have changed the king's word, and yielded their bodies, that they might not serve nor worship any god, except their own God. (Daniel 3:24–28)

There was someone in the fire who was like the Son of God. Daniel's story assures us that, though we may be thrown into the fiery furnace, we will never go in alone. Like the Savior, we will be accompanied by angels to strengthen us. The only thing that will really burn away will be the ties that bind us to this earth.

I recently heard a talk by a successful businessman, who recalled dining in a faraway city with some important business contacts. They were kidding him about his observance of the Word of Wisdom. "Go ahead," said one, "have a drink. You are far away from home and we are not in your peer group. No one will ever know; live it up a little!" The man smiled, shook his head and replied. "No thanks. I just don't think it makes much sense to own a cabin in Babylon. I'm either in, or I'm out. And I'm in my faith and out of Babylon."

What we are worshipping, we are becoming." Every moment of every day, our choices enact our loves, our desires, and our aspirations and we are molding ourselves into the God or Gods we thereby worship. That is why all talk about punishment and rewards, about justice, merit and desserts can be wrongheaded and misleading. We are not in some contest to rack up points. We will not some day wait with baited breath to see what prize or pain is meted out by some great dispenser of trophies. We cannot so trivialize life that we make of it a coliseum where we wage moral combat like spiritual gladiators for a presiding authority on high, to save or damn according to our performance. Where would be the purpose in all that? He might take the measure of our souls at any moment and deal with us accordingly, saving himself, not to mention us, a great deal of trouble. How much more meaningful is a life designed for spiritual formation rather than spiritual evaluation. All tests evaluate and life is no exception but the most meaningful and productive tests are those that assess with an eye to improvement, that measure in order to remedy and that improve and prepare us for the next stage in an upward process of advancement. For these reasons, all talk of heaven that operates in terms of earning rather than becoming is misguided. Such ideas misconstrue the nature of God, his grace and the salvation he offers.

—Teryl Givens[5]

So life in the Diaspora goes on, whether it is Babylon, Las Vegas, or Washington DC. Stories of faithful youth in strange places inspire us to reconsider our actions. Our own prophet, Thomas S. Monson, shared the story of his first experience in the Diaspora (in this case San Diego) when he went to boot camp as a young man. This good Utah boy suddenly found himself as, he assumed, the only Mormon in the camp, but soon found out, after speaking up, that there were two more. (Shadrach and Abed-nego!) He had made a decision early on that if he had to stand alone, he would. Then he brings that commitment into the present day: "Since that day, there have been times when there was no one standing behind me and so I *did* stand alone. How grateful I am that I made the decision long ago to remain strong and true, always prepared and ready to defend my religion, should the need arise."[6]

These stories are exciting and well-told, and can be meaningful in the lives of our children, many of whom are in a minority in their schools. Let's bring in the humor, let's bring in the danger and the excitement, and then bring in the message—that obedience to our covenants will set us apart in fortunate ways from the crowd and bless us with peace.

Jonah: How to Be the Worst Missionary Ever

JONAH

One way to learn is by seeing a really bad example, and the Old Testament generously offers several of those! We can use Jonah to teach our children how to be good missionaries by showing them a really poor example of one. Jonah's story is a whale of a tale. It is included in the Jewish Bible among the twelve minor prophets, who are classed as minor simply because their books are short. Ironically, though he has the worst attitude, Jonah is one of the most successful prophets in the Old Testament. So this turns all of the things that you tell missionaries sideways, and shows us again how sometimes the worst people get lucky breaks in this life.

My husband, Craig, was a great missionary and a really hard worker. Because he got along well with others, his mission president assigned him an almost comical progression of companions. One carried a bowie knife at all times! Another did not like his hair to get messy, and so if it was a windy day, he wouldn't leave the apartment. He would just simply refuse. Craig explains that the young man was too big to pick up and carry, so sometimes they just had to stay in the apartment because he wouldn't go outside! One day, when the wind was blowing and Craig's companion was refusing to leave the apart-ment, the phone rang. It was Billy Casper, the famous golfer. He said,

> God is personally invested in shepherding His children through the process of mortality and beyond; His desires are set upon the whole human family, not upon a select few. He is not predisposed to just the fast learners, the naturally inclined, or the morally gifted. The project of human advancement that God designed offers a hope to the entire human race. It is universal in its appeal and reach alike. This, however, has not been the traditional view.
>
> –Teryl Givens[7]

"Oh I'm so glad I caught you in your apartment. Could you come and meet me for lunch? I have some people I've been talking to and I'd like you to teach a gospel discussion to them." They went and had a wonderful experience teaching. So from then on, his companion would say, "See, we need to stay in the apartment all of the time, just in case the phone rings!" He was kind of a Jonah.

The story of Jonah is initially meant to be funny. The Hebrew people found everything in their scriptures, from inspiration to entertainment. Jonah (who reminds me of Eeyore in Winnie the Pooh) doesn't want to go on his mission, and is sure everything is going to go wrong. He finally has to get swallowed by a whale just to get him there! But as the scriptures tend to do, things go from comic to serious very quickly. Jonah spends three days in the belly of the whale and emerges a new man, comparing the whale's belly to *Sheol*, or death. Jonah, our comical grump, has become a type of Christ, down in the valley of death for three days, and emerging in a kind of resurrection. Some of the worst people get a chance to be a type of Christ in the Bible, which is just another expression of the condescension of God. Jonah, humbled by experience, speaks in poetry at this point.

> Nobody grows old by merely living a number of years. People grow old by deserting their ideals. . . . You are as young as your faith, as old as your doubt, as young as your self-confidence, as old as your fear, as young as your hope, as old as your despair.
>
> —Samuel Ullman[8]

"I called out to the Lord from my distress, and he answered me; from the belly of Sheol I cried out for help, and you heard my prayer" (Jonah 2:2, NET). It's a humorous story on one level, but it's also a very serious story. When we start to deny God, we begin to move away from Him, and as we do that we approach the valley of death. The closer you get to God, the closer you get to eternal life, and the further you get away from God, the further you move toward death. Sheol is not paradise; it's the Valley of Death where there's nothing. But even in Sheol, God hears you.

Now the one thing that Jonah is supposed to do is preach the gospel in Nineveh, the capital of Syria. The Ninevites are usually portrayed as really awful godless people, but in this story they all repent! They fast, they pray, and they even make the oxen and asses fast! But even though they all repent, Jonah's still grumpy; he's mad because he prophesied that they were all going to be destroyed and then they weren't destroyed (see Jonah 3:10–4:1). What a guy!

Jonah—channeling Eeyore again—goes off and sulks, and God is so merciful to him that He has a little plant grow up above Jonah to shade him (see Jonah 4:6). Then the next day, a worm comes and eats the plant (see Jonah 4:7). God is trying to give Jonah an object lesson here, but Jonah takes it as another fulfillment of his certainty that everything was going to go wrong, In effect, he says, "Oh I told you everything was horrible. The plant's gone now and I have no shade." And God says, "You care about the plant and yet don't care about keeping my word." In other words, "These people don't understand the gospel. So why is it that you have no mercy for those people and you're worried about this little plant?" (see Jonah 4:9–11). Apparently, the one person that didn't get converted on Jonah's mission was the one person who needed to be—Jonah.

For me, one of the great takeaways from the story of Jonah is similar to the lessons we learn from Daniel. We don't always get rewarded with what we want for doing what is right. But let's hope that we will continue to do what is right anyway.

NOTES

1. Bible Dictionary, "Daniel, book of."
2. *Merriam-Webster Dictionary*, s.v. "diaspora," accessed September 1, 2017, www.merriam-webster.com/dictionary/diaspora.
3. Lance B. Wickman, "But If Not," *Ensign*, November 2002.
4. Ibid.
5. Teryl Givens, *The God Who Weeps: How Mormonism Makes Sense of Life* (Salt Lake City: Deseret Book, 2012).
6. Thomas S. Monson, "Dare to Stand Alone," *Ensign*, November 2011; italics in original.)
7. Givens, *The God Who Weeps: How Mormonism Makes Sense of Life*.

8. Samuel Ullman, "Youth," in Margaret England Armbrester, *Samuel Ullman and "Youth": The Life, the Legacy* (Tuscaloose, AL: University of Alabama Press, 1993), 113.

Personal Notes

_____
_____
_____
_____
_____
_____
_____
_____
_____
_____
_____
_____
_____
_____
_____
_____
_____
_____

_____

_____

_____

_____

_____

_____

_____

_____

_____

_____

_____

_____

_____

_____

_____

_____

_____

_____

_____

_____

_____

_____

_____

_____

Chapter Nine

> ## QUEENS

Esther: Queen for a Day

"In Esther," writes scholar Jack M. Sasson, "unsubtle villains meet with brutal fates; proud partisans are fully vindicated; lovely heroines retain the affection of all; and stolid, dim-witted monarchs are there to be used by all."[1] The book of Esther ties its narrative to the reign of a Persian king called Ahasuerus, whose historical counterpart was probably Xerxes. Yet there is something deliberately fairy-tale-like about the way the story is presented, rather like the stories in the *Arabian Nights*. Take for example the description of the long procession of the "fairest maidens in the land," who were literally marinating in oils in order to replace the vanquished Queen Vashti (see Esther 2:4). The girls do not go in to the king until "she had been twelve months, according to the manner of the women, (for so were the days of their purifications accomplished, to wit, six months with oil of myrrh, and six months with sweet odours, and with other things for the purifying of the women;)" (Esther 2:12).

Wait a minute. Is it okay to talk about the scriptures and a fairy tale at the same time? Can a scriptural story be comic, and yet also be true? In a word, "yes." The scriptures are literature—some of the greatest literature ever written. This does not mean that the scriptures are not true. Literature refers to the way a text is written; the artistry with which the story, poetry, or history is presented to us. Let's take a look at how this works in the book of Esther.

> **In terms of preoccupation with self and a fixation on the physical, this [obsession with physical perfection] is more than social insanity; it is spiritually destructive, and it accounts for much of the unhappiness women, including young women, face in the modern world. And if adults are preoccupied with appearance—tucking and nipping and implanting and remodeling everything that can be remodeled—those pressures and anxieties will certainly seep through to children. At some point the problem becomes what the Book of Mormon called 'vain imaginations.' And in secular society both vanity and imagination run wild. One would truly need a great and spacious makeup kit to compete with beauty as portrayed in media all around us. Yet at the end of the day there would still be those "in the attitude of mocking and pointing their fingers."**
>
> **–Jeffrey Holland[2]**

PURIM: A TIME TO PARTY

The book of Esther, like all of the books of scripture that ended up in the canon, is included in the Bible for a series of reasons. The redactors of the biblical text had three main purposes for including this wonderful tale of a girl who saves a nation.

1. To explain the origin of Purim (not mentioned in the Torah)—the national liberation festival celebrated by all Jews in March.
2. To help the Jews understand the spirit of Purim and how to celebrate it.

3. To show an example of faithful Jewish ancestors who faced ruthless foes in the Diaspora and triumphed through righteousness.[3]

In order to do this effectively, the book of Esther is read aloud each year during the celebration of Purim. This is never done on the Sabbath, but instead is done at a special service the night before and the morning of the holiday. It is accompanied by noisy cheering (for Mordecai and Esther) and booing (for Haman) by children and adults, dressed in costumes and equipped with noisemakers. The *Jewish Study Bible* explains: "Purim is a carnivalesque holiday, replete with mock reenactments of the Esther story, partying and excessive drinking, carnivals and masquerades, and a general sense of frivolity uncharacteristic of Jewish festivals. The Talmud . . . encourages one to get so drunk that one cannot distinguish between 'Cursed be Haman' and 'Blessed be Mordecai.' Like Purim, the book is full of boisterous merrymaking—a comic farce for a carnivalesque holiday."[4]

In the spirit of the holiday, the story is told in the style of a fairy tale—with beautiful maidens, evil villains, and a plot to destroy the king, which is then foiled by the wily Mordecai. Underlying the plot is also the long-standing rivalry between the house of Saul, represented by Mordecai, and his old enemy Agag, reincarnated in Haman. The plot, structured on "improbabilities, exaggerations, misunderstandings and reversals,"[5] often strains credulity on purpose: The king builds a seventy-five-foot stake on which to impale his enemies; Esther's identity as a Jew is kept secret, though her uncle is employed in the palace; and a small minority of Jews massacre seventy-five thousand enemies in the brutal finale. Yet its referral to the royal annals of the kings—the official records on which many of the biblical texts are based—encourages us to believe that Esther truly did exist, and that such a story, though embellished in the telling, is rooted in history.

HADASSAH: GOD IS HIDDEN

The book of Esther is also unique in its curious lack of the mention of God. The afflicted Jews mourn and fast, but do not pray. God's name is not mentioned. And the traditional religious observances, such as dietary restrictions, maiden modesty, and marriage only within the covenant, seem not to be in effect. This bothered the redactors so much that in the Greek version of the Bible, there are dozens of additions that add prayers, the name of God, and more traditional behavior by Hadassah, better known as Esther. This lack of religious focus may have been intentional, since the fairy-tale nature of the narrative may have made the redactors omit more sacred references. The hidden nature of God in the book caused traditions to arise, such as the wearing of masks and the traditional Hamantaschen cookies that are made with filling hidden inside them.

Esther's story, though filled with entertaining scenes, has a serious intent. It is written to the Jews of the Diaspora, those who were strangers in a strange land. As such, it has a wonderful message to any faithful Saints who find themselves surrounded by nonbelievers. We can strengthen our own resolve to live our covenants in whatever circumstances we may find ourselves, and not just when we're surrounded by those who share our beliefs. As the *Jewish Study Bible* concludes, "The book succeeds in putting a serious message in a comic form."[6]

For me, the serious and beautiful message is that of the effect that one good woman can have on society. I read the following quote in tribute to my mother when she died recently. These are the last lines of the great novel *Middlemarch*—the story of one good woman, and how her quiet life impacts everyone she meets.

> But the effect of her being on those around her was incalculably diffusive: for the growing good of the world is partly dependent on unhistoric acts; and that things are not so ill with you and me as they might have been, is half owing to the number who lived faithfully a hidden life, and rest in unvisited tombs.[7]

Should the Scriptures Be Fun?

In the fascinating documentary *Broadway Musicals: A Jewish Legacy*, we learn that over a fifty-year period the songs of the Broadway musical were created almost exclusively by Jewish Americans: "These are the popular songs that our nation took to war, sang to their children at bedtime, and whistled while waiting for the bus; taken in total they comprise the vast majority of what is now commonly referred to as 'The American Songbook.' For example, Irving Berlin wrote the most popular Christmas song, 'White Christmas' . . . and the most popular Easter song, 'Easter Parade.' And Berlin's "God Bless America" became so popular, it nearly replaced the National Anthem."[8]

We can find the roots of this remarkable ability to bring stories to life in the Old Testament. Remember, for the Jewish people, the scriptures were everything; they were not just doctrine but entertainment as well. And the stories were not just read or told. In the case of Esther, they were acted out during the Purim festival, held every year to celebrate the victory of the Jews under her direction.

Through the centuries since, Esther's story has also been of interest to artists, inspiring a rather hilarious series of "fainting paintings," recording the terrifying moment when she faces the king with her life on the line.[9] Looking at them makes me feel a bit dizzy. . . .

All of this has me thinking, how can we make the scriptures a little more exciting and (dare we say it?) *fun* for our families? Can we stage a play or create a family musical? The scriptures were written to entertain as well as enlighten. Are we taking all of the entertainment value out of them by the way we present them?

Years ago, I was called to be the chorister in Primary. I was fairly terrified, as they usually don't have me work with the little kids; so to prepare, I attended a workshop given by the Primary General President in Salt Lake City. I was quite sure that she would encourage us to be serious and reverent about the singing time. Well, the first thing she did was make us all stand up and stack our chairs against the wall and sit on the floor. For the next thirty minutes, she had us up and marching or doing dance moves. We laughed, we sang our hearts out, and we had a wonderful time. She wasn't a bit worried about having fun while we sang about God, Jesus, and the scripture stories.

When is the last time you got everybody into makeshift costumes to act out a Bible story? Even if you are just pulling cushions off the couch to make an ark and each taking the part of an animal, the Bible stories can be fun. I have a friend who reenacted the scene of Elijah and the priests of Baal with her children; she surprised them by dumping a bucket of water on the altar and on them! Can we think of more creative ways to make the scriptures fun and memorable? Esther and the Purim festival show us that we don't always need to be solemn and serious in order to get the message across. Everybody loves to laugh.

Ruth: Patron Saint of Refugees

RUTH

The book of Ruth is unique for several reasons. First of all, this is a book about common, everyday people facing common, everyday challenges. Unlike all of the books we've seen so far, this isn't a tale of prophets or judges or kings or warriors. This is a tale of two poor women: one an Israelite and one a Gentile. They have some very difficult challenges, and they are the same challenges that many of us will face in our lives. And as we read their story, we can gain hope for good resolutions for our own problems and our own trials.

While there may not be any mighty conflicts or warriors in the story of Ruth, there are intense struggles for survival—not only physical survival, but the emotional strength to endure life's difficulties and our battles with grief. We can see our own problems and struggles here, and there's so much we can glean from it.

But perhaps one of the most unique parts of the book of Ruth is the fact that, like the book of Esther, God is really mentioned only obliquely. And He plays no intervening role in this story. In fact, by many accounts, you might say that the Lord isn't in this story at all. And yet, in another sense, the story is all about the Lord.

One way to understand the story of Ruth is to see it as a story that exemplifies the ways in which human beings can emulate the Savior, and how each of us—through sacrifice, love, and devotion—can ease the struggles of those around us and be a blessing and a redeemer to others. Ruth's intense devotion to her mother-in-law, Naomi; Naomi's machinations to bring about a union with Boaz and Ruth; and Boaz's gentle, faithful devotion to this young foreigner (Ruth), who perhaps brings nothing but need to the union, are examples of how to live lives of faith and compassion.

RUTH AS A REFUGEE

In our current sociological climate, Ruth is particularly relevant. She is a refugee—a stranger in a strange land. As of June 2017, there were 65.6 million people in the world classified as forcibly displaced. There were 22.5 million refugees, and 10 million people who were "stateless." Out of all of these suffering souls, only 189,300 people were resettled in 2016.[10] The scope of the problem is so much greater than the current solutions that the temptation is to simply look away and try not to think about each refugee as an individual child of God. The Old Testament won't let us do that. In order to teach us how important every person is, we are offered little biographies of people, like Ruth, who have no real place in society, but are precious to God.

Ruth, as a Midianite married to an Israelite, is already a person who doesn't really belong in either country. When her mother-in-law, Naomi, decides to return to her own land after the death of her husband and sons, Ruth must make a choice (see Ruth 1:5–7). Will she become a displaced person, a stranger in a strange land? Her mother-in-law, understanding how hard that will be, encourages her daughter-in-laws to stay in their own country and find new husbands (see Ruth 1:8–9). Orpah decides to stay with her people, but Ruth makes her famous statement of loyalty, and our scene is set. "And Ruth said, Entreat me not to leave thee, or to return from following after thee: for whither thou goest, I will go; and where thou lodgest, I will lodge: thy people shall be my people, and thy God my God" (Ruth 1:16).

WHAT HEBREW SOCIETY DID FOR THE REFUGEE

There were safeguards in the Mosaic law for the refugee. Aware that they had been strangers in many different societies, Jewish law protected refugees with several guidelines. Along with setting aside cities of refuge for foreigners, there were rules about how they were to be treated. Here are a few examples:

- "Do not mistreat or oppress a foreigner, for you were foreigners in Egypt" (Exodus 22:21, NIV).
- "When a foreigner resides among you in your land, do not mistreat them" (Leviticus 19:33, NIV).
- "Do not deprive the foreigner or the fatherless of justice, or take the cloak of the widow as a pledge" (Deuteronomy 24:17, NIV).

- "Cursed is anyone who withholds justice from the foreigner, the fatherless or the widow" (Deuteronomy 27:19, NIV).

One commentator explains that, though there was more fluid travel from one nation to another in biblical times, there was also less protection from a well-organized state.

> While past societies did not have comprehensive passport controls, they also lacked the fluid, prosperous economies, social tolerance, legal respect for rights, and general nonviolence that prevails in the democracies of the contemporary West. So while immigrants might enter a Greek *polis* or the Persian or Egyptian or Roman Empires without being prevented by the state, once there, they would be less safe from private violence, and might have trouble making a living, or integrating socially with the host society. There were no, or at most few, borders in the modern sense of invisible lines slicing up the world's land which it was illegal for humans *qua* humans to cross without permission. But one's rights and physical safety usually depended on being embedded in a physical kin-group or city-state, on having people who, so to speak, "got your back." Migration wasn't illegal, but it wasn't safe either.
>
> It is in this context which the Biblical texts on this topic in Deuteronomy must be read. We could deduce that foreigners could come and reside in Israel physically, as a side-effect of the lack of a passport regime before modern times, but this is also amply confirmed by the Biblical texts, which routinely refer to "resident foreigners" and explain how they should be treated. But the Law of Moses also insists that resident foreigners be treated justly and fairly.[11]

TAKING CARE OF THE WIDOWED AND THE FATHERLESS

We see in the book of Ruth that Boaz, a wealthy landowner and farmer, allows gleaners to follow the harvesters in his fields (see Ruth 2:1–3, KJV). This was a way of providing food for the poor. When Ruth and Naomi come into Bethlehem, Boaz hears about them, and realizes that they are distant relations. Without offering direct relief, he instructs his men to leave extra grain in the field for

Ruth to gather (see Ruth 2:15–16). We see a combination of social policy through the Mosaic law, cultural custom, and individual compassion in the way that Ruth and Naomi are treated by Boaz.

WHAT SHOULD WE DO TO HELP THE REFUGEE?

What is our responsibility toward the poor, the displaced, the homeless, and the refugee? This is a matter of debate in every society, and as Christians it is important that we give this careful thought. Recently the Church has issued several statements about the refugee crisis. President Dieter F. Uchtdorf, who was a refugee himself when he was young, said in an interview:

> [Regarding those who reached out to help his family and others when they were homeless] "There were so many who were willing to help regardless of religion, of race, of background, and that's what we're trying to do now," he said.
>
> The LDS church, which Uchtdorf helps lead as a member of its governing First Presidency, has called for compassion on refugees, urging its members to give what they can.
>
> The church is also donating another $5 million to assist displaced families in Europe.
>
> "If we declare to be Christians in our case as we are—as LDS, as Mormons—there is our responsibility to follow the Savior through our acts, not just through our declarations, and help," he said.
>
> But not everybody is singing this same tune. In the wake of terrorist attacks in Paris and elsewhere, a fear of refugees has spread. Some prominent voices want them left to fend for themselves.
>
> "It sounds familiar because that's how the people sometimes talked when I was a child," Uchtdorf said of the public backlash against refugees. He also acknowledges to some, the task of helping may seem overwhelming.
>
> "Can we help everyone? No," he said. "Can we do a lot? Can we help individuals? Yes."[12]

After a visit to the Czech Republic, President Uchtdorf said, "We are children of one Heavenly Father," he said. "We are all brothers and sisters. Our two great commandments are to serve God and our fellowman. We are to reach out to those in need and help them—and not just by impressive declarations, but by one-on-one help, eye-to-eye help, by lifting up those who are in need."[13]

THE ANSWER MAY BE RIGHT IN FRONT OF YOU

I have a little theory about this that I call moral proximity. I believe that God places certain people in our way that He expects us to help. That is what the story of the good Samaritan means to me; Jesus seems to be saying that we should help the person that is placed in our path and not pass them by. I call this moral proximity because I believe that I am expected to help certain people and not worry about trying to help everyone. God is watching over all of us, and another person may be expected to help someone else. Rather than be overwhelmed by how many people need help, I should do what I can to help those whom God places in my way.

> We control the disposition of our means and resources, but we account to God for . . . stewardship over earthly things.
> —D. Todd Christofferson[14]

We can waste a lot of time arguing how, or even whether, we should assist the flood of refugees in the world. I like President Uchtdorf's positive response. Like Boaz reaching out to Ruth and Naomi, he encourages us to see individuals that have been placed in our sphere of influence, and do something to help them. Here are a few things we can do to be of assistance to the stranger in our midst.

1. We can pray for guidance, rather than try to excuse ourselves. If we were to pray every day and ask God to help us be of service to the homeless and stranded in our midst, what might happen?
2. We can support the Church's efforts. We are blessed to have a humanitarian arm of the Church to assist refugees in a

significant way. There is no question that if we stay our hand and do not contribute to that effort when we can, we will be accountable someday.

3. We can try to give something to someone every day.

Last year, I set a little goal that turned out to be very instructive. I decided to try to give a little money away every day. Whether it was a dollar, or ten, or a hundred, I decided to pray every day for God to show me who might need a little monetary help.

I was amazed at how difficult this was! First, I forgot about it on many days. I would be so caught up in my errands, concerns, and duties, that I would come to the end of a day and realize that I had completely forgotten my goal. Second, on the days that I did remember, I had a hard time knowing what or how I should give. But on the days that I prayerfully thought about my goal, I had some remarkable experiences.

One day, I stopped at the ATM and quickly got some cash. As I got in my car, I noticed a young mom with three kids, one in a stroller. She was just standing there; she didn't look distressed or anything. But I had this little feeling as I started to pull away, so I pulled back into a parking spot and asked her if she was okay. "I'm just waiting for a taxi," she said bravely. "My car broke down." I started to leave, but had the feeling again. "Taxi's are expensive," I said. "Why don't you let me buy you a ride home?" I handed her a twenty-dollar bill. She started to cry and told me that she hadn't been sure how she was going to pay for the taxi. We hugged each other, and another lady standing nearby came over and hugged us too! We had a little love fest! As I drove away, I couldn't help but think that, of the five twenties I had taken out of the ATM, the one I gave to her brought me far more joy than the other four.

> "In order to get to heaven, you have to have letters of reference from poor people.
>
> –Rafael Perez[15]

I am still a dismal failure at my goal, and writing about it now reminds me how many days I have missed in the last year. But just thinking about giving a little bit of my substance away every day has been an enriching experience. And I use that pun deliberately.

Each person that appears in the Bible is there for a reason, and Ruth is no exception. We learn in the genealogies of Jesus, that she is a great-grandmother of the Savior. When Boaz reached out to a poor, homeless girl, he could not have known that he was in the presence of royalty. A stranger and a foreigner, she prefigured the woman who would, centuries later, ride into Bethlehem on a donkey, in labor and in distress. Both were queens in disguise.

> I believe that it is consistent with the laws of Heaven that one's right of reliance upon the Lord for protection against want is in direct proportion to his own liberality in sustaining the Lord's poor. There is an interdependence between those who have and those who have not. The processing of giving exalts the poor and humbles the rich. In the process, both are sanctified.
>
> –Marion G. Romney[16]

NOTES

1. Jack M. Sasson, "Esther," in Robert Alter and Frank Kermode, eds., *The Literary Guide to the Bible* (Cambridge, MA: Harvard University Press, 1987), 341.
2. Jeffrey R. Holland, "To Young Women," *Ensign*, November 2005; italics in original.
3. Jack M. Sasson, "Esther," in Robert Alter and Frank Kermode, eds., *The Literary Guide to the Bible*, 335.
4. Adele Berlin and Marc Zvi Brettler, eds., *The Jewish Study Bible: Featuring the Jewish Publication Society TANAKH Translation* (New York: Oxford University Press, 2004), 1623.

5. *The Oxford Dictionary of the Jewish Religion*, 2nd ed., s.v. "Esther, Scroll of."

6. Berlin and Brettler, eds. *The Jewish Study Bible*, 1625.

7. George Eliot, *Middlemarch: A Story of a Provincial Life* (New York: Doubleday, 1904), 752.

8. *Broadway Musicals: A Jewish Legacy*, directed by Michael Kantor, (PBS, 2013).

9. For example, see Artemisia Gentileschi, *Esther before Ahasuerus*, oil on canvas, 82 x 107.75 in., The Metropolitan Museum of Art, New York; Paolo Veronese, *The Fainting of Esther*, 306 x 198 cm., Louvre, Paris; Salomon Koninck, *Esther before Ahasuerus*, oil on canvas, 61.8 x 88.6 in., National Museum in Warsaw.

10. "Figures at a Glance: Statistical Yearbooks," *UNHCR*, accessed September 5, 2017, www.unhcr.org/figures-at-a-glance.html.

11. Nathan Smith, "The Old Testament on Immigration," *Open Borders*, May 13, 2012, accessed September 5, 2017, openborders.info/blog/the-old-testament-on-immigration/; italics in original.

12. Daniel Woodruff, "LDS leader Uchtdorf remembers life as refugee, urges compassion in migrant crisis," *KUTV*, February 4, 2016, accessed September 5, 2017, kutv.com/news/local/lds-leader-uchtdorf-remembers-life-as-refugee-urges-compassion-in-migrant-crisis.

13. Noelle Baldwin and Sarah Jane Weaver, "President Uchtdorf Recalls Being a Refugee, Asks Members to Reach Out," *Church News*, May 27, 2016, accessed September 5, 2017, www.lds.org/church/news/president-uchtdorf-recalls-being-a-refugee-asks-members-to-reach-out?lang=eng.

14. "Pursuing Zion requires living a life of purity," *Church News*, October 11, 2008, accessed September 5, 2017, www.ldschurchnewsarchive.com/articles/55171/Pursuing-Zion-requires-living-a-life-of-purity.html.

15. Mary Jordan, "If Clinton wins, Thomas Perez does, too. Only question: What job does he get?," *The Washington Post*, July 5, 2016, accessed September 5, 2017, www.washingtonpost.com/national/if-clinton-wins-thomas-perez-does-too-only-question-what-job-does-he-get/2016/07/05/d7e38480-4184-11e6-88d0-6adee48be8bc_story.html?utm_term=.ad6319db0405.

16. Marion G. Romney, "A Practical Religion" (address to seminary and institute faculty, Brigham Young University, June 13, 1956).

Personal Notes

Chapter Ten

TRIALS

Job: Why Do Bad Things Happen to Good People?

"Have you considered My servant Job? For there is no one like him on the earth, a blameless and upright man, fearing God and turning away from evil" (Job 1:8, NASB).

Why do good things happen to bad people and bad things happen to good people? This dilemma is at the heart of theology. If God causes all of the suffering in the world, how can He be worthy of our worship? These questions are presented in a dramatic tale that features a kind of "bet" between God and Satan to determine how much one good man will suffer before he gives up and curses God. Along the way, four "comforters," friends of Job, come to mourn with him after he loses everything: his children, home, possessions, and health (see Job 2:11). Their sincerity cannot be doubted; they sit down and join him in a week of fasting in sackcloth and ashes before they speak up (see Job 2:11–13), but when they begin to speak, any chance of comfort is gone. For these comforters spout the doctrine of distributive justice. In other words, they maintain that an omnipotent God causes the righteous to prosper and the wicked to suffer. According to that formula, if Job is suffering, he must be a sinner. Bildad the Shuhite has it all figured out:

Doth God pervert judgment? or doth the Almighty pervert justice? . . .

> If thou wert pure and upright; surely now he would awake for thee, and make the habitation of thy righteousness prosperous.
> Behold, God will not cast away a perfect man, neither will he help the evil doers. (Job 8:3, 6, 20)

It is easy to fall in with this logic without realizing where it leads. We speak of God blessing us when things go well, but that leads inexorably to the idea that God is cursing or punishing us when things fall apart. As a dear friend said to me when her healthy, vibrant husband was diagnosed with ALS just as they were entering retirement, "What did I do that God would punish me in this way?"

The extreme example of Job's suffering serves to illustrate where the doctrine of distributive justice leads: to the idea that justice is meted out in accordance with behavior. Even the most casual assessment of the world around us, however, shows that to be anything but true. And the tragic consequence of believing in a God who, like Santa Claus, is making a list (and checking it twice) of the naughty and nice children and rewarding them accordingly, is that when things go wrong, faith fails.

Job refuses to believe in this version of God. Though it is evident that everything has been taken from him, he resists the idea that God is punishing him for some unknown sin, or that God is just randomly sending destruction on the innocent. Both ideas are troubling on some level, and Job takes us all the way there. If God is all-powerful, are the terrible occurrences of life examples of careless neglect (at best) or random cruelty (at worst)?

> Though I were perfect, yet would I not know my soul: I would despise my life.
> This is one thing, therefore I said it, He destroyeth the perfect and the wicked.
> If the scourge slay suddenly, he will laugh at the trial of the innocent.
> The earth is given into the hand of the wicked: he covereth the faces of the judges thereof; if not, where, and who is he? (Job 9:21–24)

IS IT OKAY TO BE ANGRY AT GOD?

This is where the book of Job rises from a mere morality tale to a work of inspired scripture: Job fearlessly challenges the incorrect theology that God is punishing us when things fall apart, and demands to know just what is going on. In response to Bildad's harangue, Job speaks directly to God, avowing his innocence. Rabbi Harold S. Kushner writes that the very fact that we can see the unfairness in the world shows that we are divine in nature: "Life is not fair. The wrong people get sick and the wrong people get robbed and the wrong people get killed in wars and accidents. . . . Our responding to life's unfairness with sympathy and with righteous indignation, God's compassion and God's anger working through us, may be the surest proof of all of God's reality."[1]

Thus, our righteous indignation at life's unfairness is not an affront to God, but is a way of getting to know Him. When Job says of God, "Where, and who is he?" (Job 9:24) he has arrived at the beginning of God's version of life. As Jesus said, "This is life eternal, that they might know thee the only true God, and Jesus Christ, whom thou hast sent" (John 17:3).

WHO IS GOD, AND WHERE IS HE WHEN I NEED HIM?

Nearly all of the things we say to each other when tragedy strikes can sound like the loopy logic of Job's comforters. Statements like, "You are going through this because God knows you are strong enough to handle it," presuppose that God is the cause of the trouble. Is this so? Did God cause your illness, bankruptcy, divorce, or whatever trial has befallen you? What about the earthquake, tsunami, or tornado that destroyed your home? Does God cause these disasters? I like a card I recently received that said, "If this is all part of God's plan, then God is a terrible planner!"

The Old Testament narratives were written from the perspective of distributive justice. The authors and redactors often avow that God did such and such. For example, God hardens Pharaoh's heart so that he won't let the Israelites go (see for example Exodus

10:1). And God sends fire and destroys Sodom and Gomorrah (see Genesis 19: 24, 28). Well, if He destroyed that city, I wonder, did He destroy the beautiful city of Fukushima that was devastated by the tsunami in 2011 and then laid waste to by the failure of the nuclear reactor? I didn't live in Sodom, but Abraham negotiated fiercely to save the city just for the sake of his relatives who lived there.

I did live in Fukushima, however. I served there as a missionary through the summer and fall of 1975, and I thought it was one of the most beautiful places on earth. The people were kind, the ocean was beautiful, and the trees, as fall approached, were a riot of color. Thirty-five years later, I returned with my husband to stay with a family I knew and loved there, and found that very little had changed. But just a couple of years later, the entire city was nearly destroyed by a tsunami and then by nuclear waste, and my friends were lucky to escape with their lives. They abandoned their home and had to go and live with relatives in Tokyo. If God was responsible for that, it would be hard to think of him as a loving, merciful friend.

One great historian warns us to be careful about making assumptions when it comes to God's involvement in these types of disasters:

> Our faith tells us that there is moral meaning and spiritual significance in historical events. But we cannot be completely confident that any particular judgment or meaning or significance is unambiguously clear. If God's will cannot be wholly divorced from the actual course of history, neither can it be positively identified with it. Although we see evidence that God's love and power have frequently broken in upon the ordinary course of human affairs, our caution in declaring this is reinforced by our justifiable disapproval of chroniclers who take the easy way out and use divine miracles as a short-circuit of a causal explanation that is obviously, or at least defensibly, naturalistic. We must not use history as a storehouse from which deceptively simple moral lessons may be drawn at random.[2]

Joseph Smith taught that God is not, as the comforters' logic assumes, all-powerful. In one respect, He has relinquished His power. By granting free agency to people, He no longer controls the consequences of their choices. And in the same way, the earth itself is subject to the random fluctuations of nature. Fires, tempests, earthquakes, and more will be a part of life. Also, the pollution and corruption of the earth through the wrong choices of its inhabitants will cause more suffering. Wars, forced migrations, and the suffering of the politically oppressed, account for much of the pain and suffering in the world. God does not want these things to happen, and yet they must happen as part of the package.

> In the Garden story, good and evil are found on the same tree, not in separate orchards. Good and evil give meaning and definition to each other. If God, like us, is susceptible to immense pain, He is, like us, the greater in His capacity for happiness. The presence of such pain serves the larger purpose of God's master plan, which is to maximize the capacity for joy, or in other words, "to bring to pass the immortality and eternal life of man." He can no more foster those ends in the absence of suffering and evil than one could find the traction to run or the breath to sing in the vacuum of space. God does not instigate pain or suffering, but He can weave it into His purposes. "God's power rests not on totalizing omnipotence, but on His ability to alchemize suffering, tragedy, and loss into wisdom, understanding, and joy."[3]

HOW FAITH HELPS: COMFORT AND PEACE

And yet, the scriptures are full of examples where God intervenes in the events of life. We call these miracles. Faithful people believe in them. People without faith call them coincidences. Can we absolve God of causing the bad and yet still believe in miracles? Let's look at how this might work.

We tend to assume that we can't have it both ways; either God is involved in our lives, or He isn't. But I think the truth may be a bit messier. God is involved in our lives, and He isn't. How is He involved? He offers comfort and strength and guidance as we seek Him. And His help infuses meaning into the random events of life that otherwise would leave us bitter and sad.

One year, two of my friends battled terminal cancer. Both had good families and supportive friends. But I was struck by one of these friends who had a deep faith in God, as well as the strength to continue on. When diagnosed, she made a plan to accomplish all that she could with the months or years left to her. She made blankets for grandchildren she would never meet. She wrote letters to her children to be opened at certain milestones, such as weddings and graduations. She saw her life as an ongoing continuum where she would continue to learn and grow, and be a part of strengthening her family from beyond the grave. While she bravely underwent every treatment that could extend her life, and while she experienced a great deal of fear and uncertainty, she had peace in her heart.

My other friend—an equally wonderful and loving person—had been raised by a father who was both very religious and abusive. Her faith in a loving God was poisoned by this upbringing, and she had just managed to get along without it. But as her cancer progressed, both she and her devoted husband were unable to face the inevitable fact that she was dying. They couldn't talk about it together, nor could they discuss it with their children. No plans were made. The only thing they could do was keep on fighting up to the very day she died. She had been taught to believe wrong things about God, and so her faith didn't strengthen her when she needed it.

Though God may not make our problems disappear, he can help us face what life brings us. So, what shall we pray for? Rabbi Kushner suggests: "People who pray for miracles usually don't get miracles . . . but people who pray for courage, for strength to bear the unbearable, for the grace to remember what they have left instead of what they have lost, very often find their prayers answered. They find that they have more strength, more courage than they ever knew themselves to have."[4]

HOW FAITH HELPS: POWER AND PERSPECTIVE

Beyond comfort and peace, God (or His heavenly helpers) may actually intervene in the lives of the faithful and cause a change in the natural course of events. This appears to be a part of the process of faith. As we learn to believe in and trust God, we become privy to extra help and knowledge that can, as the scripture says, "greatly enlarge the soul" (D&C 121:42). Faithful people can grow so strong that God begins to work in tandem with them. Reading the accounts of Jesus with His disciples, we can see a training process. Jesus heals someone, and so the disciples try it, and they fail. He gently explains, "This kind goeth not out but by fasting and prayer" (Matthew 17:21). In other words, those forty days and nights that Jesus spent in the wilderness fasting, and the countless times He went away by Himself to pray, connected Him to God. He then knew when and how to intervene, and was a conduit for God's power when He did.

So when bad times come to us, we can look at Jesus and see that even a perfect man needed a lot of time alone with God to tap into the delicate balance of heavenly intervention in human events. Jesus shows us what Job's comforters should have done. In every case where Jesus encountered suffering, He offered compassion and kindness along with healing and perspective. All of us can follow His example.

"Job asked questions about God, but he did not need a lesson in theology. He needed sympathy and compassion and the reassurance that he was a good person and a cherished friend."[5]

POETRY BORN OF PAIN

The poetry of the Bible reaches its pinnacle in the book of Job. After wading through three-dozen chapters of Q and A in the book of Job, God suddenly answers Job "out of the whirlwind" (Job 38:1). And what an answer! He never deigns to answer Job's many questions about why everything is going wrong in his life. Instead, He opens a vision of His greatness to Job, as He did to Moses and to Enoch (see Moses 1, 7). Bubbling up through these verses is a joy in creation that gives me chills every time I read it. God clearly delights in His creations. Listen to His description of the warhorse:

> Hast thou given the horse strength? hast thou clothed his neck with thunder?
> Canst thou make him afraid as a grasshopper? the glory of his nostrils is terrible.

He paweth in the valley, and rejoiceth in his strength: he goeth on to meet the armed men.

He mocketh at fear, and is not affrighted; neither turneth he back from the sword.

The quiver rattleth against him, the glittering spear and the shield.

He swalloweth the ground with fierceness and rage: neither believeth he that it is the sound of the trumpet. (Job 39:19–24)

Perhaps one of the greatest gifts that sorrow gives us is the ability to pay attention. When illness strikes, we value the precious moments that we have together. When loss occurs, we cling more lovingly to those who remain. My meditation teacher told of a unique experience that she had while she was mourning the loss of her sister, who had died leaving four children motherless. On Mother's Day, my teacher, who lived in a distant state from her nieces and nephews, was overcome with grief as she thought of their loss, and hers. She went for a walk, and decided to choose the most beautiful thing she could find that morning. It was a grouping of her favorite flowers that were growing along the roadside. She said, "As I stood and enjoyed the beauty of the flowers, I consciously tied my grief to the beauty of that scene. From then on, when I was overcome with grief, my mind was also filled with the joy and beauty of those beautiful flowers, and I held my joy and grief in my heart together."[6]

Job says,

For I know that my redeemer liveth, and that he shall stand at the latter day upon the earth:

And though after my skin worms destroy this body, yet in my flesh shall I see God:

Whom I shall see for myself, and mine eyes shall behold, and not another; though my reins be consumed within me. (Job 19:25–27)

As Job learns to hold his grief, his questions, his love for God, and his faith in the redemption all together in his heart, he finds many of the answers that he seeks; in the meantime, he also discovers peace about what he does not yet understand.

TOOLBOX: INTERACTIVE DRAMA

Thomas Carlyle said that the book of Job was "the most wonderful poem of any age and language; our first, oldest statement of the never-ending problem—man's destiny and God's way with him here in this earth. . . . There is nothing written in the Bible or out of it of equal literary merit."[7]

The book of Job is part of the "wisdom literature," and follows the literary convention of the fairy tale or folk tale. The story begins with a "once upon a time" phrase—"there was a man" (Job 1:1). It is set in a vague location that is definitely non-Israelite—the land of Uz (see Job 1:1). The numbers are all very stylized—seven sons, three daughters, and seven thousand sheep and three thousand oxen (see Job 1:2–3). The characters are also stylized—Job is "perfect and upright" and he never makes a misstep (Job 1:1). We are clearly on different narrative ground here than we were in 1 and 2 Samuel with our flawed heroes, David and Solomon.

Why present this story in this way? One scholar suggests that structuring the story as a folk tale, rather than a historical account, encourages a "dramatic reading" of the book of Job.

> The book is a kind of interactive drama, which presupposes a reader's involvement. . . . Job is not an Israelite, but his experience is certainly one of those to which every Israelite could easily relate. The setting equips the author with more flexibility and boldness in drawing the scenario of the poetic core and building the hero's somewhat harsh relationship with God. Thus he can avoid a the possible scandal on the part of his orthodox audience.[8]

The book of Job might be compared to a drama where real characters from different parts of our religious history come together to explore certain important truths. So we need not worry about whether God actually had a dialogue with Satan that resulted in a bet about how Job would react if all of the benefits of obedience were snatched away. Framing the drama in this manner gives the author of the book the opportunity to explore the most fundamental question about God: namely, if God is just and loving, and also all-powerful, why do the good and the innocent suffer?

Lessons from the Front:
How to Be a Better Comforter

JOB 2–37

One of the fundamental requirements of being a Christian, we are told, is to "mourn with those who mourn . . . and comfort those that stand in need of comfort" (Mosiah 18:9). This is easier said than done, isn't it? It's very hard to know what to say when people have terrible things happen to them. So, how can we learn to be better comforters? Here are a few guidelines:

1. Avoid playing "Can you top this?"
2. Avoid explaining why this event has happened.
3. Let the mourner guide the conversation
4. Bring gifts: the Spirit, food, comfort, laughter, and love

The first two things to avoid are trying to compare the situation to anything else, and trying to explain why these things happen. Job's friends fall into both traps, and they are not helpful.

YOU THINK THIS IS BAD? WELL, HAVE I GOT A STORY FOR YOU!

When I was in college, my former roommate lost her first baby the day he was born, and she was devastated. I went to her small apartment, and accompanied her to the mortuary to see the little one, dressed in the nightie she had lovingly made. We returned to the apartment sad and discouraged. Over the course of the day, we were visited by a series of well-meaning women, each of who, it seemed, had a story to tell us about a similar or worse loss. The cumulative effect of all of these horrible experiences was not uplifting. In fact, we were sorely tempted to stop answering the door! The lesson we both learned that day was "think carefully before you share that story!" Describing a worse situation is not necessarily comforting.

Psychologist Carlford Broderick tells the story of a man who suffered a terrible tragedy. He was working in a store when a robber came in. As he turned, the robber thought he was pulling out a gun and the man was shot and paralyzed. The well-meaning Latter-day Saints who came to visit him said some remarkable things that rivaled Job's comforters. One of his very close friends said to him, "You've always been a great athlete, but you're kind of a cocky guy too. You're pretty excited when you win the game and all that kind of thing. I'm sure God's given you this experience to humble you. Then you could be a better person."

Then someone else said to him, "Well, God gave you this test and He only gives this kind of thing to people who can handle it, right?" We don't really love that when people say that to us, do we? In other words, they made kind of a hero out of him. "You are a special person because God has given you this trial."[9] That one that sounds good when you say it, but when you actually hear it, there's something about it that sounds like you won the wrong lottery. Remember when Tevye, the unlucky hero in *The Fiddler on the Roof*, says to God, "It's true that we are the Chosen People. But once in a while can't You choose someone else?"[10]

Since my husband was diagnosed with cancer several months ago, we have learned a lot about how to comfort others, as so many people have extended love and mercy to us. The vast majority of people have been wonderful, supportive, and kind. We can tell they are worried about saying the wrong thing and are desperate to say something helpful. This is so moving to us. We are never offended by anything anyone says to us; we are so grateful for the love and support. However, a few people

> We who lived in concentration camps can remember the men who walked through the huts comforting others, giving away their last piece of bread. They may have been few in number, but they offer sufficient proof that everything can be taken from a man but one thing: the last of the human freedoms—to choose one's attitude in any given set of circumstances; to choose one's own way.
> —Victor Frankl[11]

have shown themselves to be particularly competent comforters, and we are learning from them.

Soon after Craig was diagnosed, we found it exhausting to go to church because so many kind people came up and wanted to talk about the details of his disease that it was difficult. One night, a dear couple we hadn't seen for some time called and invited us to dinner. On the way to meet them, Craig said, "I'm just not sure I can talk about this one more time!" At dinner, the husband said, "You know we are interested in anything you feel like saying about your diagnosis and your treatment. But if you don't feel like talking about it, that is fine too, let's just talk about something else." It was an inspired and insightful thing to say. It left Craig free to follow his feelings that night, and we had a lovely evening together.

Another couple came to see us, and instead of bringing a meal, they brought healthy snacks. Craig had been in the hospital and was taking a lot of pain medication, which adversely affects the appetite. The dried fruit, granola, yogurt, and other munchies that they brought were his favorite things to eat.

A third couple came with gifts that were funny, but actually rather inspired. Craig was confined to a wheelchair for a couple of months, and among the gag gifts that were brought was a stick with a "grabber" on the end. It was amazing how much Craig used that thing!

Creative comforting is more than trying to fix a problem for someone else. It is trying to enter into the mindset of the sufferer and see what can be done.

USING THE POWER OF PRAYER

I love the lady who cleans my teeth. Having my teeth cleaned is an activity that I have always dreaded, but she is such a joy that I actually look forward to it! Pamela is an Evangelical Christian and a part-time minister, and I always feel blessed to be with her. Just after Craig was diagnosed, I was at the dentist's office, and I told her what had happened. Craig has Multiple Myeloma, a form of blood cancer that can destroy the bones. We were especially worried because one of his vertebrae was collapsing from a tumor, and he had to have radiation treatment, which threatened to destroy the stem cells that he would later need for a bone marrow transplant. He was in a wheelchair, in terrible pain, awaiting a surgery on his back. I told her this in a five-minute conversation. She promised to pray for me, but she meant it in a way that I hadn't experienced before. The next Sunday morning, I woke up and there was a text from her on my phone. It was a prayer. Here it is:

> Lord, I lift Marilyn and Craig up before your throne this morning. Lord, I ask you to strengthen Marilyn, dear Lord. Holy Spirit, touch her and give her peace deep within her spirit. Strengthen her heart and mind and place the right people in her path that will help her as she helps her husband. Father, I lift Craig up to your throne this morning. I wash every cell and atom in his body in the precious blood of Jesus. I ask you, Father, to preserve Craig's stem cells and place him in permanent remission from this cancer. I take authority over every evil that has tried to destroy Craig's life. Satan, the Lord rebuke you in the name of Jesus. Craig shall be healed and made whole! I command those stem cells to remain covered by the blood of Jesus. They shall not be destroyed but shall cause Craig to be healed. I dispatch angels around their home to protect and shield their lives and health. And I plead Psalm 91 over Craig's life. Commanding healing to come forth, in Jesus' name, Amen.[12]

As I read this prayer, I was overwhelmed by the Spirit. Pamela knows her Bible far better than I do, and I had to go look up Psalm 91 because I didn't even know what it says. Essentially, it says that the plague will not come near your door. If ever there was a plague in our day, it is cancer. I am humbled and grateful that in our Church we have the true order of prayer, the priesthood, and our temple covenants to strengthen us. But Pamela's prayer challenged me. Am I praying with this kind of faith for the people that I love? I'm not sure that I am. When I'm sitting with a child, talking about a challenge, am I saying, "Let's stop and pray about that right now." Am I really using the power of prayer?

The week after I received Pamela's text message, I was walking out the door after our weekly scripture class, and a woman came up and told me she was just visiting that day. She told me a little story about a terrible life situation she was facing. She'd been driving across the country, and a friend had recommended that she listen to the YouTube recordings of our class. She thanked me for those recordings, and later, I wanted to write her a little email of encouragement. When I sat down to write, I thought, all of a sudden, "Well, if my dental hygienist can do it, I can do it."

So instead of just writing an email and saying, "I'm sending thoughts and prayers, and I hope the Lord will bless you," I wrote out a prayer for the first time in my life, specifically about her. I wrote it in an email. It felt a little awkward, but she received comfort from it. Since then, I've been thinking about this a lot. Can we pray more specifically with the people that we love and bring the comfort of Christ to them through prayer?

THE COMFORTER IS ALREADY THERE

> Suffering and death are part of the everlasting drama of our relationship with our creator. Far from being an unjustifiable violation, an outrage, they exemplify and enhance our human condition. If ever it were possible . . . to eliminate suffering, and ultimately death, from our mortal lives, they would not thereby be enhanced, but rather demeaned, to the point that they would become too insignificant . . . to be worth living at all.
>
> –Mother Teresa[13]

A final thing about comforting is to remember that we are never the first responder. No matter what the situation, the Comforter is already there. When I was a young mother, an acquaintance in the ward lost her husband in a freak accident. She had three little children the same ages as mine. Her loss frightened me, and I found it difficult to know what to say, as she was living my worst nightmare. I was asked to bring a dinner to her family, and I gladly made ham and rolls—the full Mormon feast, complete with the Funeral Potatoes.

That was the easy part! Once I got to her home, I sat in my car across the street; I was simply too afraid to go to the door. I was sure I would cry, or say the wrong thing, and I just didn't want to come face-to-face with her pain. I desperately wanted to "doorbell ditch" the whole meal and run for it. But that was cowardly, and besides, what if I got caught?

Finally, I had no choice but to go up and knock on the door. I will never forget the almost tangible rush of the Spirit that flowed out to me as this new widow opened the door. Her tearstained face was shining with love. She welcomed me in and introduced me to her family members. Everyone hugged me and thanked me for the food.

> Christ's agony in the garden is unfathomable by the finite mind, both as to intensity and cause. . . . He struggled and groaned under a burden such as no other being who has lived on earth might even conceive as possible. It was not physical pain, nor mental anguish alone, that caused Him to suffer such torture as to produce an extrusion of blood from every pore; but a spiritual agony of soul such as only God was capable of experiencing. No other man, however great his powers of physical or mental endurance, could have suffered so; for his human organism would have succumbed, and syncope would have produced unconsciousness and welcome oblivion. In that hour of anguish Christ met and overcame all the horrors that Satan, 'the prince of this world' could inflict. . . .
>
> In some manner, actual and terribly real though to man incomprehensible, the Savior took upon Himself the burden of the sins of mankind from Adam to the end of the world."
>
> —James E. Talmage[14]

I had forgotten that where there is sorrow, the Comforter is already on duty. You will never go into a house of suffering or death alone. The Savior is already there and the room will be filled with angels. You only need to look and listen and see how you can be helpful. He is in charge and His healing grace will be everywhere you look. That is the real secret of comforting.

NOTES

1. Harold S. Kushner, *When Bad Things Happen to Good People* (New York: Anchor Books, 2004), 156.
2. Leonard J. Arrington, *Adventures of a Church Historian* (Chicago: University of Illinois Press, 1998), 236–37.
3. Teryl Givens, *The God Who Weeps: How Mormonism Makes Sense of Life* (Salt Lake City: Deseret Book, 2012).
4. Kushner, *When Bad Things Happen to Good People*, 168.
5. Ibid., 77.
6. Karen Sothers, personal correspondence with author.
7. Kushner, *When Bad Things Happen to Good People*, 43–44.
8. Dariusz Ivanski, *The Dynamics of Job's Intercession* (Rome, 2006), 67.
9. Carlfred Broderick, *The Uses of Adversity* (Salt Lake City: Deseret Book, 2008).
10. Joseph Stein, *Fiddler on the Roof* (New York: Crown Publishers, 1964), 54.
11. Victor E. Frankl, *Man's Search for Meaning* (Boston, MA: Beacon Press, 2006).
12. Pamela, text message to author.
13. Mother Teresa, in Malcolm Muggeridge, *Something Beautiful for God* (San Francisco: Harper & Row, 1971), 132.
14. James E. Talmage, *Jesus the Christ: A Study of the Messiah and His Mission according to Holy Scriptures both Ancient and Modern* (Salt Lake City: The Church of Jesus Christ of Latter-day Saints, 1915), 613.

Personal Notes

_____

_____

_____

_____

_____

_____

_____

_____

_____

_____

_____

_____

_____

_____

_____

_____

_____

_____

_____

_____

_____

_____

_____

_____

_____

_____

_____

_____

_____

_____

_____

_____

_____

_____

_____

_____

_____

_____

_____

_____

_____

Chapter Eleven

CONCLUSION

What Would Jesus Feel?
Emotions in the Scriptures[1]

Let's begin by asking the question that we've never really asked: is the Old Testament inspiring? Because it is a book of scripture, we have to believe that it is worth studying. But is it truly inspiring? Not everyone thinks so. There are quite a few dissenting votes from people like A. A. Milne, creator of Winnie the Pooh, said: "The Old Testament . . . has emptied more churches than all the counter-attractions of cinema, motor bicycle, and golf course."[2] However, we're going to look at why the Old Testament is, in fact, inspiring.

FIVE BASIC EMOTIONS

To examine the worth of this text, we might look at the way the Old Testament helps us understand human emotions. Since the scriptures are there to teach us to learn to live in a "right relation-ship" with God, we should gain insight into our daily lives from its pages, and the Old Testament is surprisingly helpful with that.

The Old Testament gives us detailed accounts of the lives of people who are making all sorts of mistakes, but are also doing many things right. These accounts hopefully allow us to walk through the world and not make those same mistakes because we can see the consequences in their lives. One of the things that the Old Testament has a great deal of is emotion. The God of Genesis is a God with physical elements and emotions. The people we meet are driven by passions as well.

There's action going on all the time in the Old Testament, and much of it is violent. This is no Jane Austen novel, with people drinking tea and exchanging meaningful glances; it's an action story.

Psychologists have identified six basic emotions that exist in every culture. They are fear, anger, sadness, disgust, joy, and surprise.[3] I'm interested in how these emotions are expressed in the Bible, and how they evolve from the Old Testament to the New Testament.

TURNING OUR EMOTIONS INSIDE OUT

Pixar released a wonderful movie called *Inside Out*, in which five of the basic emotions I just mentioned are portrayed as characters inhabiting the mind of a little girl named Riley.[4] (For some reason, they skip "surprise," which is really kind of surprising.) The movie makes the point that every human being is driven by these basic emotions. Can the Old and New Testaments help us move from being people who are driven by these emotions, to people who are in command of them, and even transcend them?

The characters in the Old Testament model each of these emotions, sometimes in positive ways, and sometimes in negative ways. Then, as we move into the New Testament, Jesus offers us the perfect model of these emotions, and in so doing, shows us how to deal with them. He teaches us by example what to do when we feel fear, disgust, sadness, anger, and even joy. He takes each one of these emotions to a new level, and invites us to come with Him to a life where our emotions are a blessing, not a tyrant who controls us. Let's take them one at a time.

#1 FEAR

When I think of the Old Testament, I think of fear. God is scary in the Old Testament. He kills whole populations when His anger is kindled, so you had better watch out. When Job says, "Though he slay me, yet will I trust in him" (Job 13:15), we can see why he feels that God might legitimately slay him, since everything else in his life has been destroyed.

But in the New Testament, we begin to see that perhaps much of this fear was based in a wrong interpretation of events in the Old Testament. For Jesus is a God of love. And in the New Testament, Jesus is also a model of great bravery—facing down mobs, rulers, and even His executioners with studied calm. But He candidly confesses to us that He was afraid, at least once, and that was in the Garden of Gethsemane.

He took Peter, James, and John along with Him, and He began to be deeply distressed and troubled. "'My soul is overwhelmed with sorrow to the point of death,' he said to them. 'Stay here and keep watch'" (Mark 14:34, NIV). Going a little farther, he fell to the ground and prayed that, if possible, the hour might pass from him. "'*Abba*, Father,' he said, 'everything is possible for you. Take this cup from me. Yet not what I will, but what you will'" (Mark 14:36, NIV).

In a revelation to Joseph Smith, more of Jesus's feelings from that night are revealed,

> For behold, I, God, have suffered these things for all, that they might not suffer if they would repent;
>
> But if they would not repent they must suffer even as I;
>
> Which suffering caused myself, even God, the greatest of all, to tremble because of pain, and to bleed at every pore, and to suffer both body and spirit—and would that I might not drink the bitter cup, and shrink—
>
> Nevertheless, glory be to the Father, and I partook and finished my preparations unto the children of men. (D&C 19:16–19)

So, what did Jesus do when He was afraid? He prayed for God's help and He begged for release from His suffering, but He told God that He was completely ready to do His will. And when He was able to overcome, He gave glory to the Father.

One extra help that we learn about in both the Old and New Testaments is expressed in one line: "An angel from heaven appeared to him and strengthened him" (Luke 22:43, NIV). So, with the Lord's experience in the Garden as our guide, we know that when we are afraid we can beg for release, recommit ourselves, and rely on God. And we know that angels will be near because Jesus has modeled this for us.

#2 DISGUST

If there was an emotion that Jesus resisted, it was disgust. He actually sought out people that everyone else rejected. Time after time in the Old Testament, we have lepers, the unclean, and people who do reprehensible things that are cast out. In the New Testament, these are the very people that Jesus chooses to spend His time with. He makes a particular point of it. We think of the woman who, unclean from a bleeding disorder of twelve years, reaches out and touches Him. He immediately turns and reaches out to her (see Luke 8:43–48). Every kind of untouchable being was touched by Him.

But though He never exhibited it to others, Jesus personally experienced disgust. People were disgusted with Him. He was poor, probably often dirty, and had no money. Leaders rejected Him; He was driven out of towns and turned away by respectable people. He was forced to march naked through the streets carrying His own cross. He was the object of disgust.

The following is a story from motivational speaker Dan Clark, about how damaging disgust can be.

> When I was on my mission in Ireland, I was sent with my companion to open up a city called Tralee, which had no members. One day a woman answered her door and surprisingly called us "elders" and invited us in. I noticed she had not looked

at our nametags, so I asked her what she knew about the Church. She smiled and proudly told us she was a member but had been inactive for years. I asked her if she still believed, and she told us that yes, she still had a testimony.

When I asked her why she had gone inactive, she explained that she had never been able to break her smoking habit and that every time she went to Church and the members smelled the smoke on her clothes and breath, she was made to feel guilty and unwanted. She then turned her head away for about sixty seconds. When she looked back at us, she had tears streaming down her cheeks. With her lip quivering, she sweetly and humbly replied, "I sure wish everybody's sins smelled."

Didn't Jesus invite us all to come as we are? Didn't Jesus say, "He that is without sin among you, let him first cast a stone at her" (John 8:7)? Didn't Jesus teach us to "leave the ninety and nine and go after [the one]" (Luke 15:4)?[5]

#3 SADNESS

Isaiah prophesied that Jesus would be "a man of sorrows, and acquainted with grief" (Isaiah 53:3).

In the Old Testament, there is a great deal of sorrow. People lose their families in war, are persecuted for their beliefs, and suffer all sorts of terrible fates. In the New Testament, life is not much easier. Jesus lived during a time when death, disease, and disaster lurked around every corner.

There is one moment in the Gospels that is particularly poignant. Shortly before His Crucifixion, Jesus is staying with His disciples and receives word that His dear friend Lazarus has died in the town of Bethany. Though Bethany is only a few miles away, Jesus waits two more days before He goes to Lazarus's home. By this point, Lazarus has been long buried. Martha, Lazarus's grieving sister, comes to meet Jesus and says, reproachfully, "Lord, . . . if you had been here, my brother would not have died" (John 11:21, NIV). This must have hurt him deeply.

The User-Friendly Old Testament

When they arrive at the house, Jesus is confronted by the sorrow of the people He loves. Mary repeats Her sister's reproach as soon as she sees Him.

> When Mary reached the place where Jesus was and saw him, she fell at his feet and said, "Lord, if you had been here, my brother would not have died."
>
> When Jesus saw her weeping, and the Jews who had come along with her also weeping, he was deeply moved in spirit and troubled.
>
> "Where have you laid him?" he asked.
>
> "Come and see, Lord," they replied.
>
> Jesus wept. (John 11:32–35, NIV)

What I find so moving about this is the fact that Jesus has not come to mourn Lazarus, He has come to raise Lazarus from the dead! He knows He can raise him from the dead and that the miracle is just minutes away. But when confronted with the pain in the faces of His loved ones, He weeps. Right there, in the moment, He feels what they feel.

Here's another little story from Dan Clark:

> The daughter said, "Oh, Mommy, I walked my friend Sally home. She dropped her doll on the sidewalk, and it broke all to pieces. It was awful!"
>
> Her mother said, "So you are late because you stayed to help your friend pick up the pieces of the doll and put it back together again?"
>
> She replied, "Oh, no, Mommy. I didn't know how to fix the doll. I just stayed to help her cry."[6]

#4 ANGER

God often seems angry in the Old Testament, but I try to remember that He is coming to us through the perspective of the authors and redactors. Many times in the narrative, He sounds like the angry, vengeful gods that are worshipped by the other cultures surrounding the Old Testament Saints at the time. As we move into the New Testament, Jesus shows us what the anger of God is really like. God does mete out punishment and justice, but His version of anger is controlled and His justice is distributed for a reason.

We have several examples of Jesus responding sharply to teachers and leaders who offended His sense of right and wrong. And we have the famous scene where He found unscrupulous moneychangers taking advantage of the poor people who came to the temple to offer sacrifices (see Matthew 21:12–16). But we also know that when He goes to drive the moneychangers out of the temple, he stops to braid a cord (see John 2:15). That tells us a great deal.

#5 JOY

The Bible tells us that to know God is to experience "life eternal," or the life that God has. The Old Testament offers us a basis for understanding God; in the same way that living a lifetime with a parent offers us a basis for understanding that person in a different way than just living with them as an adult would not. With our childish eyes, we look at God in the Old Testament as if everything that happens is about us. As we grow spiritually, we begin to see that there are many more issues at stake that just our little concerns. And as we move into the New Testament, Jesus invites us into a spiritual adulthood by allowing us to see into His thoughts and even His fears. It's breathtaking and life-changing.

Paul said, "When I was a child, I spake as a child, I understood as a child, I thought as a child: but when I became a man, I put away childish things" (1 Corinthians 13:11).

"Looking unto Jesus the author and finisher of our faith; who for the joy that was set before him endured the cross, despising the shame, and is sat down at the right hand of the throne of God" (Hebrews 12:2).

So we learn that Jesus looks at the joy before Him and then endures the sorrow, the anger, the fear, and the negative emotions that come through the perspective that offers. We need to keep the joy ahead of us.

Jesus's capacity for joy is as great as His capacity for suffering. In His climactic meeting with the Nephites after His Resurrection, He models pure joy for us.

> And it came to pass that when Jesus had made an end of praying unto the Father, he arose; but so great was the joy of the multitude that they were overcome.
>
> It came to pass that Jesus spake unto them, and bade them arise.
>
> And they arose from the earth, and he said unto them: Blessed are ye because of your faith. And now behold, my joy is full. (3 Nephi 17:18–20)

It goes on,

> And when he had said these words, he wept, and the multitude bare record of it, and he took their little children, one by one, and blessed them, and prayed unto the Father for them.
>
> And when he had done this he wept again. (3 Nephi 17:21–22)

We cry when we're sad and we cry when we're full of joy because those two emotions are similar in a way. They're all the way there;

> You cannot selectively numb emotion. You can't say, here's the bad stuff. Here's vulnerability, here's grief, here's shame, here's fear, here's disappointment. I don't want to feel these. I'm going to have a . . . banana nut muffin. . . .
>
> You can't numb those hard feelings without numbing the other[s]. . . . So when we numb those, we numb joy, we numb gratitude, we numb happiness. And then we are miserable, and we are looking for purpose and meaning, and then we feel vulnerable, so then we have a . . . banana nut muffin. And it becomes this dangerous cycle.
>
> —Brené Brown[7]

they are as deep as our emotions get. The movie, *Inside Out*, has as its theme the idea that there is no real joy without a component of sadness in it. Jesus is surely the model for that.

In the Bible, we meet a God who feels anger, sadness, and fear. A God who does not feel disgust at His creations, but experiences their disgust at Him. A God who, because He has emotions like our own, can help us learn to master them. A God who, because He is "a man of sorrows, and acquainted with grief" (Isaiah 53:3), has a greater capacity for joy. Neal Maxwell said of Jesus:

> If you were to collect the agony for your own sins and I for mine, and multiply it by that number, we can only shudder at what the sensitive, divine soul of Jesus must have experienced in taking upon himself the awful arithmetic of the sins of all of us—an act which he did selflessly and voluntarily. If it is also true (in some way we don't understand) that the cavity which suffering carves into our souls will one day also be the receptacle of joy, how infinitely greater Jesus' capacity for joy, when he said, after his resurrection, "Behold, my joy is full." How very, very full, indeed, his joy must have been![8]

I'm thankful for the Old Testament. I don't feel comfortable with all of it, and I don't understand all of it. But every time I go back to it, I find something new that touches me, that inspires me, and that asks me to be better than I am. I hope that the comments I have made here have spurred your thoughts and got you thinking a little differently about the text. If so, I'd like to hear about it. We have only begun to explore its depths. Drop me a line, and God bless you on your journey through this wonderful book.

marilyngreenfaulkner@gmail.com

NOTES

1. My thanks to Amy Turner for the talk, given in 2016, that inspired this chapter.
2. A. A. Milne quoted in, Gregory A. Boyd, *The Crucifixion of the Warrior God: Interpreting the Old Testament's Violent Portraits of God in Light of the Cross*, vols. 1–2 (Minneapolis, MN: Fortress Press, 2017), 33.

3. Neel Burton, "What Are Basic Emotions?," *Psychology Today*, January 7, 2016, accessed September 5, 2017, www.psychologytoday.com /blog/hide-and-seek/201601/what-are-basic-emotions.
4. *Inside Out*, directed by Pete Docter (Burbank, CA: Walt Disney Studios, 2015), DVD.
5. Dan Clark, "The Four Steps on the Stairway to Heaven," (Brigham Young University devotional, September 30, 2014), speeches.byu .edu/talks/dan-clark_four-steps-stairway-heaven/.
6. Ibid.
7. Brené Brown, "The Power of Vulnerability," filmed June 2010 in Houston, TX, TED talk video, 20:19.
8. Neal A. Maxwell, "But for a Small Moment" (Brigham Young University devotional, September 1, 1974), speeches.byu.edu/talks /neal-a-maxwell_small-moment/.

Personal Notes

_____

_____

_____

_____

_____

_____

_____

_____

_____

_____

_____

_____

_____

_____

_____

_____

_____

_____

_____

_____

_____

_____

_____

_____

_____

_____

_____

_____

_____

_____

_____

_____

_____

_____

_____

_____

_____

_____

_____

_____

_____

_____

_____

_____

_____

_____

_____

_____

_____

_____

_____

_____

_____

_____

_____

_____

_____

_____

_____

_____

_____

_____

_____

_____

_____

_____

_____

_____

_____

_____

_____

_____

_____

_____

_____

_____

_____

_____

_____

_____

_____

_____

_____

_____

_____

_____

_____

_____

_____

_____

_____

_____

_____

_____

_____

_____

_____

_____

_____

_____

_____

_____

_____